D0984080

Rising Stars

AND

Fast Fades

SUCCESSES AND FAILURES OF
FAST-GROWTH COMPANIES

W. Keith Schilit

LEXINGTON BOOKS
An Imprint of Macmillan, Inc.
NEW YORK

Maxwell Macmillan Canada
TORONTO

Maxwell Macmillan International
NEW YORK   OXFORD   SINGAPORE   SYDNEY

Library of Congress Cataloging-in-Publication Data

Schilit, W. Keith
   Rising stars and fast fades : successes and failures of fast-growth companies / W. Keith Schilit.
     p.   cm.
   ISBN 0-02-927892-9
   1. Success in business. 2. Business failures. I. Title.
HF5386.5384 1994
650.1—dc20   93-40135
                                               CIP

Copyright © 1994 by W. Keith Schilit

All rights reserved. No part of this book may be reproduced or transmitted in any form or by any means, electronic or mechanical, including photocopying, recording, or by any information storage and retrieval system, without permission in writing from the Publisher.

Lexington Books
An Imprint of Macmillan, Inc.
866 Third Avenue, New York, N.Y. 10022

Maxwell Macmillan Canada, Inc.
1200 Eglinton Avenue East
Suite 200
Don Mills, Ontario M3C 3N1

Macmillan, Inc. is part of the Maxwell Communication Group of Companies.

Printed in the United States of America

printing number
1   2   3   4   5   6   7   8   9   10

to Bradley Reed Schilit,
who epitomizes fast growth

Contents

Preface

After four years of off-again/on-again, find-some-more-information/get-rid-of-some-information, on-the-go writing, I finally felt that this book was complete. So I left it in the capable hands of Beth Anderson and her talented team at Lexington to put this work into production.

Then, wouldn't you know it, I stumble upon another company that compels me to do some more editing, even though I thought I had already completed writing this book twice before. Yet the more I thought about it, I realized just how special this company was: in many ways it summarized everything that I had already written about successful fast-growth companies. Why not use it as an introduction to the basic principles, identified in this book, that differentiate the "rising stars" from the "fast fades." So let me introduce you to *Chico's FAS,* a tremendously successful retailer of women's apparel, with whom I've had the pleasure of being associated for the past year.

Chico's began as a small Mexican folk art and leather goods shop on lovely Sanibel Island, on the west coast of Florida, in the fall of 1983. From its modest beginnings, its founders—Marvin and Helene Gralnick—along with some outstanding recent additions to its management team, have grown Chico's into one of the most exciting specialty retailers in America and one of the rising stars of the 1990s. Consider the following:

- Over its ten-year history, Chico's has grown from nothing to a $40 million business, a sevenfold gain from its sales level of 1988). From its one tiny store in Sanibel in 1983, Chico's is preparing to open its one hundredth store within months of its tenth birthday.
- In March 1993 Chico's completed a very successful $20 million initial public offering (IPO). Within about three months

its stock price doubled, making it one of the most successful NASDAQ companies as well as one of the most successful IPOs during that time period. Its stock price has been strong ever since.

- Chico's sales per square foot have been increasing steadily over the years to its current level of around $500 of sales per square foot.
- Chico's comparable-store sales have been increasing at a dramatically higher rate than the industry averages. On an annual basis, the company has *averaged* double-digit comparable-store sales increases over the past five years, often increasing 15 percent or more in a given month. This has come during a time when retailers have been performing so poorly that they are thankful for *any* increase in comparable-store sales.
- Chico's profit margins are among the highest in its industry. The company had 60 percent gross profit margins and double-digit net profit margins over the past year.

It is not surprising that Chico's founders were recently named "Entrepreneurs of the Year" for the state of Florida in the *Inc.* magazine/Ernst & Young competition.

In later chapters of this book I employ a framework to distinguish success stories from failures based on eight factors. Although the fine people at Chico's did not read this book ahead of time, somehow they adhered to these principles in building their outstanding company. Some examples are listed below.

Nichemanship. Chico's has a very well-defined niche market—style-conscious women aged thirty to fifty-five—and it locates its stores in upscale shopping areas throughout the nation. Moreover, although the opportunity does present itself from time to time, the company has generally resisted the temptation to get into unknown areas; rather, Chico's has "stuck to its knitting" and done what it does best: sell casual clothing to its well-defined target market.

Sustainable competitive advantage. Chico's is known as a provider of moderately priced, distinctively designed clothing (in other words, good value for high quality). Certainly value retailing is a trend for the 1990s, which has enhanced Chico's competitive advantage. And since Chico's realizes that providing great value may not be enough of a competitive advantage for the years to come, it has strengthened its position by gaining additional advantages in terms of innovativeness, attention to cost control, unique designs, speed of distribution, and attention to customer service. Combined, these competitive advantages keep the company quantum leaps ahead of other specialty retailers.

Superior product/service quality. Chico's private-label merchandise is typically high quality, 100 percent cotton, and designed for easy care. But designing and manufacturing a high-quality product is not enough; you also have to love the product. Not surprisingly, the Chico's people have an intense love for their product. In fact, almost everyone who works for the company—including the chairman of the board, *him*self—will typically be found wearing Chico's clothing, even though no rule says that they have to do so. Even more impressive is the company's service quality. Chico's fashion consultants routinely go that extra yard for their customers, calling the latter when new styles come into the store that complement Chico's ensembles that they had purchased previously. In addition, Chico's employees are all continually reminded that they can do "whatever it takes" to make a customer happy, regardless of what it costs. So, if a customer needs a particular outfit tomorrow, Chico's (thanks to Federal Express, which is one of Chico's role models) will make sure that the customer has it on time, even though Chico's has to absorb the costs. The Chico's people all realize that if going that extra yard costs the company a few hundred dollars (or even more), then it's a very small investment to make to get a customer for life. In fact, in today's market environment, retailers cannot afford *not* to go that extra yard, regardless of the cost. Nonetheless, Chico's stands out as one of the few companies to adhere genuinely to this value system.

Innovativeness. Chico's is known throughout its industry as an innovative retailer. This shows in its boutique-store layouts. It also shows in the exclusively designed private-label products that carry the "CHICO'S" trademark. In an industry where the successful companies must stay well ahead of the competition or be also-rans, Chico's is always designing years into the future. The company spots early fashion trends throughout the world, then brings the ideas back to its exceedingly capable design team, which has been under the guidance of Helene, Heidi, and Mary over the years. With lightning speed, those designs are produced in Chico's manufacturing facilities overseas and then distributed to the stores in time for the latest season. In addition, the company is innovative in its marketing efforts (for example, invitations to private sales and membership in its "Passport Club" for its most loyal customers) as well as its human resource efforts (for example, rewards for outstanding sales accomplishments, and stock option and stock purchase programs).

Strong cultural foundation. Chico's culture, which is certainly a product and a refinement of its top management, can hardly be described; it has to be felt. The typical Chico's employee goes to work every day feeling that she is working for the most outstanding company in this country. They love their work. They love their designs. Their spirit, which is captured by their slogan "We are family," does not just touch its people; it moves them! Better yet, that feeling and enthusiasm rubs off on its customers as well. Marvin, one of the founders of Chico's, articulates it clearly when describing such potential threats as competitors copying Chico's unique design styles: "They can steal our designs, but they can't steal our souls." It is just this feeling that is shared by everyone with whom I come into contact in the Chico's family—from top management to Karin, the company's first employee (who is still spreading the value system today), to Steve, the construction supervisor (who spends his time on planes introducing strangers to Chico's), to the wonderful sales associates (who are lovingly referred to as the "Chiclettes").

Valued customers, valued employees. Everybody who walks into a Chico's store is valued. Not only is it a fun experience to shop there, but the Chico's fashion consultants make it user friendly. Rather than displaying merchandise by traditional groupings of pants, tops, and dresses, it is stacked casually and is grouped in coordinated "color areas"—in other words, it is arranged in the same manner that it is worn by its loyal customers. And why shouldn't they be loyal? Customers are never rushed. It is not unusual to see stores open an hour past closing time, since the doors do not close until the very last customer has been served. Also, everybody who works there is valued every bit as much as its customers. It is difficult to land a job at Chico's; the company is very careful in its selection efforts, and just as careful in its orientation and training efforts. But once an employee has joined the company, that family feeling—which is about as fitting a term as possible—is obvious. It is not surprising that many Chico's employees were customers who fell in love with the company and wanted to work there. It has been said that a loyal customer is your best salesperson. Certainly Chico's is living proof of that, in more ways than one.

Quality management. The management of the company is as impressive as you can find. The spirit of the company was created by Marvin and Helene Gralnick, refined by Barry and Michal Szumlanski (another reason they really mean it when they say "We are family"), and enhanced by Charlie Kleman and Jeff Zwick. Marvin and Helene were the visionaries who got the company off the ground and turned impossible dreams into reality for their Chico's family. (They also were astute enough to realize that you can make a lot more money selling blouses, dresses, and pants than you can selling Mexican folk art.) Barry paved the way for the company's expansion and is a vital force in the company's growth today. Michal is the motivational genius behind the sales force. Charlie is an absolute master of financial controls. (He has also demonstrated that accountants certainly need not be dull.) And Jeff, who blends the qualities of leader, visionary, innovator, coach, motivator, buyer, seller, singer, songwriter, cowboy, and spokesman, has overseen the growth of Chico's while strengthening the culture that was created by Marvin and Helene. Somehow these six individuals, with very different backgrounds but with a common value—to make Chico's the greatest place in this country to shop and to work—have been the perfect blend of leadership to make Chico's such a success story.

Venture capital support. During its early years, as the company grew it was able to get some informal funding, which catapulted its growth significantly. Chico's would certainly not be in the position it is today had it not gotten that funding to fuel its growth.

Chico's is just one success story. Who are the other successful fast-growth companies of today? What accounts for their success? How can you predict which companies will be the fast-growth success stories of the future? How can you distinguish the "rising stars" from the "fast fades"? These are the questions addressed in this book, which takes an in-depth look at the "winners" and "sinners" among fast-growth companies and provides easy-to-use information for investors, customers, employees, and managers of such companies. For investors, I explain how to spot the early indicators of success, as well as the red flags that could signal imminent disaster. For (existing or potential) customers or employees, I explain what to look for when dealing with these companies. And for managers, I explain how to take steps to ensure that a company is headed for the winner's circle, rather than the loser's pit.

Interestingly, there are no magic formulas or secrets for success. Rather, the better-performing fast-growth companies generally employ some fairly basic managerial principles that can be utilized by most managers and recognized by most investors. The main focus of this book is on describing these basic principles that can be applied to any fast-growth company.

PART I

The Fast-Growth Companies

1

Fast Growth

Wal-Mart, The Limited, Home Depot, Liz Claiborne, Federal Express, and Microsoft are among the most successful fast-growth companies in the United States. They have all been more than generous to their customers, their employees, their investors, and the communities in which they do business. So if you have invested in any of these companies, you have probably done quite well financially. If you have purchased anything from any of them, you have probably been pleased with the products that they offered and the service they provided after the sale. If you have worked for any of them, you have probably been very happy with your job. And if you have dealt with any of these companies in any other way, you have probably been favorably impressed with them.

For example, under its late founder Sam Walton's carefully laid out strategy and inspirational leadership, Wal-Mart has grown over a thirty-year period from a start-up in Bentonville, Arkansas, to a $52 billion success that is extremely well regarded in any community in which it does business. Several years ago, one of my good friends was fortunate enough to hear Walton address a group of retailers. He was so excited by Walton's remarks that when Wal-Mart went public in 1970, he invested $1,000 in the little-known discount retailing chain. Today that $1,000 investment in Wal-Mart is worth over a million dollars—a thousandfold increase on his investment! There are also countless Wal-Mart "associates" (as the employees are called) who have become millionaires as a result of their commitment to that company.

From an investment standpoint, Wal-Mart has few equals in terms of its long-term performance. Yet there are some other success stories that should raise eyebrows. Investors who were fortunate enough to invest in such companies as Home Depot (which increased in value by over 7,000 percent during the 1980s), Liz Claiborne (up 3,400 percent over that time period), Adobe Systems (up 1,600 percent), LA Gear (up 1,400 percent), or Autodesk (up 1,200 percent) at the time—or shortly after—these companies went public did exceedingly well. In the case of Home Depot, a mere $15,000 investment in the early 1980s would have enabled an investor to become a millionaire by the time the decade had ended.

What do we know about the successful and unsuccessful fast-growth companies? What are the characteristics of their growth activity? Why do some fast-growth companies succeed while others become dismal failures? Are there common characteristics of success and of failure? As these growth-oriented companies continue to grow, do they get "leaner and meaner" in the process—or, as is the case with so many former football players, do they simply get fatter and slower? What is their fate after the growth slows down? These are the questions addressed in this book.[1]

Fast-Growth Companies

There are different degrees of fast growth (or *hypergrowth*, a term often applied to these companies). As a general guideline, we can classify companies as fast-growth firms if they have experienced consistent 50 percent or greater annual growth over several years during their history. Typically growth does slow down eventually—perhaps to 20 percent or 30 percent per year for such companies.

The most extreme cases of growth are typically among early-stage, "turbocharged growth" companies such as those included in the *Inc.* 500 annual listing of the fastest-growing privately held corporations in the United States. A recent listing included such names as the following:

- CEBCOR (Chicago, IL), a provider of employee leasing services
- Devon Direct Marketing & Advertising (Malvern, PA), a provider of advertising services
- Gainey Transportation Services (Grand Rapids, MI), a provider of long-haul, dry-van trucking services
- Ocean State Coordinated Health Services (Warwick, RI), a provider of cost-managed health care services
- Cogentrix (Charlotte, NC), which owns and operates cogeneration facilities

Unless you live in the above cities, work for these companies or use their services regularly, or are fanatic about reading every business periodical that comes your way, you are probably unfamiliar with these names. Yet they are some of the high-growth success stories of the past few years and may turn out to be the superstar performers over the coming decade. All of the companies named above increased in size by at least a hundredfold during the late 1980s, and one of them—Cogentrix—grew by a thousandfold (or 100,000 percent!) over that same period. To put this growth in the proper perspective, a typical mom-and-pop retail store generating $500,000 to $600,000 in sales in a year that grew by 100,000 percent over a five-year period would then be comparable in size to many of the Fortune 500 companies. If Cogentrix were to sustain its 100,000 percent growth rate from the 1985–1990 period for the subsequent five years, it would generate annual sales of $130 billion by 1995, which would make it comparable in size to the largest corporations in the world. But this will not happen, for there are three certainties in life: death, taxes, and slowdowns among fast-growth companies.

A bit less dramatic than the high-flying firms just mentioned are the *Inc.* 100: small, publicly held companies that have often been experiencing a "meager" 100 percent or so annual growth rate. Many *Inc.* 100 alumni have gone on to become more established, successful high-growth companies.[2] Some examples are Apple Computer, Compaq Computer, Federal Express, Liz Claiborne, and Sun Microsystems, all of which are relatively young companies (most less than twenty years old) that are multibillion-dollar businesses.

Fast-growth companies are not just early-stage, high-tech businesses. They include retailers, low-tech manufacturers, and numerous other companies that have grown dramatically in rather mundane industries.

It's Not Just for the Small and Young

Typically, fast-growth companies are smaller, entrepreneurial organizations in early stages of development (roughly 5 to 15 years old). There are several large hypergrowth companies (billion-dollar-per-year companies such as Wal-Mart, Apple, and Compaq), however, as well as several fairly old companies (like the 150-year-old Cross Pen Company) that have characteristics similar to smaller, faster-growing entrepreneurial companies. When we think of large established companies, we often think of layoffs (during the 1980s, the *Fortune* 500 eliminated nearly 4 million jobs) and plant closings. Yet many larger companies have been sources of jobs as they have grown and have had a dramatic positive impact on the economy.

Fast-Growth in Low-Growth Industries

It is also important to examine growth relative to an industry. For example, steel manufacturers Worthington Industries and Nucor have been growing at the rate of 16 percent and 11 percent per year, respectively, since the early 1980s. Although these growth rates might not seem spectacular, they are five to ten times the industry average. For that reason, we can view these steelmakers as fast-growth companies.

Unglamorous Growth

The conventional thinking is that to be successful, companies must operate in attractive, exciting, high-growth sectors in high-tech regions. This will often be the case. As the reader will see in the next few chapters, however, there are winners *and* losers among such companies. For example, such stars as Microsoft, Apple, Compaq, Autodesk, and Intel certainly typify successful high-tech companies. But Columbia Data Products, Vector Graphic,

Kaypro, and Osborne Computer, to name just a few, demonstrate how even companies in high-growth sectors in high-tech regions can fail.

Even more interesting is the fact that there are numerous successful companies that have operated in rather unglamorous sectors in low-tech regions. In addition to such classic success stories as Wal-Mart, there is also Unifi (of Yadkinville, NC), which produces texturized polyester yarn; A. T. Cross, a leader in the writing instruments field; and Dunkin Donuts, a national chain of donut shops. These examples demonstrate how low tech companies in seemingly unglamorous sectors can excel.

There is great excitement but also great risk associated with "hot" companies in glamorous industries. This is particularly evident in high-tech industries, where competition can be exceedingly intense. For instance, the moment one computer company designs a breakthrough product, a dozen other companies will soon be spending tens or hundreds of millions of dollars designing one that can outperform it. This is less likely to occur in mundane, low-tech industries.

And just because a company is in a low-growth industry does not mean that the company itself will not grow. Marriott, for example, was growing at 20 percent per year in the 1980s while the hotel industry as a whole was growing at the rate of only 2 percent. This accounts for why its stock price increased by 1,200 percent during that decade. Consequently, successful companies in unglamorous industries often stand a much better chance of avoiding competition and in becoming star performers than do their more glamorous counterparts. For example, Safety-Kleen, which sells solvents to clean greasy machine parts, increased in value by more than tenfold during the 1980s. Loctite, which sells adhesives, quadrupled in value during that time.

Growth, Success, and Failure

Fast-growth companies include both success stories and failures. Nearly one hundred thousand American businesses fail every year—an average of nearly two thousand in a given week. That failure is especially pronounced among smaller (and often growing) businesses, since they are often lacking in resources and less able to withstand a weaker economy; customers' defaults on debts often result in their own default of subsequent debts. In 1992 alone General Motors, Ford, IBM, and DuPont, four of the industrial giants of the twentieth century, lost a total of $40 billion, but they are still around. In contrast, smaller companies with massive losses often die altogether.

A company's well-being is most at risk during its faster growth. During that time the company must invest heavily in expanding its plants and operations, in purchasing inventory, in hiring personnel, and so forth. That is also when competition is often most severe and the presence becomes highly visible to competitors, customers, and suppliers, etc. Thus, continued growth becomes a task in itself. And, continued profits becomes a monumentous effort. People Express Airlines, for example, a success in the early 1980s, failed largely due to its reckless growth.

Similarly, as Kinder-Care Learning Centers grew significantly over the 1980s, it launched a rather disastrous, junk-bond-fueled diversification attempt. By January 1991 the company, being squeezed for cash, stopped paying interest on its debt and began an effort to restructure in order to avoid bankruptcy. Under investment-banker-turned-CEO, Tull Gearreald, however, Kinder-Care has taken several steps to improve the quality of its centers. Although some bondholders would rather see the funds funneled to repay debt, the general feeling is that the only way for them to get their principal paid back is to make the company more healthy.

Successful Versus Unsuccessful Fast-Growth Companies

Obviously, sheer growth is not enough for success. After all, such seemingly successful companies of the early 1980s as ZZZZ Best, Pizza Time Theatre, Psych Systems, Wedtech, Kaypro, Vector Graphic, and People Express Airlines have all filed for bankruptcy and ceased operations. There are two important features relevant to distinguishing successful from unsuccessful companies. First, one must take into account qualitative as well as quantitative performance indicators. This is especially important for early stage ventures with high start-up costs (such as costs associated with research and development), which may be outstanding companies even though they have not been profitable yet. This was certainly the case with during the first few years of operation of Genentech, which has often been regarded as one of the best managed and most admired companies in the biotechnology industry.

Second, it is important to evaluate the performance of companies over the long term. Thus such measures as long-term appreciation of the price of a firm's stock, long-term profitability (return on investment, growth in earnings per share, and so forth) and corporate reputation (in terms of innovativeness, quality of management and personnel, community and social responsiveness, and the like) can be used to assess success. Regarding stock market performance, it is important to recognize that share prices for fast-growing companies can vary significantly on a week-to-week (or even day-to-day) basis. With good news, a stock price can soar; however, the stock market is quite unforgiving upon hearing bad news: witness the recent one-day stock price declines of more than 20 percent for LA Gear, 30 percent for Oracle Systems, and 50 percent for Digital Microwave. When one evaluates a company's long-term performance, however, one ignores the sometimes dramatic short-term fluctuations in stock prices.

Appreciation in stock price over the long term is often a good measure of performance

---

Clear (and Not So Clear) Winners

The criteria for successful fast-growth companies are often quite nebulous. The most straightforward indicators of companies that can be classified as successful are attractive earnings growth and stock price appreciation over a sustained period of time. Such companies as Wal-Mart, The Limited, Compaq, Microsoft, Home Depot, and Liz Claiborne clearly fit into this category. For example, Compaq's dramatic increase in stock value since it went public in 1983, coupled with its twenty-five-fold increase in sales and its substantial increase in profits, would be considered a success story.

But there are also a few special cases that one can refer to as *turnarounds*—companies that were failing and then been set back on the right course, usually as a result of a change in management. Such turnarounds as Remington Products (under Victor Kiam) and North American Tool and Die (under Tom Melohn), should be viewed as successes.

Clear (and Not So Clear) Losers

Some unsuccessful companies are also readily identifiable. For example, computer maker Kaypro, which went public in 1983 and subsequently went bankrupt, would be labeled a failure. Such other now-bankrupt computer companies as Osborne Computer and Vector Graphic would also be considered failures. Even more dramatic is the case of Worlds of Wonder, a fast-growth company that went public at a $400 million market value. Its stock price soared from $18 per share to $29 per share on the first day of trading. Within months, though, the company was bankrupt—an obvious characteristic of failure.

Similarly, consider Silk Greenhouse of Tampa, Florida, a high-growth success story that ran into trouble in 1989 as a result of its massive expansion. Stores did not open on schedule, inventory costs rose significantly, and cash flows were hampered, all of which contributed to a dramatic decline in the stock price. The company consequently scaled back its expansion efforts, but its stock had lost almost all of its value by that time. It was a case of too little, too late; the company went bankrupt within months. Such is the humbling nature of "hot" stocks in "hot" industries—the ones that get mounds of favorable publicity and that every investor you come across seems to succumb to the pressure to buy. Certainly, the prices of such stocks can do well in a very short time. But as quickly as they rise, they are still susceptible to falling—and they will probably drop in price a lot more quickly than they rose.

Other companies can be classified as unsuccessful based on weak earnings and/or dramatic declines in the value of their stock over a sustained period of time. For example, Home Shopping Network (HSN), of Clearwater, Florida, went public at a market capitalization of $250 million. On its first day of trading, the stock price skyrocketed from $18 to $44. Within nine months HSN had a market value of $3 billion, despite a huge level of debt (approximately 300 percent) of equity and other ominous signs. Shortly thereafter, as the hype associated with this company began to disappear, its stock lost 90% of its value. More recently HSN has faced a host of problems, not the least of which was an order to pay GTE of Florida and a subsidiary $100 million for libel and slander in a legal battle. (After an appeal, HSN settled with GTE for $4.5 million.)

Interestingly, all the unsuccessful fast-growth companies just mentioned were, at one time, doing quite well. They were apparently unable to control their growth, however, and subsequently they fell on more difficult times. Why have these failures occurred? Were they because of management? Were they due to the role of the investors in these companies? Probably they resulted from a combination of factors that will be discussed throughout the book. Among these were probably numerous errors and misjudgments over a long period of time. As noted by a San Francisco–based venture capitalist in referring to some of these failures, "There's been a lack of tough-minded checking out of deals. People get into situations with entrepreneurs or companies that they soon realize aren't going to work out, but once you start, you often find a deal takes on a life of its own."[3]

Growing Pains

Even the best companies suffer from growing pains. For example, superstar performer Sun Microsystems had a $20 million quarterly loss in 1989, its first deficit in more than five years. Sun had introduced a new series of products that was affected by delayed shipments caused by component shortages and problems with Sun's management information system. Fortunately, a solution of strict cost controls and a streamlined organization remedied the problems quickly enough to continue the company's successful growth strategy. The important lesson is that the successful fast-growth companies have generally been able to bounce back from their shortcomings, while the unsuccessful companies often fail completely when significant problems begin to arise.

Business and Personal Success

Business success or failure can often directly influence personal success or failure. Consider Tony Bykerk, a telecommunications entrepreneur who built K & B Engineering into an Inc. 500 company in just a few short years. Bykerk had a $2 million house, a fifty-three foot yacht, and a few luxury cars; he also had a drinking problem, a troubled marriage, and some real problems at the office. Although sales were growing at a tremendously rapid rate, profit margins were declining.

Remarkably, Bykerk was able to solve all these problems. He took care of his drinking and marital crisis; sold the house, boat, and cars; and consolidated his business from 450 employees to 85, and from sixteen offices to four. He survived in both his personal and business lives. As Bykerk noted, "Growth was a narcotic."[4]

Success Is a Long-Term Notion

Success—especially as related to investments—is difficult to define, particularly with speculative investments such as those in fast-growth companies, which are often smaller in market value or market capitalization and which often fluctuate significantly in market or stock price (sometimes even from day to day). Thus it is critical to focus on the long-term outlook for a company.

From an investment perspective, one thing is quite evident when it comes to examining fast-growth companies: over the long term, quality, rather than hype or temporary market conditions, prevails. As Peter Lynch, one of the greatest stock pickers of recent times, recently noted in his best-selling book *One Up On Wall Street,* "In the end, superior companies will succeed and mediocre companies will fail, and investors in each will be rewarded accordingly." Consequently, day-to-day fluctuations in stock price can be disregarded. A basic measure of success is consistent appreciation in the price of a company's stock *over a number of years.* Moreover, success is measured relative to the overall stock mar-

ket. Many fast-growth companies perform quite wel
dramatic short-term rise in the overall stock market.
high quality company (such as Wal-Mart or Home Depot or Liz
Claiborne or Compaq or Apple or Microsoft), however, to outperform the stock market consistently over a long time horizon.

---

*Over the long term, quality, rather than hype or
temporary market conditions, prevails.*

Looking Ahead

There are countless examples of successful and unsuccessful fast-
growth companies. In the next chapter I discuss the impact that
such companies have had and examine their patterns of growth.
Then, in Chapters 3 and 4, I describe the nature of growth in high-
tech and low-tech businesses and introduce several examples of
success and failure of fast-growth companies.

In Part II I examine in detail the factors that have contributed to
the success of the better-performing fast-growth companies. I devote one chapter to each of the following eight characteristics:

- *Nichemanship* (creating specific, focused, differentiated markets)
- *Sustainable competitive advantage* (selling product features,
  quality, value, and so on)
- *Superior product/service quality* (communicating quality to
  the customer or client)
- *Innovativeness* (winning through new product development
  or through new ways to reach the market)
- *Strong cultural foundation* (creating the value system that
  pervades the organization)
- *Valued customers, valued employees* (being close to customers and employees)
- *Quality management* (such as having a visionary chief executive officer)
- *Venture capital support* (funding as well as managerial assistance by experienced investors)

Initial Thoughts on Fast Growth:
Important Summary Points

1. Some examples of fast-growth success stories are Wal-Mart, The Limited, Liz Claiborne, Home Depot, Federal Express, Apple Computer, Compaq Computer, and Sun Microsystems.
2. Many fast-growth companies have *not* been successful; some examples are ZZZZ Best, Pizza Time Theatre, Kaypro, Vector Graphic, Osborne Computer, People Express Airlines, Silk Greenhouse, and Worlds of Wonder.
3. There are great performers, such as Safety-Kleen and Loctite, in unglamorous industries.
4. The appreciation in the value of a company's stock over the long term is a good measure of performance of the company.

2

The Impact of Fast Growth

Why Growth Is Important

There are some good reasons to encourage businesses to grow. Research suggests that (1) most businesses filing for bankruptcy have less than one hundred employees; (2) survival rates double for companies that have grown; (3) companies that have grown the most aggressively have survival rates of nearly 80 percent; (4) a company needs about $500,000 in sales annually to escape from the "zone of vulnerability"; and (5) the chances of survival and prosperity increase dramatically when annual sales exceed $1 million (note that only 3% of the 18 million businesses in the United States have annual sales of more than $1 million).[1]

Sustained earnings growth is a primary determinant of increased stock price.

Thus growth tends to affect favorably the success of a business. More important, however, is the fact that as a company's sales grow, earnings tend to grow as well. It is sustained earnings growth that is a primary determinant of increased stock price, or the increased value of the company, over the long term. Consequently, when sales increase rapidly, the investor can often expect the stock price to do the same. It will be the growth in *earnings,* rather than in sales by itself, that will dictate whether the company will be a long-term winner.

Companies that grow are more likely than those that do not not only to survive, but to excel. Companies that do grow and prosper have impact throughout the economy. Specifically, the successful fast-growth companies have contributed significantly to new job creation, economic development, personal and community success, innovative technologies, and managerial excellence.

Opening New Markets and Creating Industries

Clearly, the growth of a company is most significant at the inception or early stages of an industry. In fact, many companies have grown as a result of their ability to open up industries. This was evidenced by Head in skiing equipment, by McDonald's in fast food, by Federal Express in overnight delivery, by Digital Equipment in minicomputers, by Apple in personal computers, by Intel in semiconductors, and by Genentech in biotechnology.

Changing Bureaucracy

Some fast-growth companies have been responsible for changing the way we live and work. For example, Federal Express, an $8 billion-per-year company based in Memphis, Tennessee, grew at better than a 30 percent annual rate over the last part of the 1980s and effectively controls the overnight delivery industry in this country. The company, which resulted from an economics term paper written by its founder, Frederick Smith, while he was at Yale (he earned a grade of C on the paper), has even forced our stuffiest bureaucracy—the U.S. Postal Service—to inaugurate Express Mail, one of its first real innovations since it started parcel post service in the early twentieth century. This trend of the private sector getting involved in typically public-sector services has been a tremendous opportunity for entrepreneurial companies in transportation services, education, health care, trash removal, street repair, fire protection, vehicle towing, sewer cleaning, graffiti removal, and many other areas.

Creating Personal Wealth and Success

Fast-growth companies have also been responsible for the personal financial success of many entrepreneurs as well as the investors in these companies. This has resulted in additional taxes (on earnings, capital gains, and so forth), greater philanthropic endeavors, and higher economic status of the communities in which these ventures are located. There has been massive wealth resulting from some of these entrepreneurial companies, with several entrepreneurs being ranked among the wealthiest individuals in the world. For example, Leslie Wexner borrowed $5,000 from an aunt in 1963 to start a sportswear store. Today, as a result of the expansion of The Limited and its associated stores, Wexner's personal fortune is estimated at approximately $2 billion. His philanthropic activities are recognized nationally, and the personal fortunes of the investors in The Limited have grown handsomely as well.

Similarly, Bill Hewlett and Dave Packard, founders of the company which bears their names, are billionaires who have established foundations to enable them to share their wealth with those in need of financial resources. And 1992 presidential candidate H. Ross Perot, whose net worth was estimated at about $3 billion after he sold his company Electronic Data Systems (EDS) to General Motors, has been a strong supporter of educational and other social causes.

Doing Social Good

On a much smaller scale, Ben Cohen and Jerry Greenfield, founders of Ben & Jerry's Homemade, a gourmet ice cream company based in Waterbury, Vermont, have made their entrepreneurial success a model for social change. The company is well known for its participatory management approach, its periodic company-wide employee meetings, and its unique compensation practice in which the salary earned by the highest-paid employee (Mr. Cohen, the chairman, who is paid about $100,000 a year) is limited to five times the salary of the lowest-paid full-time worker. (Compare that to the average compensation of CEOs at major American corporations, which is nearly one hundred times the average factory worker's salary.) In addition, Ben & Jerry's gives 7.5 percent of its pretax income to charity, which is about four times the national average and is one of the highest percentage rates of any company in the United States.

Enhancing Corporate Reputation

Some fast-growth companies have been exceedingly successful in terms of reputation, long-term profitability, and innovation. For example, in *Fortune* magazine's annual survey of the most admired corporations in America, Liz Claiborne and Wal-Mart have been ranked not only significantly higher than any of their competitors, but consistently in the top ten of all corporations.[2] Liz Claiborne, which was a small, entrepreneurial company as recently as the 1970s and is now the largest women's apparel company in the world, increased its sales by an average annual rate of nearly 40 percent over the last part of the 1980s (versus an industry average of 8 percent), while its earnings per share have grown by 37 percent (versus 17 percent) and its return on equity by 45 percent (versus 19 percent). Surprisingly, unlike other companies that have burdened themselves with significant debt to foster their growth, Liz Claiborne has taken on very little debt in the process: its debt-to-equity ratio has been less than 4 percent, as compared to an industry average of more than 40 percent. Wal-Mart has not done poorly either, as is evidenced by its 40 percent compounded annual growth and its one thousandfold increase in stock price since the early 1970s.

Several fast-growth companies have had a tremendous advantage over their larger counterparts in terms of product quality and innovation. Quality consultant A. Blanton Godfrey, for example, referred to Sun Microsystem's line of products as "definitely the best workstations in the world. Even the Japanese use them."[3] Like Liz Claiborne, Wal-Mart, and Sun Microsystems, such companies as Compaq, Federal Express, Nordstrom, and Apple Computer have been listed among the best-managed American companies in other surveys. As noted by Daniel Benton, computer analyst for Goldman Sachs, "Compaq is a case study in management excellence. It is the only company in the world that has established a brand name better than IBM's."[4] Incredibly, this comment was made in 1987, when Compaq was only four years old.

Despite some turbulent times, Compaq's reputation eventually became even stronger.

Developing Innovative, High-Quality Products and Services

The Limited has been recognized as one of the most admired and most innovative organizations in its industry. One measure of success in retailing is the movement of inventory, which is generally a function of the distribution process; most firms need to place orders six months in advance. The Limited, though, tracks customer preferences through point-of-sale computers on a daily basis. It then restocks its inventory by sending orders by satellite to plants in the United States as well as in South Korea, Hong Kong, Singapore, and Sri Lanka. The goods are then sent back to the company's home base in Columbus, Ohio, four times per week. Within forty-eight hours they are sorted, priced, and prepared for shipment in the company's highly automated distribution center, then shipped out to the company's more than three thousand stores. Despite The Limited being able to do something in one week that it takes its competitors six months to accomplish, the company's hard-driving, entrepreneurial founder, Leslie Wexner, described this restocking process as "not fast enough for the '90s."[5]

Similarly, Genentech (in South San Francisco, CA) has developed such innovative new products as t-PA, a clone of one of the body's own enzymes that dissolves blood clots in the treatment of severe heart attacks. Medtronic (in Minneapolis, MN), which has always been at the leading edge of technology, is a world leader in pacemakers. The same is true for Microsoft in computer software (for example, its Excel spreadsheet) and operating systems (for example, DOS and Windows), Tandem in distributed database management technology; Intel in microprocessors; Convex Computer in mini-supercomputers; and Cray Research, in supercomputers.

Creating New Products, Spin-Offs, and Start-Ups

Many successful early-stage fast-growth companies have given rise to other new ventures, both as spin-offs and as "intrapreneurial" efforts within the company. These spin-offs have often been as successful as the companies from which they were formed. For example, Tandem Computer was formed by several executives from Hewlett-Packard, which itself is considered one of the greatest entrepreneurial success stories of all time. Similarly, Data General evolved from Digital Equipment Corporation (DEC) and has become one of the latter's leading competitors in selected market segments.

An example of new ventures forming within an entrepreneurial fast-growth company is seen at Cypress Semiconductor, a $250 million company based in San Jose, California, and started by T. J. Rodgers in 1982. Although Cypress is an early-stage venture itself, the company creates separate start-up companies within the Cypress umbrella for new product lines. Each of the four companies formed over Cypress's first eight years of existence is run as a separate entity: there is a president of each company, and the employees have stock in their new venture. Apparently Cypress has benefited by this, as is evidenced by the company's average growth rate of well over 100 percent since the late 1980s. Moreover, at a time when the semiconductor industry has been hit with a severe slump, characterized by plant closings and layoffs, Cypress has expanded its manufacturing efforts by purchasing one of Control Data's factories.

Patterns of Fast Growth

Most of the quick-growing companies that I examined have followed a similar pattern of growth from start-up to further development. They enjoyed several years of spectacular growth in revenues during their early years, which put them in an attractive position for either an initial public offering (IPO) or an acquisition by a larger company. This allowed them to obtain a significant cash infusion intended to enhance further growth.

Going Public Versus Other Exit Routes

Going public is often seen as an attractive alternative not only for a company but also from the standpoint of early-stage investors (such as venture capitalists), because a ready market will then exist for the latter to get their original investment out of the business. That this can be a very profitable arrangement for investors has been evidenced by such IPOs as those for Lotus Development, Apple Computer, Compaq Computer, Microsoft, and Genentech, to name just a few.

I should not, however, overstate the importance of the IPO market as a means of "cashing out." Although IPOs generally get the greatest publicity and are best known by the public, there are other, more commonly used exit routes for companies, most notably corporate acquisitions. The number of IPOs has fluctuated significantly in the early 1990s depending upon the climate of the public equity markets, whereas the number of acquisitions has grown steadily since the early 1980s.

There have been significantly more corporate acquisitions than IPOs for venture-capital-backed companies in just about every year over the past decade.

Corporate Acquisitions

In some industries (notably biotechnology), corporate acquisitions have increasingly become the norm. In 1988, for example, according to data provided by The Wilkerson Group, there were 344 acquisitions among medical and biotechnology companies, compared to only 29 IPOs in this industry.

What is responsible for this? Since the early 1980s more than two hundred biotechnology companies have gone public, yet only a handful have made money for the public investors. Corporate acquisitions by pharmaceutical companies and companies in related industries have been successful, however, because the acquirers (who understand the technology better than does the general public) have gained valuable technologies through this process. For example, Diamond BioSensors of Ann Arbor, Michigan, which makes blood diagnostic products, was purchased in the late 1980s by Mallinckrodt, a St. Louis–based chemical company, for $30.5 million. Five years earlier, a New York–based venture capital firm, CW Group, and other investors provided Diamond BioSensors with $9 million of funding.

Venture capital firms well versed in biotechnology have recognized that entrepreneurial companies who concentrate on developing a limited number of sharply focused products that have already had some initial positive testing will be prime candidates for corporate acquisition. In such a situation, everybody benefits: the entrepreneurial company receives the corporate funding to continue its product development and commercialization; the acquirer gains new technology that can strengthen its existing product line; and the investors realize significant financial gains. This can be contrasted to the scores of upstart biotechnology companies, with poorly focused products at premature stages of development, that went public during the early 1980s. In those cases everybody lost out; many have gone out of business, while others are still—ten years later—in the product development stage, with little chance of commercial success.

Recently, several prominent acquisitions of hypergrowth companies in other industries have taken place. They include the following.

- K-mart's $320 million purchase of PACE Membership Warehouse (Aurora, CO), an operator of discount warehouse clubs
- Wal-Mart's purchase of Super Saver Warehouse Club, another operator of discount warehouse clubs
- Reebok International's $180 million acquisition of its former rival, Avia Group International (Portland, OR)
- Control Data Corporation's acquisition of VTC (Bloomington, MI), a manufacturer of high-performance integrated circuits.

Because it is difficult to obtain financial information about such companies after they have been acquired, I will not focus on them in this book.

The Mad Rush for IPOs

The tremendous success of the IPO of Apple Computer, which raised $110 million in 1980, demonstrated that the public equity markets could be receptive to IPOs of early-stage technology stocks. This was confirmed by subsequent IPOs of Vector Graphic, Altos Computer, ASK Computer Systems, Pizza Time Theatre, and Cetus. It also enabled early-stage private investors (venture capitalists) to realize that companies, especially those in high-tech industries, could receive ten or twenty times their initial investment in just two or three years, rather than five to ten years for typical venture capital investments. That prompted a stampede to the public equity markets during the 1980s.

Between 1980 and 1983 the number of new issues nearly quadrupled, while the value of those IPOs increased by ninefold. Even more dramatic is the difference between the number and value of IPOs and those only a decade earlier. In 1974, there were only 15 IPOs, which raised a total of $100 million. In 1983, 888 IPOs raised $12.6 billion.

In 1974, 15 IPOs raised $100 million. In 1983, 888 IPOs raised $12.6 billion.

It was relatively easy to go public in the early 1980s. With the dramatic increase in quantity, however, came a corresponding decrease in the quality of new issues. As Benjamin M. Rosen of Sevin Rosen Management, one of the most astute venture capitalists in the nation, noted in referring to the dramatic increase in the number of issues going public in 1983, "That was a terrible period. . . . We were all guilty. Anything that wiggled could either get venture capital or go public and did, and a lot of people are paying the price for that. But the interesting thing about that is that quality did prevail."[6]

Burgess Jamieson, general partner of Sigma Partners in San Jose, California, said, "People say power corrupts, but I think it's money that does the trick. . . . We have the symptoms of the heightening of greed among venture capitalists and entrepreneurs. I suppose greed is okay up to a point, but it's like wine. A glass is pleasant; a bottle will have a different effect."[7]

Failure Follows Success

The euphoria came to an end in 1982 with the demise of Osborne Computer. On first look, it appeared that the company had all the essential ingredients for success: a bright, articulate leader in Adam Osborne; an exciting breakthrough product in its portable computer; and an eager group of investors that included Ken Oshman, founder of ROLM, and Jack Melchor, an experienced Silicon Valley venture capitalist. Yet, the public offering that was to occur never did, as a result of problems in production, cash flow, and management. Eventually the company filed for bankruptcy amid a battery of lawsuits.

Osborne was soon followed into the bankruptcy courts by such previously highly regarded companies as Victor Technologies and Pizza Time Theatre. And other once-successful companies (such as Fortune Systems, Diasonics, Vector Graphic, Xonics, and Evotek) that had each previously received several million dollars of venture capital were struggling. These events were instrumental not only in destroying the IPO market in 1983 and 1984, especially for high-tech issues, but also in depressing the stock prices of already publicly held technology companies. Another important negative outcome was the demise of scores of smaller, newer venture capital firms.

The situation was quite similar to that of the late 1960s and early 1970s. That period had also witnessed a tremendous boom in emerging companies, many of which had well-publicized (and well-hyped) IPOs. Despite initial rises in their stock prices, many of these companies soon crashed as a result of their fundamental weaknesses. A significant potential problem in such a situation is that since there is a direct link between the public and private equity markets, episodes of unwarranted increases in the value of the stock of several corporations could have a dramatic negative impact on the venture capital industry and on entrepreneurial activity as a whole.

IPOs: The Pros and Cons

Of course, some companies have done exceedingly well after their IPOs—for example, Federal Express (Memphis, TN) in overnight delivery; Compaq Computer (Houston, TX) in personal computers; Reebok (Canton, MA) in athletic shoes; Adobe Systems (Mountain View, CA) in computer systems; and Microsoft (Redmond, WA) in computer software. Other former superstar growth companies have had dramatic declines in their stock prices after their IPOs, including Continuing Care (Canton, MA), a marketer of home health care equipment; Home Shopping Network (Clearwater, FL), a television retailer; and New World Pictures (Los Angeles, CA), a television and motion picture producer. Some, including Pizza Time Theatre, Wedtech, and Vector Graphic, have failed altogether.

IPOs have had some tremendous benefits. They have provided entrepreneurs with status as well as personal fortune, as has been the case with founders Bill Gates of Microsoft, Steve Jobs of Apple Computer, Mitchell Kapor of Lotus Development, William Poduska of Apollo Computer, and Elisabeth Claiborne Ortenberg of Liz Claiborne. They have provided a source of capital, usually at a more attractive valuation to the entrepreneur than has generally been the case for more sophisticated private investors.

There have been some significant problems, however, associated with IPOs. Specifically, they have generally resulted in a loss of control of the venture (in terms of percentage of stock ownership) for the entrepreneur. They have also been exceedingly time-consuming in terms of audits and reporting requirements and expensive, with costs starting at $250,000 and increasing with the size of the offering. In addition, they force the company to carry out its business under the careful scrutiny of public investors, who often have a much shorter time horizon than the entrepreneur or the private investors. Nonetheless, companies will often be under pressure by early-stage investors to go public in order for the latter to cash out their earlier investments.

Impact of Fast Growth: Important Summary Points

1. Growth tends to affect favorably the success of a business. But it is sustained earnings growth, not growth alone, that determines the increased value of a company.
2. Fast-growth companies open new markets and create industries (for example, McDonald's, Apple); change bureaucracy

(for example, Federal Express); create personal wealth and success (for example, The Limited, Hewlett-Packard, EDS); enhance corporate reputations (for example, Wal-Mart, Liz Claiborne, Federal Express, Nordstrom); develop innovative products and services (for example, Sun Microsystems, Genentech, Medtronic, Microsoft, Intel, Cray Research); and create new spin-offs and start-ups (for example, Hewlett-Packard, Cypress Semiconductor)

3. Typically, fast-growth companies have either gone public or have been acquired by larger corporations, even though corporate acquisitions are a more popular means of "exit" than are IPOs (especially in such industries as biotechnology).

4. There was a dramatic increase in the number and value of IPOs in the early 1980s, especially among technology companies.

5. Although many IPOs increased dramatically in value shortly after going public, several of them eventually collapsed as a result of weak business fundamentals.

3

High-Tech Growth

When we talk about successful fast-growth companies, we often think of such high-profile technology companies as Apple, Microsoft, and Genentech. This chapter examines the high-tech companies that have been growing at phenomenal rates. (Chapter 4 explores the growth of low-tech companies.)

Classic High-Tech Hypergrowth: The Computer and Office Automation Industry

Since the early 1980s, high tech has become fashionable, and high-tech stocks—especially in the computer industry—have become the glamour stocks on Wall Street that typify the entrepreneurial dream. Apple Computer, which was founded by whiz kids Steven Jobs and Stephen Wozniak in Cupertino, California, has grown from a start-up company in the mid-1970s to a profitable and highly innovative $7 billion company. Of course, Apple is not alone in this regard, as evidenced by the success of Compaq, Sun Microsystems, Conner Peripherals, and Cypress Semiconductor, among others.

Ralph Gomory, the former head of research at IBM and current president of the Alfred P. Sloan Foundation, predicts that computers will be one hundred times cheaper by 2010.[1] This suggests that we are still at an early stage of development in the information revolution, even though (according to Link Resources) there are more than 40 million home computers in the United States, or about one for every three adults. Over the coming years, informa-

Computer Sales 1991

Segment	Size of Segment	Industry Leaders	Market Share
Personal computers	$68 billion	IBM	15.6%
		Apple	9.7%
		Hewlett-Packard	1.6%
		Digital Equipment	0.2%
		Others	72.9%
Mainframes	$30 billion	IBM	58.1%
		Unisys	6.9%
		NEC	5.6%
		Others	23.9%
Minicomputers	$29 billion	IBM	19.6%
		Digital Equipment	15.6%
		Hewlett-Packard	5.5%
		Bull	5.2%
		Others	54.1%
Workstations	$6 billion	Sun Microsystems	27.5%
		Hewlett-Packard	26.0%*
		Digital Equipment	20.5%
		IBM	2.4%
		Others	23.6%

*Includes revenues from Apollo Computer, which was acquired by Hewlett-Packard in 1989.
Source: Dataquest.

tion will be processed faster and our lives will be affected more dramatically than we can ever imagine.

It has been predicted that computers will be one hundred times cheaper by 2010.

Fast-Growth Computer Companies

In recent years, approximately 30 to 40 percent of the *Inc.* 100 companies (the fastest-growing small public companies in this country) have been in computers and related industries. More impressive than that is that more than a dozen start-up companies

Sales Per Employee (As a Measure of Productivity), 1990

Digital Equipment Corp.	$104,375
Hewlett-Pacckard	143,837
IBM	182,305
Sun Microsystems	214,638
Apple Computer	451,648

in the computer industry also have attained *Fortune 500* status since the early 1970s. Such success stories, which include Compaq Computer (Houston, TX), Tandem Computer (Cupertino, CA), Sun Microsystems (Mountain View, CA), Seagate Technology (Scotts Valley, CA), Intel (Santa Clara, CA), and Cray Research (Minneapolis, MN), have been about more than companies; they have been about the emergence of industries. They have also paved the way for newer, smaller start-ups—such as Adobe Systems (Mountain View, CA), Chips & Technologies (San Jose, CA), and Cypress Semiconductor (San Jose, CA)—to become the success stories of tomorrow.

WORKSTATIONS. The growth of these high-tech companies has been nothing short of sensational. Sun Microsystems, for example, which began in 1982, is now a $4 billion-a-year company, and a leader in technical workstations with nearly a 30 percent market share. Under the leadership of founder and CEO Scott McNealy, Sun has been the leading company in its industry in sales growth, averaging more than 100 percent growth per year during the late 1980s (versus the industry average of just over 10 percent) and the second leading company in its industry in earnings per share (EPS) growth, with an average of nearly 90 percent per year (versus a loss for the average company in this industry). To state another way, Sun's EPS growth has been more than twice as high as that of IBM, Hewlett-Packard, and Digital Equipment combined, while its sales growth has been about triple the rate of those three giants in the computer industry.

Sun's early 1990s strategy is similar to the one IBM used when it created the standard design for personal computers with its PC. Sun has created a hardware design, called SPARC, and is inviting other computer companies to build clones. By standardizing the design, it will force the manufacturers to compete on price and performance, which can be advantageous to Sun. In addition, Sun has become a recognized leader in the workstation segment of the computer industry, thereby prompting software developers to write programs for the Sun models. There are more than two thousand software applications for the SPARC architecture, many of which have been written by such major software companies as Lotus, Ashton-Tate, and WordPerfect. The more software that is available, the more workstations Sun can sell, thereby making it even more appealing for software companies to continue to develop applications for Sun. Sun also stays ahead of its competition by offering new products every six months or so, at correspondingly lower prices. These developments are likely to result in the continued growth of this innovative leader in workstations, a firm that is merely ten years old.

Interestingly, it was Apollo Computer, not Sun Microsystems, that pioneered the workstation in the early 1980s. Led by William Poduska, Apollo grew dramatically during its early years. When it went public in 1983, it has a valuation of four times its annual revenues. Shortly thereafter Apollo's lead in the marketplace began to dwindle, largely as a result of Sun's strategy of engineering its system for AT & T's Unix operating system. Apollo began to lose both market share and money. In 1989 Apollo was sold to Hewlett-Packard for $476 million, a value less than its sales for 1988.

PERSONAL COMPUTERS. Compaq Computer's early success under founder and CEO Rod Canion was just as remarkable, if not more so, as that of Sun Microsystems. Compaq, which began in 1983 (when it generated an astounding $111 million in sales in its first full year of operation, largely because of the strong relationships it established with its retailer network), became a $2 billion company by the time it was only five years old and nearly doubled in size in the next five years to its 1993 level of nearly $4 billion. As of 1993 its net profit margin exceeds that of its biggest rival, IBM, and its EPS growth is the highest in the industry, having increased at a 40 percent rate since 1988. Its return on equity has been approximately 30 percent per year, which is comparable to that of

Apple, and about that of Hewlett-Packard and Sun Microsystems combined.

Unfortunately success can often come to a quick halt, especially for high-visibility, high-growth, high-tech businesses such as Compaq. For example, 1991 was a tough year for Compaq, which faced its first-ever layoffs, shedding 12 percent of its twelve thousand workers. Perhaps Compaq did not take the clone makers seriously enough. Lost market share prompted the ouster of founder Rod Canion, who was replaced as CEO by Eckhard Pfeiffer.

COMPUTER SOFTWARE. Microsoft (of Redmond, WA) is considered by many to be the leading computer software company in the world. It was founded in 1975 by William Gates III along with a schoolmate, Paul Allen, who wrote a version of the BASIC programming language to run on early microcomputers. Earlier, at the ripe old age of fifteen, Gates, who began working with computers in the seventh grade, had formed a company (called Traf-O-Data) with Allen to analyze auto traffic patterns in Seattle using a computer that had the recently introduced Intel 8008 microprocessor chip.

In the early 1980s Microsoft acquired the disk operating system (DOS) to be used on IBM personal computers and their compatibles. Today, more than 120 million personal computers use Microsoft's MS-DOS software. Microsoft's average annual growth in sales and profits were approximately 60 percent between 1988 and 1993, and its operating system, word processing, spreadsheet, and data base products have been huge successes. Microsoft outsells its three largest competitors—Lotus, Novell, and WordPerfect—combined; its market valuation is comparable to that of IBM. Consequently its investors and managers have

Market Share for Software 1991

Microsoft	30.0%
Lotus Development	10.9%
Novell	8.4%
WordPerfect	7.0%
Borland	6.6%
95 others combined	37.1%

benefited by the company's success. The most notable individual success is the thirty-seven-year-old Gates, the largest single shareholder, whose 45 percent stake in the company was worth $350 million when Microsoft went public and over $6 billion in 1993—not bad for a dropout from Harvard who taught himself computer programming as a teenager.

Will the Growth of the Computer Industry Continue?

According to **Venture Economics,** there was more than a 60 percent decline in venture capital investments in the computer hardware industry during the last half of the 1980s. Such declines in early-stage investments in computer companies could indicate a slowdown in the growth of the computer industry. Several case examples will illustrate why this decline in such investments has occurred. Symbolics (of Cambridge, MA), a manufacturer of artificial intelligence computers, went public in 1984 at $6 per share. By 1986 the stock price had increased to more than $15. The next three years, however, were marked by losses and a restructuring, and consequently the stock dropped to below $3 per share.

Perhaps the best recent example of companies in this industry not reaching their expected potential involves the formation of Stardent, a manufacturer of graphics workstations for scientists and engineers. Stardent is the result of the merger of two of the best financed, yet most disappointing, computer start-ups in history—Ardent Computer, which raised $108 million thanks in part to the backing of Kubota, Ltd. (Japan), and its former rival, Stellar Computer, which raised $60 million. As of 1993, a public offering for Stardent may still be far away.

There are other reasons for the declining level of investments in computer hardware. One of the problems in the computer hardware industry is that most of the niches are already filled; moreover, those niches that remain will probably not offer the explosive growth opportunities of such earlier niche players as Apple, Microsoft, or Compaq. In addition, the life span of products has shortened dramatically. Computer companies are replacing product lines every one or two years, rather than every four to five years, as they had previously done.

A problem in the computer hardware industry is that most of the exploxive-growth niches are already filled.

Perhaps the biggest concern among venture capitalists is the risk/return balance of such investments. As was seen with Ardent Computer and with Stellar Computer, the start-up capital could be enormous: up to $100 million or more. The investors of these funds do not even know if there will be a product; even if one is developed, the market can be uncertain and the competition fierce.

WHAT'S NEXT? One of the biggest question marks in the computer industry in the 1990s is Steve Jobs's latest venture, NeXT, Inc. The company is well capitalized: early-stage investments came from Jobs ($7 million), Stanford University ($658,000), and H. Ross Perot ($20 million). More recently, Canon invested $100 million for 16 percent of the company, giving NeXT a valuation of $625 million before it sold its first unit. Yet at a Technologic Partners Conference in 1988, a majority of the high-tech entrepreneurs and investors who were polled predicted that the company would not reach the $500 million mark in sales. It may be difficult to dispute the logic of their forecast; however, many would be reluctant to bet against the intellect, the vision, and the motivation of Jobs.

Nonetheless, NeXT has been laden with problems ever since the company was founded in 1985. After several delays the coal-black NeXT computer was introduced, but not until 1988. Even then, it did not sell well because the software was not done. Fortunately, Jobs was savvy enough to listen to his customers. When they wanted a floppy disk drive, he added one; when they wanted lower prices, he lowered them. The result: sales of $30 million in 1990, $130 million in 1991, and $140 million (with a small profit!) in 1992.

Throughout most of its history, NeXT has tried to take on Apple's Macintosh and Sun Microsystems' work stations, but to no avail. It made a significant decision to shift direction in 1992 after finally recognizing that it should get out of the computer hardware business in order to concentrate on software development (its NextStep operating system). Unfortunately, NeXT had already invested about seven years and $100 million in hardware development. If NeXT does emerge as a success, it will likely come from its software sales.

UPS AND DOWNS IN THE COMPUTER INDUSTRY. Even the great companies in this industry have their ups and downs. For example, the stock price of IBM, which in the mid 1980s, was referred to as "the bluest of the blue chips," has declined by 70 percent since 1986. Just as dramatic is the case of Digital Equipment Corporation (DEC), another leading company in the computer industry. In 1986 *Fortune* magazine named Ken Olsen, DEC's founder and CEO, "America's most successful entrepreneur." After all, Olsen had taken DEC from a start-up company to a $14 billion global power over a thirty-year period, largely as a result of technical superiority and Olsen's decentralized management style. Olsen, however, was ousted in 1992: DEC was accused of having lost sight of its customers, while its stock price had lost more than 85 percent of its value (dropping from a high of more than $200 per share).

Health Care

The health care and biotechnology areas have recently become prominent growth industries; 15 to 25 percent of the *Inc.* 100 companies have been in these areas over the last few years. The 1980s and 1990s have witnessed the tremendous growth of such health care procedures as electronic shock wave lithotripsy (ESWL) for breaking up kidney stones, magnetic resonance imaging (MRI), cardiac catherization, coronary arteriography, and phototherapy. Consequently several venture capital firms have been eager to invest in companies in such sectors of the health care industry as outpatient clinics, health maintenance, and medical diagnostics. This has been prompted by the successes of several companies in the health care field that went public during this time.

Nellcor (of Hayward, CA) is a manufacturer of patient monitoring systems. Nellcor raised $75,000 through self-funding and $1 million through private sources, followed by a $3 million investment (for a 35 percent ownership position) by Technology Venture Investors, a prominent venture capital firm. In 1983 Nellcor's first product—the N-100, which monitors oxygen in a patient's arterial blood during surgery—was brought to market. As of 1993 the N-100 is found in more than half the seven thousand hospitals in this country, which has resulted in Nellcor capturing about two-thirds of this industry while growing at a compounded annual growth rate of more than 100 percent over recent years.

An Aging Population Provides Opportunities

Several entrepreneurial companies have taken advantage of the shift in age of the U.S. population. Such industries as health care management, outpatient care, rehabilitation centers, nursing homes, and home health care have not only grown substantially but have become some of the fastest-*changing* industries in this country. For example, HealthCare Compare (of Downers Grove, IL), which implements health care cost management services, and HealthSouth Rehabilitation (of Birmingham, AL), a developer and operator of rehabilitation centers, are two companies that are less than ten years old and have had compounded annual growth rates of more than 100 percent between 1988 and 1992.

Home Health Care Experiences Significant Growth

One notable area of growth in health care and delivery has been in home health care, which doubled in size between 1988 and 1992 and, according to Frost & Sullivan, is expected to double again by 1997. Home respiratory care is close to being a $1 billion industry; diagnostic cardiac units is a $100 million business; intravenous infusion systems are a $50 million business; and breathing monitors is a $20 million industry. One of the more interesting companies in this sector is MEDphone Corporation (of Paramus, NJ), which manufacturers a phone-linked computer system that enables health care professionals to make "electronic house calls." The cost to the patient is around $7,500 to purchase the unit and

$300 to $500 per month to lease. The device, which is automatically connected via a telephone to a hospital or a physician's office, has electrodes that can be hooked up to a patient's chest. Thus, the health professional can deliver an electronic jolt directly to a patient over the telephone line. MEDphone is now developing a cellular telephone model that will be marketed to police, fire, and ambulance services.

Several other companies have developed (or are currently developing) home health care services. For example, MiniMed Technologies (in Sylmar, CA) and Infusaid (in Boston, MA) plan to market small pumps that can be surgically implanted in patients to dispense insulin in a controlled manner throughout the day. Tokos Medical Corporation, which public in 1990, has a product called Term Guard, which allows for home monitoring of uterine activity for pregnant women in danger of a premature delivery; the product cost the patient $75 a day, as compared to the $600 daily cost for monitoring in a hospital. Buddy Systems (of Northbrook, IL) rents computer consoles to postsurgical patients at a cost of $30 a day; the consoles monitor vital signs and transmit the information to the hospital via telephone. All of these products allow patients to receive quality care at home, generally at a much lower cost than a typical hospital stay.

Health Care Companies Going Public

One measure of the success of companies in the health care field is that over the past few years, several have gone public. In addition to HealthCare Compare and HealthSouth Rehabilitation, which were discussed earlier, these include New England Critical Care (of Marborough, MA), a home health care company; HMSS (of Houston, TX), a home intravenous treatment company; and Redicare (of Newport Beach, CA), an operator of outpatient medical centers.

Of course, not all ventures have achieved their expected level of success. An example is Diasonics, which manufactures nuclear magnetic resonance imaging machines. It was launched with the assistance of three venture capital firms (F. Eberstadt & Co., Hambrecht & Quist, and L. F. Rothschild Unterberg and Towbin) that paid approximately $1 per share for eight hundred thousand shares of the company. The company went public in 1983 for $22 a share, raising more than $100 million in the process. Within a few years, however, Diasonics ran into trouble and lost most of its value.

Overall, nonetheless, the early success of companies in the health care field have prompted the growth of ongoing investments. Such investments are a strong signal that this industry is on target for continued growth. Due to the technical nature of medical care, several venture capital firms have become specialists in the industry or in just one portion of it. For example, CW Group, a New York–based firm, specializes in health care and biological sciences. CW recently invested in Athena Neurosciences (San Carlos, CA), which is developing diagnostics and therapeutics for Alzheimer's disease and other disorders of the central nervous system, and National Rehabilitation Centers (Nashville, TN), an operator of rehabilitation centers.

The Growth of the Biotechnology Industry

In the early 1980s, biotechnology was one of the glamour industries among private and public investors. Venture capitalists David and Isaac Blech, for example, have funded about a half dozen biotech companies. The biggest financial success among their biotech investments has been Genetic Systems (of Seattle, WA), a pioneer in the application of antibodies. In addition to their investment in the company, the Blechs helped raise $48.5 million in subsequent limited partnerships, private placements, and public offerings. Genetic Systems went public in 1981 for $1.25 per share. Five years later, Bristol Myers purchased the company for stock worth $10.50 per share, netting the Blech brothers $30 million.

Biotech stocks became hot issues on Wall Street. Genentech, of course, is the best-known story in this industry. On the day the company went public on October 14, 1980, its stock soared from an IPO price of $35 to $89. Soon companies like Cetus, Biogen, Amgen, and Centocor, were seen as attractive investment opportunities by public investors, even though most investors knew virtually nothing about the technologies of these companies.

Shortly thereafter there was a major consolidation in the biotechnology industry, with dozens of companies being acquired by larger chemical and pharmaceutical companies—Hybritech by Eli Lilly, and DNAX Research Institute by Schering-Plough, among others—and many more failing to live up to their potential. Liposome (of Princeton, NJ), for example, was launched in 1981 to develop an effective drug delivery systems using liposomes, which are water-filled, fatty membranes. The company, however, spent $65 million over its first 10 years without having developed a marketable product.

Today in Biotechnology

In 1993 there are about eleven hundred companies in the biotech industry. According to a recent study by Ernst & Young, less than 25 percent of these companies are profitable. Most of them do not even have a product yet.

There is, however, tremendous promise in this industry. Current sales of biotech-based drugs are between $1 billion and $2 billion annually; that should triple by 2000. Yet public sentiment has not been supportive of this industry, probably because of promises of too much, too soon. As noted recently by James Swartz, general partner of Accel Partners (of Princeton, NJ), a venture capital firm that has invested in this industry, "It took more than a decade before the transistor was embodied into any significant commercial product and another decade before transistor-based circuits were applied to computers. Drugs and pharmaceuticals, even the non-biotech types, have a development cycle of 10 to 15 years."[2]

Consequently venture capitalists, who by nature maintain a long-term perspective, have recently made significant investments in biotechnology. For example, Biosource Genetics Corporation (of Vacaville, CA), founded in 1987, creates complex chemicals through genetic engineering. Its first product is melanin, the pigment that gives human skin its color. The product has tremendous commercial applications, as it could be used in sunscreens to provide more effective protection against skin cancer. Biosource was backed by two scientists/venture capitalists, Helen Leong and David Berliner, who had earlier helped launch Advanced Polymer Systems (of Redwood City, CA).

One thing is clear about the newer biotech companies. Unlike the early 1980s, when start-up and early-stage biotechnology companies were extremely diversified—for example, Cetus Corporation in its early years—the successful new biotech companies are narrowly focused. For example, Applied Microbiology (of Brooklyn, NY), which has focused on just two products, has had corporate sponsorship from such American pharmaceutical giants as Pfizer and Merck. Applied Microbiology's alliance with Pfizer has enabled the smaller venture to develop a mouthwash, which Pfizer will market, that contains an antibacterial agent to help prevent and treat gum disease.

Unlike the early 1980s, when start-up and early-stage biotechnology companies were extremely diversified, the successful new biotech companies of today are narrowly focused.

There is an important point related to the cyclical nature of this industry. In industries such as biotechnology, which can quickly come into and go out of favor, timing is critical when it comes to raising capital. As noted by Ronald Cape, cofounder of Cetus Corporation, "The time to take hors d'oeuvres is when they're passing them around."[3]

Telecommunications

The breakup of AT & T in 1984 and the dramatic growth of such sectors of the telecommunications industry as cellular communications and communications networks have been responsible for scores of successful fast-growth companies in this industry. This is evidenced by recent IPOs of companies in the areas of cellular telephone systems (for example, Cellular Communications), communications equipment for workstations (for example, Microcom), multifunction communication networks (for example, Network Equipment Technologies—business based in Redwood, CA, that was ranked first on the 1990 *Inc.* 100 list due to its 400% growth rate from 1985 to 1989), and pay telephones (for example, Intellicall). Each of these companies was founded after 1983 and is typical of the large number of telecommunications companies included in the Inc. 100.

Among hot growth companies at an earlier stage of development is Intermedia Communications of Florida (ICI), a Tampa-based company founded in 1987. ICI, which raised $20 million in an IPO in 1992, provides corporate customers with an alternative way to connect to long distance carriers. The company has already set up fiber optic networks throughout the state of Florida. Successes like that of ICI have prompted several venture capital firms to invest in telecommunications companies, which suggests that this industry will continue to grow. A few firms have become so specialized that they invest only in this industry. One such example is Communications Ventures (of Menlo Park, CA), which was started in 1987. The firm tends to limit its investments to telecommunications companies in the seed and start-up stages. Communications Ventures generally invests approximately $500,000 in such ventures, as it did with its recent investment in Pair Gain Technologies, a company based in Torrance, CA, that has created specialized digital communication lines for telephone companies.

Green Industries

Another recent growth industry that has had its share of technology companies is environmental waste management. Entrepreneurial companies in this field often have greater growth prospects and offer more controlled risks than other types of companies.

Demand for environmental products and services has grown as governmental regulations have become stricter. Consequently, investors have been eager to take part in the growth of these companies. For example, Burr Egan Deleage & Company recently invested in Galson Remediation Corporation, based in Syracuse, NY. Galson has a patented chemical treatment technology to clean up dioxins and PCBs that offers tremendous advantages compared to incineration, the alternative method. Similarly, In-Process Technologies (of Sunnyvale, CA), a developer of a patented industrial waste processing system that converts toxic gases to nontoxic materials, has received approximately $2 million in venture capital funding.

Of course some investors exert caution when it comes to funding environmental companies, partly because of their lack of knowledge or experience in this industry, and partly because of regulatory concerns. It is always dangerous to invest in an industry in which demand is dependent upon government regulation; just as regulation has promoted the growth of environmental and waste management companies, so could regulatory changes negatively affect the long-term outlook for this industry.

High Tech and High Growth . . .
But Not Always High Profit

There has been tremendous growth of high-tech companies in recent years. Apple, Compaq, Sun Microsystems, and Genentech, are just a few examples to illustrate this.

Of course, growth alone will not ensure long-term success for these technology companies. The stories of the successes and failures of fast-growth companies in the computer industry suggest that being in an attractive, visible, high-growth industry is not enough. More important are the characteristics of the particular company in a given industry. One fast-growth company can be a tremendous success, whereas another can be a dismal failure. For example, although there was a boom in the computer industry in the early 1980s (the time during which Apple became a success) Fortune Systems lost 90 percent of its market value from 1983 to 1984. More extreme is the case of computer maker Vector Graphic, which, like Apple, grew rapidly during the early 1980s. Although Vector's sales jumped an average of 15,000 percent—from $400,000 in 1977 to $25 million in 1981—in the years just prior to its initial public offering, it could not sustain its rapid growth and eventually filed for bankruptcy in 1985.

Growth alone will not ensure long-term success for technology companies.

In the biotechnology area, many investors were turned on by the high growth and the hype surrounding biotech companies in the early 1980s. Most of the companies that were touted by brokers because of their "proprietary positions," their "technological capabilities," or their "superior product potential," however, never lived up to their expectations. In fact, investing in biotechnology (rather than investing in *quality* biotechnology companies such as Genentech or Amgen) turned out to be a great way to lose money during the decade.

A Look Ahead

There has certainly been tremendous growth among technology companies. Several low-tech companies (often in so-called low-tech regions), however, have experienced comparable growth and, in many cases, far superior returns for their investors. Chapter 4 examines such low-tech, fast-growth companies.

High-Tech Growth: Important Summary Points

1. Some examples of high-tech fast-growth successes in computers and office automation are in selected niches such as workstations (for example, Sun Microsystems), personal computers (for example, Compaq), and computer software (for example, Microsoft).
2. In the late 1980s and early 1990s there has been a steady decline in venture capital investments in the computer hardware industry.
3. The health care industry has benefited tremendously from social and demographic changes, such as the aging population and the popularity of home health care.
4. Selected fast-growth niches in health care and biotechnology include cost management (for example, HealthCare Compare), rehabilitation centers (for example, HealthSouth Rehab), patient monitoring (for example, Nellcor), home health care (for example, MEDphone, MiniMed, Tokos), and biotechnology (for example, Genentech, Amgen).
5. Other fast-growing technology industries include telecommunications (prompted by the breakup of AT & T) and environmental concerns (prompted by regulations).

4

Low-Tech Growth

High Tech Is Not Synonomous with High Growth

From some of the success stories described in the previous chapter, one may be seduced into believing that economic development and employment growth has been, and will continue to be, solely in high-tech industries. This is clearly not the case. In fact, according to management guru Peter Drucker, between the mid-1960s and the mid-1980s high-tech companies accounted for only 5 million (out of the total of approximately 35 million) new jobs in this country—or the same number lost by Fortune 500 companies over that period.[1] Moreover, some of the biggest flops in the 1980s and early 1990s have been high-tech, high-growth businesses such as Columbia Data Products, Vector Graphic, and Kaypro. Thus we must look beyond the "hot" growth industries, especially in the high-tech area, to the specific characteristics of a particular company within an industry to determine if it is a potential star performer.

Low Tech, High Growth: Catfish and Carts

Of course, high technology businesses are a vital part of our economic growth. Perhaps more typical of fast-growth companies nationwide, however, is Delta Pride Catfish of Indianola, Mississippi. Neither the company nor its location would suggest anything remotely high tech. Yet Delta Pride, which was founded in 1981, is a profitable enterprise that generates over $100 million in sales a year.

Similarly, consider Carts of Colorado (of Commerce City, CO) which has become the leading seller of pushcarts in the United States. In 1984, brothers Stan and Dan Gallery (who were in their twenties at the time) invested $3,600 in New York City to buy a couple of hot dog carts, which they brought to Colorado. They generated $300 to $400 per day per cart at construction sites and $1,200 to $1,500 per day per cart at weekend outdoor events, with food costs equal to approximately 20 percent of sales. Feeling that they could be more profitable if they built their own carts, the brothers did so at a cost of approximately $750 apiece. Before long, they had a fifteen-cart fleet. Due to problems encountered with the health department of Denver, they were forced to redesign their carts with new cooling units, a high-capacity burner, and hot and cold running water. The Gallery brothers were soon approached by a customer who wanted to purchase a cart. They priced the cart at $5,200 and, to their surprise, received an order from the customer for three carts. Over the next few years, these vendors-turned-manufacturers sold "mobile vending sites" to such respected corporate clients as Coca-Cola, Marriott, Disney, Pizza Hut, and Oscar Mayer. Carts of Colorado is generating about $10 million in revenues annually from the sale of carts.

Defying the Odds in Low-Tech Industries

Anyone who is remotely interested in technology products has to admire the high-tech companies that have created not only products but entire industries. Yet it can be even more interesting to examine the successful companies that have defied the odds by launching businesses in highly competitive low-technology industries. Just consider the success of such companies as Bandag (Muscatine, IA), a tire retreader; Safety Kleen (of Elgin, IL), which develops cleaning systems for parts and tools; and Loctite (Hartford, CT), an adhesives company. Each of these high-growth, low-tech companies is generating about $500 million per year in revenues and has been doing so very profitably (with net margins of more than 10 percent) in what some people refer to as unattractive industries.

Obviously stores were selling women's clothing before The Limited came into existence, and they were selling toys long before

Toys 'R' Us entered the picture. Yet such specialty retailers have been incredible successes in the 1980s and 1990s. High-tech lovers may be disheartened to find that the *Inc.* 500 and *Inc.* 100 lists have included—in addition to the high-tech superstars—public relations firms, photographers, printers, photocopying companies, skateboard manufacturers, tobacco distributors, and recreational vehicle dealers, all of which have grown at much faster rates than most high-tech start-ups in Silicon Valley. Service companies are particularly appealing for their investment value, since they can be profitable almost immediately. Technology and manufacturing companies, in contrast, generally are not, due to their high start-up costs.

Some Blockbusters

There are countless examples to support the notion that the *real* growth in the U.S. economy has come from rather mundane industries, often in what are thought of as low-tech locations. A good example would be Blockbuster Entertainment (of Fort Lauderdale, FL), a nearly billion-dollar-per-year operator of video rental stores that controls 15 percent of the U.S. market. Blockbuster, which is ten times larger than its next-largest competitor, has grown under the leadership of H. Wayne Huizinga, who had earlier built Waste Management Corporation into the nation's largest trash hauler. (He has also since been awarded a major league baseball franchise, much to the dismay of myself and my fellow residents of the Tampa–St. Petersburg area, who lost out in the bid to Huizinga's Miami group.) Huizinga invested $18 million in Blockbuster between 1986 and 1987, when the company was a small Dallas-based chain of stores. Within months it grew from 20 stores to 130, and it has since grown by an additional tenfold.

The success of Blockbuster is largely attributable to recurring revenue streams from the rental of video cassettes. The company could buy cassettes for $40 apiece and then rent them out for $3. After thirteen rentals, which can take just a few weeks, each cassette generates attractive profits. This is essentially the same concept that Huizinga was using at Waste Management: the company would make money from renting out trash bins, many of which had been put out on the streets a decade earlier and are still generating revenues, without any expenditures on them.

Blockbuster Entertainment is not the only blockbuster among low-tech businesses. Other success stories among so-called mundane industries would include the following:

- Rocking Horse Childcare Centers (Cherry Hill, NJ), an operator of day care centers
- Cash America Investments (Fort Worth, TX), an operator of pawnshops
- One Price Clothing Stores (Duncan, SC), an apparel retailer
- Rally's (Louisville, KY), an operator of drive-through restaurants

Each of the above companies has grown by a compounded annual rate of more than 100 percent from the late 1980s to the early 1990s.

As noted earlier, however, fast growth does not necessarily translate into success; several of the fastest-growing companies in the nation, which would fit very nicely on the above list of low-tech "superstars," have had their share of problems. For example, Silk Greenhouse (Tampa, FL), a retailer of artificial flowers and plants, and WTD Industries (Portland, OR), a lumber processing company, are just two examples of businesses that have recently experienced dramatic declines in their stock prices due to nonexistent earnings.

Social and Demographic Trends Provide Opportunities for the Growth of Low-Tech Businesses

Food for Thought

A significant growth sector in our economy is in restaurant chains, as evidenced by Eateries (Oklahoma City, OK), which develops and manages full-service restaurants, and Discus (Bloomington, MN), which develops and operates Fuddruckers, a chain of hamburger restaurants. The 100 percent annual growth rates of these two restaurant firms have been largely a response to the migration of people to high-growth poulation centers, as well as the emergence of dual career households.

Of course, not all such restaurant chains have been successful. Kelly Johnson, which was a $95 million company in 1984, went bankrupt a year later when it overestimated the market for Mexican food. Thus social trends provide a company with an opportunity; however, Part II of this book makes clear, it takes much more than merely an opportunity for the business to succeed.

Catering to the Dual Career Household

Approximately 50 percent of all families in the early 1990s can be considered dual career (that is, they are headed by two employed adults). This number is likely to increase to approximately 75 percent by 2000 or shortly thereafter. These dual career households have been largely responsible for the explosive growth of Liz Claiborne, which makes high-quality but affordable clothing for professional women. Liz Claiborne realized the needs of business and professional women at a time women were entering the work force in record numbers; the company took advantage of this emerging trend and practically created an industry around it. The result for stockholders who purchased shares in the company at its IPO in 1981 was a 3,400 increase in the value of their stock—twelve times better than the performance of the overall stock market during a booming bull market–over the course of nine years. Moreover, parents in the dual career households have begun having families, which has certainly helped Toys 'R' Us, with its huge selection of toys for kids, and Kinder-Care Learning Centers, the nation's first day care chain (although, as noted in Chapter 1, Kinder-Care has faced a host of problems since the late 1980s).

Jocks and Reeboks

The fitness craze, which has also been readily seen among young professional couples, resulted in the success of Nike during the late 1970s and early 1980s and later in the explosive growth of Reebok and LA Gear. Investors in LA Gear saw their stock appreciate fourteenfold over a four-year period subsequent to its IPO in 1986.

Baby Boomers

America has 76 million members of the baby-boom generation. Baby boomers have been characterized as *prosumers*, a name meant to identify them as more proactive than mere passive consumers. This market has helped the home supplies stores, which target either do-it-yourselfers or, in the case of the less handy types who simply want to save contractors' markups on materials, the buy-it-yourselfers. Home Depot (Atlanta, GA), with annual sales of about $7 billion, has been a superstar in this industry. A typical Home Depot store generates more than $20 million in sales annually ($400,000 per week), with net profit margins of about 4 percent, as compared to the 1 percent to 2 percent margins of its competitors. Of course not every home supplies company will be as successful as Home Depot, as evidenced by the failure of Mr. How, a division of Service Merchandise, which folded in 1986.

Wal-Mart Leads the Way Among Low-Tech Superstars

Many of the fast-growth companies have grown dramatically through successful retailer expansion efforts, particularly when they have undertaken a niche strategy. (I will discuss this at greater length in Chapter 5.) The classic entrepreneurial success story among retailers is, of course, Wal-Mart, founded by the late Sam Walton. Although the leading business publications love to point out how the success of this company brought considerable wealth to Walton and his family, it is much more important to point out how the success of Walton and his associates has brought huge wealth to the public investors in Wal-Mart. As of the beginning of 1993, Wal-Mart had the second highest market valuation of all corporations in the United States.[2]

Wal-Mart itself does not represent a new idea in retailing. The company is a discount retailer, based in Bentonville, Arkansas, rather than one of the nation's high-growth cities (such as San Diego, Tampa, Phoenix, or Austin). Wal-Mart grew from a $45 million business to a $1.6 billion business during the 1970s, and then to a $26 billion business during the 1980s and to a $52 billion business today, primarily through opening up stores in secondary market locations throughout the South. Wal-Mart's sensational growth has skyrocketed the company into the number one spot among all retailers. Between 1988 and 1992 Wal-Mart's average growth in sales, earnings per share (EPS), and return on equity (ROE) were above 30 percent, two to three times the averages for its industry. Each of those performance measures is comparable to that for Apple Computer, one of the superstar performers in the personal computer industry, during the same time period.

The Best of the Rest

Wal-Mart is now considered a blue-chip company, having grown well beyond an early-stage venture. There are a few other successes that are not too far behind Wal-Mart. For example, The Limited, (of Columbus, OH), the specialty retailer of women's clothing founded by Leslie Wexner, has had even more impressive statistics. During the 1980s The Limited's return for its investors were the highest of any retailer. The company, which is now a $7 billion-per-year business, has increased its sales, EPS, and ROE each by an average of about 40 percent between 1983 and 1992; these are about three times the industry average and better than any other major apparel retailer.

Similarly, Toys 'R' Us, a $7 billion retailer of toys and games based in Paramus, New Jersey, has had an average ROE of more than 20 percent between 1983 and 1992. Toys 'R' Us recently opened a $40 million six-hundred-thousand-square-foot distribution center in Rialto, California, that can accommodate eighty-thousand pallets. The center can hold 45 percent more merchandise than the company's existing warehouses, although it takes up only 70 percent of the space. Laser scanners identify the cartons for easy access to merchandise, allowing the company to get the toys out to the stores faster while keeping handling costs low. The result is that Toys 'R' Us can offer its merchandise to customers at much lower prices than its competitors, resulting in increased sales.

These success stories are indicative of such other fast-growth specialty retailers as Circuit City Stores (Richmond, VA), a $3 billion retailer of electronics whose average EPS grew by about 30 percent—or about triple the industry average—between 1988 and 1992, and The Gap (San Bruno, CA), a $3 billion apparel retailer that, despite recent problems with overly optimistic inventory levels, also increased its EPS by an average of about 30 percent during the same five years.

More Niche Strategies in Retailing

Other smaller specialty retailers that have followed a niche strategy, focusing on a clearly defined target market, have grown at an equally rapid pace. (This will be discussed in more detail in Chapter 5.) For example, Office Depot (Boca Raton, FL), an office supplies retailer founded in 1986, generates nearly $2 billion in annual sales. Egghead, a software retailer based in Bothell, Washington (near Microsoft's headquarters), that went public four years after opening its first computer software retail store in 1984, has grown to about 140 times its original size of $5 million. Businessland, a billion-dollar business based in San Jose, California, and CompuAdd, a somewhat smaller business based in Austin, Texas, are two microcomputer retailers founded in 1982 that have also achieved early success in this industry. Bill Hayden, sole shareholder of privately held CompuAdd, concentrated primarily on cost and price to expand a mail-order computer retailer from a start-up in 1982 to a $100 million company in just five years, with growth continuing since that time. CompuAdd has been a leader in terms of cost efficiency and productivity, with an average of $400,000 in sales per employee.

Dell Computer, CompuAdd's major competitor and a neighbor in Austin, also achieved early success in its mail-order computer retail business. The company went public after three years in business in 1988 amid a tremendous amount of hype. Despite its sensational growth, Dell has had its share of trouble. For example, believing that sales would continue to grow at their meteoric pace and that its costs for parts would continue to increase, Dell made the mistake of loading up on inventory toward the end of 1988. As sales slowed and the prices for the parts actually declined, it took about a year for Dell to sell off the excess inventory at sharply discounted prices.

How Have Retailers Fared in Recent Years?

During the last half of the 1980s, several major retailers went bankrupt (for example, Federated-Allied, which owns Bloomingdale's, Abraham & Strauss, and Jordan Marsh) or have been laden with enormous debt as a result of leveraged buyouts (for example, Macy's). As noted recently by Jerome Chazen, CEO of Liz Claiborne, which supplies women's apparel to many of these troubled stores, "I've been in this business for 40 years and this is the most disquieting time I've ever seen."[3]

Nonetheless, during this same time many of the faster-growing retailers had very healthy-looking financial statements. They spent heavily on expansion while maintaining a low level of debt, and they have fared quite well during turbulent times. Wal-Mart has been a stellar performer; The Limited, although some of its divisions have had subpar performance in the early 1990s, has had no operating debt; The Gap, despite recent up and down years, spends less than 1 percent of its sales on interest payments; and even JC Penney, whose performance during the 1980s was turbulent, has a strong cash flow position. As noted by one of JC Penney's suppliers, "They pay their bills on time. Do you know what that's worth today?"[4] Interest payments for the successful retailers were generally less than 2 percent of sales, while they spent the equivalent of approximately 6 percent of sales on capital expenditures for expansion. In contrast, in 1989 Macy's lost nearly $200 million on $7.2 billion in sales while spending only 2 percent of sales on capital expansion and nearly 10 percent of sales on interest payments.

Some retailers have had roller-coaster existences over the 1980s and early 1990s. Consider Patagonia, a retailer of outdoor products that sells its merchandise by catalog as well via its nine company stores and its more than twelve hundred dealers worldwide. Patagonia, founded by Yvon Chouinard, was a $3 million business in 1979 that grew to more than thirty times that size over the next decade. Aside from its staggering growth, it was well known as a model for corporate responsibility: it had a day care center and a subsidized cafeteria, and the company would conduct an annual environmental audit and impose an "earth tax" for environmental concerns. Chouinard would spend eight months each year away from the company, trekking and mountain climbing to test the company's products and to come up with new ideas. Certainly product quality was enhanced—as was the price of the products. With customers demanding low prices and with competitors keeping their prices low, Patagonia's sales began to flatten, and its profits began to decline during the late 1980s. Apparently the company missed the warning signals, continuing to expand its work force as it had during the early to middle 1980s. Inventory piled up and had to be sold at a loss, and the company laid off 20 percent of its workers. By 1989 Patagonia had declared Chapter 11 bankruptcy; the company was subsequently sold to a group of former employees.

Often entrepreneurs, like Chouinard, assume that sales will always continue to grow. They are under the illusion that they can continue to increase personnel, administrative costs, inventory, and product design and development costs indefinitely. Unfortunately, as was evident with Patagonia, if sales do *not* continue to increase, huge losses can be the reality.

There are big winners and big losers in retailing, with the gap between the two groups widening. The successful ones, which have generally been the fastest-growing companies in the industry, have made long-term strategic investments. Their sales per square foot have increased while operating costs as a percentage of sales have declined. This has resulted in lower prices for the customer, thereby increasing sales for the company. Conversely, for the larger, less successful retailers, sales per square foot have decreased, resulting in higher operating costs that make it more difficult for them to be price competitive and still be profitable. One strategy, albeit unsuccessful, that many of the large, slow-growth retailers have employed has been to put merchandise continually on sale. The problem is that although this will result in increased short-term sales, it has not been part of a profitable long-term plan.

The Impact on Suppliers

Of course, retailers have grown along with their suppliers, many of which are entrepreneurial success stories in their own right. A good example is Liz Claiborne, which has grown from a $230 million business in 1983 to a $2 billion company ten years later. In the 1980s Liz Claiborne was ranked second among *all* corporations listed in a *Forbes* ranking based on EPS growth (with an average annual rate of 43 percent) and was ranked first in ROE (with an average annual rate of more than 50 percent).

Two other good examples are in the athletic shoe industry: Reebok International (Canton, MA) grew at better than a 100 percent annual rate in the 1980s to become a $3 billion company in the 1990s; and LA Gear (Los Angeles, CA) founded in 1979, grew at a 170 percent compounded annual rate between 1985 and 1989. Although it has experienced some ups and downs in its stock price since 1990, LA Gear was one of the leading stock market performers in both 1988 and 1989, increasing in value by 367 percent and 185 percent, respectively, in those two years. Although Reebok's most recent performance has also been far from exceptional, the company has done quite well over the long term, having experienced average annual increases in sales growth, EPS growth, and ROE of 200 percent from 1984 to 1988 while maintaining an extremely low debt-to-equity ratio of 2 percent (versus 26 percent for the industry).

Great Opportunities in Franchising

Like retailing, which can grow dramatically as new stores open up nationwide, franchising has become a tremendous growth opportunity for the franchisors (who develop the product or service concept); and the franchisees (who operate the individual franchise units or locations, paying royalties to the franchisors for marketing and technical support and for the use of their trade name).

Top Franchises in the United States, 1992

---

1. Computertots
2. The Krystal Co.
3. Beaux Visage
4. Candy Express
5. General Nutrition Centers (GNC)
6. Family Haircut Store
7. Major Wok
8. Heel Quik
9. American Leak Detection
10. Checkcare Systems
11. Fastsigns
12. Check Express
13. Mrs. Fields Cookies

Source: Success magazine.

Franchises represent a fairly low-risk opportunity: only 3 percent of new franchises fail within their first year and only 5 percent by their eighth year, failure rates far below those of typical early-stage businesses. In the early 1990s franchising is a $200 billion industry—larger than the entire U.S. food industry—with more than two thousand franchises and four hundred thousand establishments.

A good example of the growth of franchising is TCBY Enterprises (Little Rock, AR), an entrepreneurial company founded in 1979 that is now the nation's largest frozen yogurt chain. TCBY has been very profitable while growing at better than a 100 percent annual rate since the early 1980s. Similar growth has been characteristic of such other emerging fast food restaurant franchises as Subway (Milford, CT), one of the nation's fastest-growing franchisors with approximately five thousand franchise units, and Domino's Pizza (Ann Arbor, MI) and Little Caesar's Pizza (Farmington Hills, MI), each of which has more than one thousand franchised units.

Several other industries have witnessed comparable growth of entrepreneurial companies with franchise operations. These include RE/MAX (Englewood, CO) in real estate, Mail Boxes Etc. (San Diego, CA) in business services, Nutri/System Weight Loss Centers (Willow Grove, PA) in health and fitness, Sylvan Learning Centers (Montgomery, AL) in education, Ugly Duckling Rent-A-Car (Tucson, AZ) in car rental, Blockbuster Entertainment (Fort Lauderdale, FL) in video rental, and Precision Tune (Sterling, VA) in auto maintenance.

Fast-Growth Companies of the 1990s

A strong argument can be made that low-tech service businesses have become the big growth industries of the late 1980s and the 1990s. The growth of businesses and of new jobs has not been restricted to Silicon Valley in California and Route 128 near Boston. As noted in Chapter 1, at the top of the *Inc.* 500 list of high-growth privately held companies for 1990 was Cogentrix (Charlotte, NC), a developer and operator of cogeneration facilities, which grew by an incredible 151,681 percent (from $133,000 to more than $200 million in revenues) over the previous five years.

Not far behind Cogentrix are several other *Inc.* 500 companies with 10,000 percent or greater five-year growth:

- CEBCOR (Chicago, IL; 1990 listing; 40,000 percent growth), which provides employee leasing services
- LGB (Chula Vista, CA; 1990 listing; 19,000 percent growth), a manufacturer of swimwear
- Golden Cheese Company of California (Corona, CA; 1990 listing; 12,000 percent growth), which manufactures cheese and other dairy products
- United Staffing (Troy, NY; 1991 listing; 19,000 percent growth), which provides employee leasing services
- Rockwell Construction (Coral Springs, FL; 1991 listing; 15,000 percent growth), which provides general contracting services
- Damark International (Minneapolis, MN; 1991 listing; 15,000 percent growth), which operates a catalog business
- Veragon (Houston, TX; 1992 listing; 40,000 percent growth), which manufactures and sells diapers
- Indeck Energy Services (Buffalo Grove, IL; 1992 listing; 19,000 percent growth), which operates cogeneration power plants

Low-Tech Growth: Important Summary Points

1. There has been significant growth of low-tech companies.
2. Social and demographic trends have provided an opportunity for the growth of many of these companies (for example, Eateries, Liz Claiborne, Toys 'R' Us, Home Depot).
3. Perhaps the most significant growth among low-tech companies has been in retailing (for example, Wal-Mart, The Limited, Toys 'R' Us, Circuit City, The Gap).
4. Several smaller specialty retailers have been successful by pursuing a specific market niches such as office supplies (Office Depot), computer software (Egghead), and computers (CompuAdd)
5. Franchising, another high-growth industry, currently accounts for $200 billion per year in revenues for companies such as TCBY, Subway, Domino's Pizza, and Little Caesar's Pizza.

Our Purpose: How to Differentiate Successful from Unsuccessful Fast-Growth Companies

There are numerous stories of such successful fast-growth companies as Compaq Computer, Sun Microsystems, Microsoft, Liz Claiborne, Home Depot, and Wal-Mart. There are countless more stories of such unsuccessful fast-growth companies as People Express, Vector Graphic, ZZZZ Best, Worlds of Wonder, and Silk Greenhouse. The critical question is what differentiates the successful companies from the unsuccessful ones. Although one can say that there are some rules for success for fast-growth ventures, it is common for entrepreneurs to say that their companies broke every rule in the book when they got started. Many such companies have not only survived but grown to be star performers.

After extensive analysis of well over one hundred fast-growth companies, however, I found that the successful companies could, in most cases, be distinguished from the unsuccessful ones based on the following eight factors:

1. *Nichemanship* (creating specific, focused, differentiated markets)
2. *Sustainable Competitive Advantage* (selling product features, proprietary technology, quality, value, and so on)
3. *Superior Product/Service Quality* (communicating quality to the customer or client)
4. *Innovativeness* (winning through new product development or through new ways to reach the market)
5. *Strong Cultural Foundation* (creating the value system that pervades the organization)
6. *Valued Customers, Valued Employees* (being close to customers and employees)
7. *Quality Management* (such as having a visionary chief executive officer)
8. *Venture Capital Support* (funding as well as managerial assistance by experienced investors)

Most successful fast-growth companies do not display *all* of these factors, but they tend to be strong on several of them. Similarly, unsuccessful companies tend to display very few of these desirable traits.

The remainder of the book explores the aforementioned distinguishing factors in further detail. Throughout Part II of this book I will devote one chapter to each of the eight factors noted above and provide several examples to illustrate what makes a successful fast-growth company.

Characteristics of Successful Fast-Growth Companies

5

Nichemanship

Strategy for Established Companies:
Growth, Acquisition, Diversification

The 1970s, 1980s, and 1990s have witnessed a dramatic increase in the size of American corporations as a result of acquisitions and product/service diversification. A typical example of this occurred in March 1987 when, shortly after GM decided to shut down eleven plants due to overcapacity in the production of automobiles, Chrysler acquired AMC. On the same day, USAir acquired Piedmont. Mergers abound in American industry.

The casual observer might question the prominence of merger activity among large corporations. After all, most research studies addressing this issue suggest that mergers have *not* been effective. Michael Porter of the Harvard Business School reported that more than half of the acquisitions of thirty-three large American corporations between 1950 and 1980—and three-fourths of those in unrelated fields—were eventually sold off.[1] Similarly, a study by McKinsey & Company of mergers between 1972 and 1983 involving the two hundred largest corporations in the United States found that only 23 percent of all acquisitions—and 8 percent of those in unrelated areas—were successful, as measured by an increase in shareholder value.

Economies of Scale: The Case of the Experience Curve

Why, then, has there been such a movement toward acquisitions? One explanation is as follows: in many industries, as you produce more units, the costs to produce each unit decreases because the total labor, equipment, space, and overhead costs are spread out over more units. This is the essence of so-called economies of scale.

Only 23 percent of all acquisitions yield an increase in shareholder value.

Strategic planners have developed a concept known as the *experience curve* that supports this notion. It suggests that as production doubles, costs per unit tend to decrease by approximately 20 to 30 percent. Naturally, this favors large corporations with sizable production runs; such corporations can produce more units, thereby lowering their costs per unit and allowing them either to

---

The experience curve suggests that as production doubles, costs per unit tend to decrease by 20 to 30 percent.

---

charge less than smaller corporations for the same units (that is, to take on a low-cost, low-price strategy) or to realize greater profit margins per unit. For example, Budweiser, which has maintained the highest level of sales in the beer industry, also has the lowest cost per unit and thereby the highest operating margin per unit among its competitors.

Can Small Companies Survive?

We might, therefore, expect only large companies with high levels of sales to be profitable. Professor Porter of Harvard, however, has demonstrated a very interesting relationship that exists between the number of units produced and the profitability of the company.[2] As suggested below by the right side of the U-shaped curve in the graph, large producers can be profitable due to economies of scale. Thus, they can be quite successful in employing a low-cost, low-price strategy to generate high market share. Consistent with the research cited above, however, small producers (including most fast-growth companies) with well-differentiated products that compete in specialized (or "niche") markets are often

---

Small producers with well-differentiated products are often far more profitable than their larger competitors.

---

far more profitable than their larger competitors. Companies that do not possess a high market share and are undifferentiated—those "stuck in the middle" in the graph—tend to be very unprofitable.

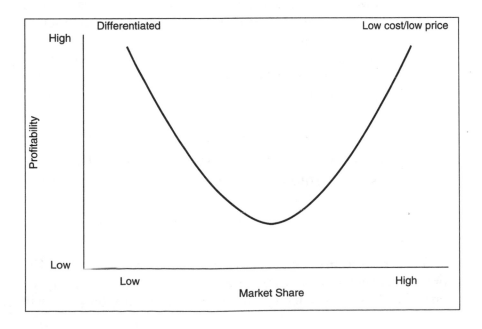

Strategy for Fast-Growth Companies: Creating Niches

The research just cited suggests that differentiation (based on targeting a specific market) or *nichemanship,* is often a smart strategy, especially for smaller businesses. Consider Malcolm Swenson of Swenson Stone Consultants (Grantham, NH), who has taken nichemanship to its limits. The company helps developers select and buy the right stones for their projects—for example, it arranged to import three hundred thousand square feet of rare red granite from Europe for Bell Atlantic's new tower in Philadelphia. Swenson keeps tabs on major quarries and stone processing plants throughout the world and assists developers in finding the desired size and color of hard-to-find stones.

More than one hundred companies in the computer and office automation industries have gone public in recent years. The successful ones have succeeded in clearly defining a market niche; for example, Apple Computer succeeded largely because it initially focused on the educational market for its product. Kaypro and countless others failed in this regard and have since gone out of business.

High-tech companies typically beget new high-tech companies, with the newer companies becoming direct competitors of their predecessors. The result is that dozens of companies can enter an industry within months; despite 40, 50, or 60 percent or higher growth in the industry, there may be a 100, 150, or 200 percent increase in the number of companies entering it. Consequently, there is not enough profit to go around.

High-tech companies beget their own direct competitors, but often there is not enough profit to go around.

When this occurs the niche-oriented companies (such as Cypress Semiconductor and LSI Logic) may do fairly well, but the ones that lack a clear niche and compete primarily on price will often suffer. Consequently, when there is a shakeout in an industry, fast growth often becomes nothing more than a precursor to failure. This is precisely what happened in the personal computer industry to Columbia Data Products, Osborne Computer, Vector Graphic, and Kaypro.

Thus, especially in its early stages, it is critical that the company develop a focused business definition or strategy. This is the strategy that brings the greatest profits to fast-growth businesses, and it often results in higher levels of profit than are realized by larger, more established companies. The Strategic Planning Institute, using its Profit Impact of Marketing Strategy (PIMS) data base—an extensive, confidential set of data from more than three thousand business units throughout the economy—found that the average return on investment for large ($1 billion or greater), less differentiated businesses was 11 percent, while the average return for smaller (less than $100 million), differentiated businesses was 27 percent, or almost three times higher.

The successful fast-growth companies are not just *following* niche strategies; rather, they are *creating* niches or markets. Regis McKenna, the leading marketing expert in Silicon Valley, notes the following:

> In fast changing industries, marketers need a new approach. Rather than thinking about sharing markets, they need to think about creating markets. Rather than taking a bigger slice of the pie, they must try to create a bigger pie. Or better yet, they should bake a new pie.
>
> In [market-creating] strategies, managers think like entrepreneurs. They are challenged to create new ideas. The emphasis is on applying technology, educating the market, developing the industry infrastructure, and creating new standards. The company with the greatest innovation and creativity is likely to win. . . .
>
> If companies think only about sharing the markets, they will never get involved in emerging businesses. They'll take a look at the business, decide that the "pie" is too small, and move on to other possibilities.
>
> That is exactly what happened to the personal computer market for inexpensive computers in the mid-1970s. At the time, these computers were used primarily by hobbyists—that is, enthusiasts who enjoyed tinkering with the machines. . . .

But a few companies, companies such as Apple and Tandy, looked at the business with a market-creation mentality. They looked beyond the hobbyists and saw that small bussinessmen and professionals might eventually use the machines—if only the machines were designed and marketed a bit differently. Rather than focusing on what was they focused on what *might be*.[3]

There are successful niche creators in just about every industry. These would include The Limited, Nordstrom, and The Gap in retailing; ServiceMaster and Caremark in health care; Williams-Sonoma in distribution; BancOne and Barnett Banks in financial services; LSI Logic and Cypress Semiconductor in semiconductors; Sun Microsystems, Compaq, and Apple in computers; and Worthington and Nucor in steel. There is even a new language associated with niche companies: terms such as *superregionals, minimills, minilabs, store within a store,* and *boutiques,* were not around a decade ago.

In a recent study by Donald Clifford and Richard Cavanagh of McKinsey & Company, it was found that more than 90 percent of the highly profitable midsize (sales of $25 million to $1 billion per year) growth companies were niche creators that competed by segmenting the market and catering to the special needs of one market segment.[4]

Key to a Successful Niche Strategy: Develop a Product/Market Focus

Nichemanship involves developing a clear product/market focus, or a well-defined strategy.[5] An investor, employee, or anyone else who may be interested in a fast-growth company knows that a business has a clear strategy or focus when it addresses the basic question, "What business are we in?" This question can be broken down into three elements:

- What is our product or service?
- What is our industry?
- What is our target market?

The answers to these questions become evident when speaking to customers, visiting company locations, reading the CEO's letter to stockholders in the annual report, or keeping abreast of articles in trade or business publications.

No company, especially an early-stage or emerging growth venture, can be all things to all people.

No company, especially an early-stage or emerging-growth venture, can be all things to all people. Thus, having a clear, sharply defined product/market focus (or strategy) is critical for a forgrowth company—or just about any other company, for that matter.

Taking Advantage of an Opportunity

Nichemanship will often involve taking advantage of opportunities as they arise. Consider the case of Liz Claiborne. Elisabeth Claiborne Ortenberg and her husband, Arthur, started a small sportswear clothing company with a $200,000 loan from family and friends and another $50,000 in personal savings. Elisabeth, then forty-seven, had more than twenty-five years experience in clothing design. Ever since that time, Liz Claiborne has grown spectacularly, all the while being recognized as one of the outstanding corporations in this country. Ever since the initiation of the survey about 10 years ago, it has been ranked consistently as one of the ten most admired corporations by *Fortune* magazine.

Liz Claiborne's strategy has been to target the business and professional woman. Moreover, the company has developed a strong customer orientation by providing versatility and affordability in styles that enhance excellent figures while they camouflage imperfect ones. Timing was critical to the growth of this company, which coincided with more women taking professional positions.

Most people acknowledge that it was Elisabeth Ortenberg herself, who was responsible for the dramatic success of the company. As noted recently by Jerome Chazen, currently chairman of the company, "She has an eye (for fashion) as finely tuned as a musician with absolute pitch."[6]

Niche Retailers Have Succeeded

One important common feature of the successful fast-growth retailers is that they have employed niche strategies by focusing on specific, targeted customer groups. Just walk into any Home Depot, The Limited, Toys 'R' Us, Circuit City, or Sports Unlimited store and you will see how these companies successfully target their efforts. For example, Home Depot, America's largest warehouse chain for do-it-yourself products, grew by more than one hundredfold in terms of revenues between 1983 and 1992 to become a $7 billion company. Home Depot's founder and CEO, Bernard Marcus, describes the company's focus as follows:

> In some cases, we have 25,000–30,000 people walking through a store in a week, 50% of whom are women. We could sell them anything. If we wanted to put panty hose at the front register, we'd sell a fortune in panty hose. But we don't. We don't want the customer to think we're a discounter, a food store, a toy store, or anything else, because it would confuse her. The perception of the customers always has to be, when they think of a do-it-yourself project, they think of Home Depot.[7]

Interestingly, even these niche retailers, who have consistently outperformed the industry giants, are specializing in targeted subsegments. Witness, for example, The Limited's narrowly focused stores, which include Limited Express, Lane Bryant, Victoria's Secret, and Abercrombie & Fitch. Similarly, The Gap's Banana Republic subsidiary has had great success.

Retailing companies have become very attractive investments, since they tend to go from start-up to exit much more rapidly and with much less capital than do technology companies. Expansion in the retail area can be done very efficiently, especially if retail stores work out attractive arrangements with the major national mall operators (such as the Rouse Company and DeBartollo). For example, The Limited's massive expansion in major malls over the past decade has not only made founder Leslie Wexner a multibillionaire but served as the role model for other smaller retail stores looking to expand. It seems as though every upstart retailer wants to be "the next Limited" or "the next Gap" or "the next Toys 'R' Us." Several are, to some extent, already on their way, including Costco Wholesale Corporation (Kirkland, WA), Price Club (San

Diego, CA), Office Depot (Boca Raton, FL), Egghead (Bothell, WA), and One Price Clothing Stores (Duncan, SC).

Let us examine some of the niche markets in which fast-growth retailers have made their mark.

Membership Warehouse Companies

One of the most phenomenal growth area in retailing (as well as in low-tech industries as a whole) has come from the membership warehouse companies. Targeting customers who prefer low prices to service, these companies are now a $25 billion per year industry that is expected to grow more than 20 percent per year for the next few years. The oldest and largest company in this sector is Price Club (of San Diego, CA), a $7 billion company that was founded in 1976 and was ranked above all other corporations in EPS growth (with a ten-year annual average of 49 percent) by *Forbes* magazine in the early 1990s. There are three newer large membership warehouse companies, each of which was founded after 1982 and generates more than $500 million a year in revenues: Costco Wholesale Corporation (Kirkland, WA), a $7 billion retailer whose 100 percent annual growth rate during the late 1980s exceeded even that of Compaq Computer; Pace Membership Warehouse (Aurora, CO), which also had a 100 percent average annual growth rate over the latter part of that decade; and Wholesale Club (Indianapolis, IN), whose average annual growth rate during that time was 75 percent. Costco, which was founded in 1983, was initially capitalized with $7.5 million in venture capital; it subsequently raised more than $200 million in private and public debt and equity. Costco's sales of $101 million from seven stores in its first full year of operation (1984) were comparable to that of Compaq Computer's incredible $111 million. Within two years, Costco was a $750 million company with twenty-two stores. By its fifth year of operation in 1988 the company had more than $2 billion in sales from forty-three stores and it had $3 billion in sales in 1989, making its growth pattern more impressive than that of Compaq, Sun Microsystems, Apollo Computer, Businessland, Reebok, or any other company in history, high tech or low tech.

The success of Price Club, Costco, and the others has resulted in a newer entrant in this industry: Sam's Wholesale Club, a division of Wal-Mart. Some suppliers of the membership warehouse companies—such as Jan Bell Marketing (Fort Lauderdale, FL), a jewelry distributor whose stock price increased by 250 percent in 1988 but has since declined somewhat; and Advanced Marketing Services (San Diego, CA), a book distributor—have experienced comparable growth.

Sporting Goods

Toys 'R' Us revolutionized toy retailing. Circuit City revolutionized electronics retailing. And, sporting goods superstores such as Sports Unlimited (Sports & Recreation Inc.) and Sports Authority have revolutionized this fragmented $30 billion industry.

Sports Authority (of Fort Lauderdale, FL) is the largest of the "superstore" (stores that are thirty thousand square feet and larger) sporting goods chains. It is also one of the hottest retailing chains in the country, a textbook example of how to launch a start-up properly. The company was started by Jack Smith, former chief operating officer of Herman's, a national sporting goods chain. In December 1986 Smith was approached by venture capitalists who wanted to create a chain of warehouse-style sporting goods stores. Smith was interested, but he insisted that the company have more of an upscale (rather than a warehouse) image and that it attempt to compete on selection rather than price. The revised focus, plus the experience of Smith and his quality management team, was enough to entice several venture capital firms to invest $18 million. The company is expected to generate $1 billion in sales in 1995.

While Sports Authority (a division of K-mart) targets larger cities, Sports Unlimited has been successful by targeting smaller metropolitan areas. Apparently that strategy has paid off handsomely for Sports Unlimited, whose stock price nearly doubled in value within a few months of its IPO in 1992.

Another good example in the sporting goods industry is Sports-Town (Atlanta, GA), a discount sporting goods store founded in March 1987 by Tom Haas. The company raised $7 million from a group of investors almost immediately, followed by another $20

10 Largest Sporting Goods Chains

	1991 Sales (in millions)	Share of Market	Number of Stores	Average Store Size (sq. ft.)
1. Herman's	$650	2.1%	260	10,000
2. Oshman's	310	1.0	185	13,000
3. Big 5	300	1.0	137	n/a
4. Sports Authority	241	0.8	36	38,000
5. Sportsmart	216	0.7	25	40,000
6. McSporting Goods	170	0.6	80	n/a
7. Academy Corp.	156	0.5	27	n/a
8. Sports Unlimited	139	0.5	19	40,000
9. Gart Bros.	130	0.4	54	n/a
10. Dunham's Athleisure	112	0.4	50	n/a
Total	2,424	8.0	873	

Source: Sports Trend; Lehman Bros.

million within one year. At a time when funding for start-ups was so scarce, how did Haas get his foot in the door? He started out by doing everything right; he had a strong background in the field, a solid management team, and a business plan. In addition, Haas cultivated the necessary contacts to secure the financing: "Anyone who has been in business for a few years winds up having friends in the business community. And some of them have ties to the capital markets. . . . Every time we visited a venture group, the circle widened because they had two or three people they wanted us to talk to."[8]

In contrast, Robert McNulty (who had earlier started Home-Club, which was bought by Zayre for $151 million in 1986) was far less successful in his venture into discount sporting goods. The investors in his SportsClub venture, which followed on the heels of HomeClub, lost $35 million on this venture after it filed for bankruptcy in 1988 and subsequently liquidated its assets.

Office Products

One of the high growth areas in specialty retailing is in office products, an industry that (including office furniture and computers as well as office supplies) generates more than $100 billion annually in retail sales. There are three relatively new players in this field, each of which has gone public since the late 1980s. Staples (Newton, MA), started in 1986, is the pioneer in the industry. It received its initial venture capital infusion of $4.5 million from Bain Capital, of Boston. The other two are Office Depot (Boca Raton, FL), which has stores throughout the South, and Office Club (Concord, CA), which has stores along the West Coast. If the growth of each continues as expected, they will soon be closing in on one another's turf. All three of these companies, which generate a very appealing $450 to $500 per square foot in sales, were seen as relatively safe early-stage investments.

The growth of these companies is certainly startling. Office Depot generated $1.9 million in sales in 1986, its first year. It received its first round of funding (from Alan Patricof Associates, Adler & Company, Chemical Venture Partners, First Century Partners, Northwood Ventures, Oak Investment Partners, and others) in 1987, and realized sales of $33 million in that year. In 1988 the company went public, and sales quadrupled to $132 million. Office Depot's growth rate was three times that of its chief rival in the Southeast, WORKplace (St. Petersburg, FL). Recently acquired by Staples and a phenomenal success story itself, WORKplace grew from a $2 million company in 1986 (comparable to Office Depot) to a $40 million company in 1988 (one-third the size of Office Depot).

Category Killers Win Out

In recent years, Sears and several of the other giants in retailing have been experiencing a slump in same-store sales. Other large retailers for example, Federated-Allied have either disappeared or have gone into bankruptcy.

The problem among large retailers is that there's tremendous overcapacity—surplus retail space that has resulted in retail vacancies and even in bankruptcies. According to Management Horizons, a division of Price Waterhouse, in 1993 there is 18 square feet of retail space per person in the United States, double the figure for 1982. Average sales per square foot, however, have declined by more than 15 percent during that time. Consumers cannot spend money as fast as the stores are being built: according to the International Council of Shopping Centers, while the number of malls increased by 22 percent between 1986 and 1989, the number of shoppers going to malls increased by only 3 percent.

Retail space per capita has doubled while retail sales per capita have fallen.

Thus competition in the retail area is incredibly intense. A recent study by Management Horizons concluded that more than half of all retailers in 1993 will be out of business by the end of the decade. There are too many stores that are too much alike. And as if oversupply of retail stores is not enough of a problem, the mail order business, which offers tremendous convenience to shoppers, has skyrocketed since the early 1980s. Catalog companies mailed out 14 billion pieces of mail in 1992, double the amount of ten years earlier. This means that successful retailers must differentiate themselves in some way, whether by product mix and/or by the nature and quality of their service—which is exactly what the better-performing fast-growth retailers have done. Such "category killers" as Home Depot, Circuit City, and Toys 'R' Us have had phenomenal success as malls expanded, and such specialty retailers as The Gap have been experiencing double-digit gains in same-store sales.

Even the successful retailers run into problems. For example, despite huge increases during the 1980s, sales growth for Toys 'R' Us in the early 1990s has slowed, and its earnings have been flat. Moreover, most of the growth in recent years has come from adding stores, not from same-stores sales. Toys 'R' Us has been facing stiff competition, especially from the much larger Wal-Mart, which now controls 10 percent of all toy sales in the United States.

Similarly, consider The Gap. From 1989 to 1991, while other retailers were hurting, The Gap reported record earnings and double-digit gains in same-store sales by offering "good style, good quality, good value." But ever-greater pressure on providing value—as defined by its customers—has forced The Gap to lower prices, thereby hurting margins. In addition, copycats have been able to knock off its fashion designs. Consequently, in 1992 and 1993 The Gap has suffered from virtually no growth in same-store sales and declining profitability. Nonetheless, the company has had two shining stars during that time, namely, Gap Kids and Banana Republic.

How the Successful Retailers Do It

There are two important characteristics of the successful niche retailer: (1) having formula that and can be duplicated and (2) experiencing real growth in sales and profits as indicated by same-store figures.

Wal-Mart, The Limited, and The Gap all became successful in one location, then duplicated that successful formula hundreds of times, city by city. This suggested continued growth in sales and profits for each, as well as continued appreciation in its stock price. During the 1980s the stock prices of Wal-Mart and The Limited increased by more than fiftyfold, and that of The Gap increased by seventyfold.

The second important factor is increased sales in *existing* stores, rather than merely as a result of building new stores. Once expansion slows down, profitability will rely on the company's ability to generate additional same-store sales. For example, Home Depot, in the midst of its rapid expansion, increased weekly sales *per store* by 124 percent during the two years prior to its going public. It therefore is not entirely surprising that Home Depot was the most successful IPO of the 1980s.

Niche Strategies of Other Service Businesses

Small Business Services

Two excellent examples of niche creators in the service sector are Automatic Data Processing (ADP) and ASK Computer Systems. The two companies are similar in their initials and in their focused target market, small businesses. Yet they differ considerably in the nature of the services that they provide.

ADP has been successful largely as a result of its well-defined niche: providing small businesses with payroll services. In essence,

ADP provides peace of mind to its clients by guaranteeing that their payrolls will be met on time. Although ADP has expanded its operations since its early days, its acquisitions have been clearly focused, all taking advantage of its strength in computers and communication networks.

Small manufacturers have a need for an integrated system to coordinate and control their inventories, purchasing, Research and Development, and production. Yet up until the mid-1970s, that need went unfulfilled. Sandra Kurtzig founded ASK Computer Systems in 1972 to develop assorted business software applications to fill that void. Its big break came in 1978 when it developed a program, which ran on Hewlett-Packard minicomputers, that could help small manufacturers run a plant. Sales and profits soared, and the company went public in 1981. Within two years, Sandra Kurtzig's personal stake was valued at nearly $70 million.

Health Care

The health care industry has its share of successful niche creators. Consider Humana, (Louisville, KY), a company with expertise in controlling hospital costs. Led by David Jones and Wendell Cherry, the top management team of Humana (which, as happens on many occasions, got started on the golf course rather than in a corporate planning meeting) became enamored with the growth potential of the nursing home industry. The company became the largest nursing home company in the country by the late 1980s, with the stock price rising tenfold in just one year. As its core business began to mature, the company sought to expand in other areas. It was fairly unsuccessful in its decision to enter the mobile home park industry, an unrelated niche market that it expected would be similar to nursing homes. A decision to enter the hospital business (a more closely related niche market), accompanied by a sell-off of nursing homes, was far more successful.

Humana's initial success was prompted largely by its ability to identify a niche and exploit opportunities in that niche. Over the years, however, Humana has experienced its share of turbulence. Thus, having a well-defined niche is a good starting point; managing the growth of a business in a particular niche involves much more.

Another growth company in the health care industry is Charter Medical Corporation, which began as a real estate business in Macon, Georgia. It moved into the property development area, building shopping centers and later nursing homes, which eventually led to managing the properties. After it took advantage of an opportunity to purchase a few psychiatric hospitals, Charter recognized that it had found a profitable business as well as an emerging growth industry; a trend was developing in our country to treat emotional problems via short-term stays in rehabilitative treatment centers rather than long-term (or lifelong) stays in remote institutions. Charter began to pursue this niche by building and managing small psychiatric treatment centers located in proximity to patients' homes. Moreover, Charter began to develop specialized programs and facilities (for drug abuse, alcoholism, adolescent problems, and so on) within its already specialized niche. It also began to advertise its facilities, thereby diminishing the negative stigma attached to psychiatric facilities. As competitors have followed its lead, they ironically have strengthened Charter's efforts. Charter has grown explosively into a multibillion dollar company with psychiatric hospitals located throughout the country.

Laboratory Companies

There have been several niche creators among technology companies. In the biological sciences, Charles River Laboratories identified a market for high-quality, genetically pure laboratory rats and filled that market need. In 1993 it is the leading company in the United States in producing research animals.

In a somewhat similar industry, Millipore has become a leader in microporous membrane technology. Initially the company had an outstanding proprietary technology; it could separate microscopic particles of any size from just about any liquid. But how could this be applied to industry? Allowing its future customers to define its products and markets, Millipore sent mailings to microbiologists and followed these up with field seminars. The result was a tremendous number of ideas on how to use the Millipore membrane. Millipore used several of these ideas to customize its products to meet its customers' needs and to create specific subniches in which to operate.

Computers and Office Automation

In the field of computers and office automation, niche creation has become the norm. Cray Research, for example, a nearly billion-dollar-a-year company, has always focused on a limited market that would purchase its multimillion-dollar supercomputers. Cray sells its computers to academic and research institutions, government and other nonprofit organizations, and some corporations that need state-of-the-art equipment. Cray has certainly had it ups and downs in terms of earnings and stock price since the late 1980s. Yet despite the fact that its customers are often on limited budgets, over the long term Cray has been a very successful company.

LSI Logic (Milpitas, CA), under chairman Wilfred Corrigan, has grown from a start-up in 1980 to a Fortune 500 company despite operating in the fiercely competitive semiconductor industry. Its strategy has been to manufacture custom chips that perform specialized functions, rather than to make inexpensive commodity-type chips. Due to the high frequency of change in the computer industry, LSI builds "gate arrays," which are semifinished chips that need a few last-minute instructions to be customized. This has sped up the production process considerably for this $700 million-per-year semiconductor company.

A fast-growth powerhouse in the semiconductor industry is Cypress Semiconductor, which has been extremely successful in its strategy of pursuing the high-end niche. As noted by the company's CEO, T. J. Rodgers, "We will take the top 3% to 10% of a market. That's it. There's always a customer who will pay more for the fastest or best made product."[9] The result has been 60 percent gross margins for this $250 million technology leader. Even during the chip recession of the late 1980s, Cypress was experiencing 37 percent annual growth and 15 percent net profit margins. Even the best companies, however, have their troubles; in the case of Cypress, price wars eventually led to losses for the company.

Niche Creators

Of course, low-tech companies have also done quite well as niche creators. For example, A. T. Cross has penned some impressive profits in the high-quality writing instruments market, and Dunkin' Donuts, with its focused product line, has soaked up impressive returns in its niche.

Another organization that hardly rates as a glamour company, is Safety-Kleen Corporation, which supplies solvent to dissolve grease from machine parts and tools. The company got its start in 1968 when some investors paid $25,000 for a company that had a few customers and the rights to a degreasing machine. Management then developed a business with a clear definition: providing a low-cost, ecologically sound way to clean greasy parts and tools at service stations, machine shops, and industrial companies. The company, now called Safety-Kleen, developed a system that included pick-up, recycling, and replacement of dirty solvents. The company has since grown to a very profitable $500 million worldwide business. Investors are quite willing to treat this unglamorous company as a glamour issue, as evidenced by its stock generally trading at more than thirty times earnings.

Similarly Unifi, under founder and CEO G. Allen Mebane, has been exceedingly successful by focusing on a specific, yet seemingly unattractive niche. In the early 1980s, strategic planners would have had a field day with Unifi. They would have seen a low-market-share, low-growth business and would have recommended selling it off. Unifi invested heavily in the seemingly unprofitable texturized polyester yarn business, however, making the company into a world leader in that segment while several larger corporations pulled out. Its competitors were unable to compete successfully against a more dedicated, flexible, and aggressive smaller company. In 1993 Unifi is a very profitable $500 million per year business.

Sticking to the Knitting

Successful niche creators generally adhere to a philosophy of "sticking to the knitting"—that is, staying with what they do best. For example, Stew Leonard, who runs America's largest grocery store, quickly recognized that 20 percent of the items in a typical store brought in 80 percent of the revenues. So Stew Leonard's has concentrated on just that 20 percent, generating more than $100 million in sales in just one location and sales per square foot that are ten times the industry average.

Another good example of "sticking to the knitting" is exhibited by Dunkin' Donuts. The company was founded by William Rosenberg, who began the business by selling coffee, sandwiches, and snacks during lunch and coffee breaks from his pushcart. He built up a small chain of doughnut stores during the 1950s and began franchising them in the Northeast. The real growth spurt, however, took place when the founder's son entered the picture. Bob Rosenberg had graduated from the Cornell University School of Hotel Administration and the Harvard Business School; perhaps his greatest asset, however, was that he had spent virtually his whole life working for the business.

Growth took off under the younger Rosenberg, although sometimes it took off in the wrong direction. The company's vending machine and franchise operations grew. Soon it got into other businesses, including a hamburger chain and a fish-and-chips operation. This uncontrolled growth took its toll on the company. With profits falling and with franchisees complaining, Dunkin' Donuts sold off many of its unrelated businesses and got back to its core operations—coffee and donuts. By the mid-1980s the company was generating over $500 million a year from more than one thousand three hundred shops located around the world, and by the early 1990s it had opened up more than four hundred new stores.

In the insurance industry, Progressive (Mayfield Heights, OH) has demonstrated the importance of sticking to the knitting. Progressive, a fast-growth billion-dollar-per-year property and casualty insurance company, has been profitable for quite some time. The company, which utilizes an extensive data base on the lifestyles and driving habits of drivers, specializes in writing policies for so-called high risk drivers. Nonetheless, Progressive has made some mistakes when it has failed to stick to what it does best. In the late 1980s, for example, the company began writing policies for trucking and transportation insurance, which turned out to be a market that the company could not handle.

THE NOT SO FRIENDLY SKIES. A contrast between America West Airlines and Mesa Airlines, two fast-growth regional airline companies, also illustrates the importance of sticking to the knitting. Despite its dramatic growth to become a billion-dollar company in its first eight years of operation, America West (Phoenix, AZ) was unprofitable throughout most of its history and filed for bankruptcy in the early 1990s. Mesa (Farmington, NM) has been profitable from the start, although it has not grown at nearly the rate of America West. Mesa, which began operations as a shuttle service between Farmington and Albuquerque (which are 148 miles apart), has remained small and focused, while America West strayed somewhat from its niche.

A common problem of commuter airlines is that they often want to become "majors." In essence, they then give up what they did best—creating and filling a niche. Commuter airlines can be successful if they look for routes where small carriers can be profitable. The large carriers must be able to fill jumbo jets because they have exceedingly high costs for computer systems and other expenses, but the commuter airlines can do quite well by filling a large percentage of seats on thirteen- and nineteen-passenger planes. That was Mesa's approach.

Because manufacturers make it so easy to obtain aircraft, small commuter airlines will often be tempted to expand too rapidly. Thus the one-time successful niche creators in this industry that have given in to the temptation of growing too fast, thereby surrendering their competitive advantage due to nichemanship—like People Express (which was swallowed up by Texas Air after suffering significant losses) and America West—have had their share of problems. (People Express is discussed in further detail in Chapter 6.)

The backgrounds of the top managers at America West and Mesa are noteworthy. Ed Beauvais, founder of America West, was formerly an airline industry economist who in 1981 raised $20 million to start his airline company, all the time with the vision to grow very big. Larry Risley, founder of Mesa, was a mechanic running an aircraft maintenance company who pledged his house and a passenger airplane as collateral for a $140,000 bank loan, which was used to purchase one commuter plane and for working capital.

UTILIZING CORE COMPETENCIES. Recently, the terms *core competencies* and *modular corporation* have been used to describe companies that stick to what they do best. The general feeling is that successful companies take advantage of their primary skills—be they in

Research and Development, manufacturing, marketing, or any other area—while they "outsource" or subcontract noncore activities. Consequently, as has been well illustrated by Dell Computer's ability to steal customers from IBM, those companies can hold down costs by not having to invest in selected fixed assets. Furthermore, they can direct their energy to where they have a competitive advantage.

To illustrate, the strengths of Nike and Reebok are in designing and marketing technologically advanced, fashionable footwear. Nike owns one small factory, while Reebok owns no plants; they contract production to suppliers in Taiwan, South Korea, and other Asian countries. The result is that Nike and Reebok have been experiencing returns on assets of more than 15 percent in the early 1990s, well above industry averages.

Also consider Dell, Gateway, CompuAdd, and Sun Microsystems. These four computer companies either buy their products ready-made or purchase all parts from suppliers and then simply assemble the machines. Dell, in particular, concentrates on its core competencies—marketing and service—and spends lavishly on training salespeople and service technicians; it has no manufacturing plants. The result is that Dell takes in $35 in sales for every dollar of fixed assets (versus $3 for Compaq). In contrast, IBM and Digital Equipment have been producing parts in-house, which may have contributed significantly to their disappointing lack of profits in the early 1990s.

Edging Out

Sticking to the knitting often provides a company with a sound, focused strategy. Yet as companies grow, it becomes increasingly easy to lose sight of that focus, with results that can be disastrous. When the successful fast-growth companies do expand, they do so by a carefully planned expansion process (that is, by controlled growth). These companies "edge out" into related businesses, often by either bringing their existing products into new markets or bringing new products into their existing markets.[10] Consequently they merely extend the niche strategy that made them successful in the first place. Alternatively, several companies have failed by adhering to a strategy of uncontrolled diversification. For example,

Baldwin United, formerly a leading producer of pianos, attempted to diversify into insurance and other financial services. The result was bankruptcy.

The success of an edging-out strategy is supported by a recent survey by David Birch of MIT, which found that businesses that are growing do so not by encouraging innovation in their existing facilities but by adding new branches via franchises (for example, Holiday Inn), retailer expansion (for example, Wal-Mart and The Limited), or service expansion (for example, Citicorp). These large companies simply take a successful formula and copy it.

THE LIMITED'S UNLIMITED SUCCESS. The Limited often seems anything but limited. The company was so named when the company's founder, Leslie Wexner, opened a small store in Columbus, Ohio, whose selections were "limited" to cheap but trendy women's sportswear. This occurred in the mid-1960s when Leslie borrowed $10,000 after he was fired from the family's clothing store in Columbus by his late father, Harry Wexner. During that time Leslie Wexner has certainly demonstrated that he has much more business savvy than his father. In 1969 the company, which was a six-store chain, went public; in 1993 it has three thousand three hundred stores in the United States. Despite weaknesses in the retailing industry, growth has not slowed down.

The Limited's strategy has clearly been one of edging out. The more than half a dozen niche-oriented chains under its umbrella include the following:

- The Limited (targeted for women in their twenties)
- The Limited Express (for teenagers)
- Victoria's Secret (for wearers of sexy lingerie)
- Lane Bryant (for big women)
- Sizes Unlimited (for budget-minded big women)
- Lerner New York (for working women)
- Henri Bendel (for upscale women)
- Abercrombie & Fitch (for preppy men)

Anybody who has ever taken a walk in a mall will recognize these names. Often there will be three or four of these stores in a single mall location.

THE LIMITED FINDS LIMITS. As successful as The Limited was in its edging-out strategy during the 1980s, the company has not behaved like a star performer during the last couple of years. Although sales and earnings for the corporation as a whole have risen consistently and Victoria's Secret in particular has excelled, growth in three key divisions—Limited Stores, Limited Express, and Lerner's—has been disappointing. The basic problem is that The Limited has taken a step away from doing what it traditionally has done best; in essence, it has lost touch with its customers.

Under its former president, Verna Gibson, The Limited stores were expert in dressing the masses. Somehow, changes—generally for the worse—began taking place shortly after her departure. For example, high-tech lighting, chrome, mirrors, and marble floors became the focal point in stores, creating a marked contrast: the better the store looked, the greater the gap between the surroundings and the *perceived* quality of the goods.

EDGING OUT IN STEEL. Successful fast-growth companies often take small steps rather than giant leaps; this is a vital component of an edging-out strategy. Consider Nucor, a highly profitable steel manufacturer. In the early 1970s, CEO Kenneth Iverson pioneered the use of minimills, the cost efficiency of which enabled Nucor to attract the low margin end of the steel market (including such products as I-beams and decking). As its success caused other steel makers to copy Nucor's minimill process, the low margin end of the market became glutted.

This forced Nucor to alter its original strategy and go after the higher-margin $20 billion flat-rolled steel market, which included products such as steel pipes and auto parts. To pursue this market, Iverson in 1986 sketched out a rough blueprint for a steel plant that would rely on a new technological process that was developed in Germany. The process, called thin slab casting, would have a tremendous cost advantage over conventional methods of steel processing. In 1989 Nucor opened the first plant of this kind in the United States. As of 1993 Nucor can turn out steel at a cost of $250 per ton, which is 15 to 20 percent cheaper than traditional steel making methods. More recently, Iverson (who is still CEO) began planning for products of the 1990s, with the intention of edging out into other related markets.

EDGING OUT GEOGRAPHICALLY. In 1987 Blockbuster Video had 238 stores. Over the next five years, the company increased the number of stores to more than 3,000 worldwide, two-thirds of which are in the United States.

As the video rental industry has matured in the United States, Blockbuster has looked for new avenues of growth. Its strategy has been to expand geographically—throughout Europe and Japan. Blockbuster recently acquired Citivision, Britain's biggest home video company. That ultimately resulted in 800 stores in Great Britain and established a foothold for expansion throughout Europe. In Japan, Blockbuster's expansion opportunities have resulted from a joint venture with Den Fujita, who runs the McDonald's subsidiary in that country and has a stake in Toys 'R' Us there as well.

Too Narrow a Niche Can Be Dangerous

Of course, just like too much of any good thing can turn out wrong, so may too specific a niche. Consider, for example, Regent Air, which offered a luxury cross-country flight at a round trip cost of $3,240. At that price, the market was extremely limited; the company shut down in 1986.

Investors in toymaker Worlds of Wonder (WOW) also found out that having too narrow a focus could be a risky strategy. WOW focused on a single product line—a teddy bear named Teddy Ruxpin that came to life through technology that synchronized eye, nose, and mouth movements to a voice on a preprogrammed cassette tape. WOW had positioned Teddy Ruxpin with a character background and ongoing storyline, building a product line that included related characters, storybooks, cassette tapes, clothing, and various accessories around the main character. WOW believed that the marketing of the related items would help extend the life cycle of the product line, but as consumer tastes changed, WOW was left with its one product and with few buyers. The company went bankrupt the year after its IPO. Thus while WOW had a clear and direct focus, it was wrong to put all its eggs in one basket, especially in the faddish and trendy toy business.

Losing Sight of Niches Can Spell Disaster

Losing sight of niches can often be disastrous for companies. For example, in the early part of the twentieth century Henry Ford changed the shape of the American automobile industry with his $360 Model T. The low-cost, mass-produced, undifferentiated ("You can have any color you want, as long as it's black") Model T, although a tremendous initial success, gradually lost market share to General Motors, which was able to offer a more diverse product line. Interestingly, in the 1990s it is Ford rather than GM that enjoys advantages in terms of distinctive features, unique styling, and superior product quality. Apparently Ford has learned something from its earlier mistake of losing sight of its niche market.

Nichemanship often serves as a fundamental component of the strategy of fast-growth business. Companies that fail often do so by losing sight of their niche. Yet even having a well-defined niche is merely a starting point from which a fast-growth company may excel. As the reader will see in the coming chapters, those companies in well-defined niches that can sustain a competitive advantage and showcase innovative and high-quality products and services often are the most successful in their industry.

Nichemanship: Important Summary Points

1. Large, established companies can be successful by following a low-cost, low-price strategy; successful fast-growth companies, in contrast, have generally followed a niche-creation strategy (for example, The Limited, BancOne, Cypress Semiconductor, Sun Microsystems, Worthington Industries).
2. There are opportunities for successful fast-growth companies to pursue niches in high-tech sectors (for example, Charles River Laboratories, Cray Research, LSI Logic, Cypress Semiconductor) as well as such low-tech sectors as retailing (for example, Toys 'R' Us, Egghead, Costco, Sports Authority, Staples), other services (for example, ADP, ASK,

Charter), and Unglamorous industries (for example, A. T. Cross, Safety-Kleen, Unifi).

3. The appropriate way for niche-oriented growth companies to diversify is by "edging out" into related businesses (for example, The Limited, Nucor).
4. Several growing companies have failed by losing sight of their niche or by having too narrowed a niche (for example, Worlds of Wonder).

Sustainable Competitive Advantage

Around the turn of the century, a salesman named King Gillette, working with an engineer named Nickerson, came up with a product to solve an ordinary problem for men. The product, which took six years to develop, was a safety razor. This would replace the straight razor, which previously was the only way men could shave themselves each morning if they wanted to look presentable. Within two years after their development, Gillette was selling two hundred thousand safety blades per year, thanks to an aggressive advertising campaign.

Gillette soon landed a major client: the United States government, which supplied soldiers with the shavers so that they could fit gas masks on their face. This made American men very comfortable with the Gillette razors, and it actually created a social norm in our society—the clean-shaven look. By 1926 there were twice as many razors as phones and more razors than light bulbs in this country. In the early 1990s Gillette sells 2 billion blades per year worldwide.

An attractive feature of just about any company, and particularly fast-growth companies, is that "something extra" in a product or service that provides the company with a decided advantage over its competitors. Like Gillette, this may include being first to market with a product. (This notion is discussed further in Chapter 8, which deals entirely with innovativeness.) Alternatively, a competitive advantage may be a proprietary technology, a new product feature, a cost or technical advantage, brand-name recognition, superior quality, better performance for the money, or some other significant benefit for the user of the product or service.

The absence of a competitive advantage may spell disaster for a company. Vector Graphic, like Apple, was a computer manufacturer founded in the mid-1970s. But unlike Apple, Vector had no real competitive advantages in terms of proprietary technology. Like many other competitors, Vector designed, developed, and marketed microcomputer systems with accompanying software for small businesses. Since there were few barriers to entry, dozens of companies just like Vector competed for that market and for the scarce profits in the newly emerging microcomputer industry. Vector, as well as its investors, turned out to be big losers in this competitive battle.

Spotting Trends Early

Often companies can grow at a phenomenal rate by sensing changing technologies and prospering with the growth of that technology. Thus investors can certainly benefit by monitoring technological, social, political, and economic trends carefully. Mc-Caw Cellular Communications, for example, was a leading player in the area of cellular communications just as cellular communication was beginning to expand.

During the mid-1980s, Home Shopping Network (HSN), which sells consumer goods over cable channels, was perfectly situated to benefit from the explosive growth in cable subscribers. As a result, it experienced a rapid increase in sales. Of course, HSN soon found that growth of a market alone does not guarantee long-term success, as evidenced by a later steep decline in its stock price.

Proprietary Advantages

Successful fast-growth companies often demonstrate their competitive advantage with a unique product that is of a proprietary nature—for example, by copyright, trademark, patent, or by some other exclusive arrangement, that is publicly available and can be readily monitored. Two classic examples of growth companies benefiting from their proprietary positions are Polaroid, with its instant printing process, and Xerox, with its "xerography" or photocopying process.

Apple's Early Success

More recently, Apple Computer had a tremendous advantage over others with its proprietary technology. The company made numerous errors in its early stages but was able to succeed because the market was forgiving for a company with such a technology edge.

One of the key reasons for Apple's success over its early years was its software support. Dan Bricklin of VisiCalc wrote the first spreadsheet program for personal computers; it was designed for the original Apple model. By 1983 there were fifteen thousand computer programs for the Apple, most of which were written by independent entrepreneurs. Apple's most successful product was the more recently developed Macintosh, the first computer to provide an extremely user-friendly atmosphere. This was a significant competitive advantage over any other personal computer available in the market.

Enhancing a Proprietary Advantage

Compaq Computer has taken on an interesting strategy that enabled it to sustain an 80 percent annual growth rate during the 1980s. The company has traditionally invested approximately only 4 percent of its revenues in research and development (as compared to between 8 percent and 14 percent for IBM, Apple, and Sun Microsystems, for example) and has invested minimally in its own sales force, relying instead on its strong relationship with its retail dealers. Consequently its cost structure is low, which has enabled it to invest heavily in marketing. Compaq routinely brings hundreds of its major accounts to Houston to comment on new products that will later meet their needs. Thus although Compaq can introduce new models significantly faster than its competitors, the company's innovative edge is often more closely related to its marketing than to its technology. In essence, its marketing efforts have enhanced its technological capabilities. This has enhanced Compaq's value in the eyes of investors.

Software Stars

Two successful fast-growth computer software companies with proprietary technologies are Autodesk and Microsoft. Autodesk has benefited from its proprietary software and copyrights and from its AutoCAD trademark, which has had substantial brand-name recognition. In five years since going public in 1985, Autodesk increased in value by 1,200 percent, thereby becoming one of the most successful IPOs of the 1980s.

In some ways, software king Microsoft has been more successful. The company developed most of its software products internally using proprietary development tools and methodology. Yet Microsoft's strategy has not been limited to having a proprietary advantage. Microsoft has become a high-volume, low-cost producer of goods that generate recurring revenues in much the same way as razor blades do for Gillette. This has enabled Microsoft to capture a substantial part of the software market for both IBM-compatible and Apple PCs and to bring considerable fortunes to its investors. Microsoft, which generated $3 billion in revenues in 1992, has been valued recently at about $25 billion, which is comparable to the market valuation of IBM, even though IBM's sales were twenty times those of Microsoft.

Biotechnology

A company with a proprietary technology has, in essence, a monopoly over its competition. This is especially important for high-tech companies. Genentech was able to establish such a monopoly

---

A company with a proprietary technology has, in essence, a monopoly over its competition.

---

in the biotech industry. An early indicator of this was the fact that it had filed more than two hundred patent applications by the time it went public in 1980. The stock market often rewards technology leaders; those investors who purchased Genentech at the time of its IPO doubled their money in just one day. Much more important, however, was that the long-term investors in Genentech realized a better than 1,000 percent stock appreciation by 1987. (The stock eventually declined somewhat following the 1987 stock market crash.)

Innovation

Personal Computers: Compaq and Its Competitors

Innovation is pronounced in the personal computer industry. This is an industry where Compaq has played David to IBM's Goliath. Compaq developed a portable personal computer when it was founded in 1982 and became an immediate smash; IBM followed, but years later. Similarly, Compaq was first to sell personal computers with the newest and most powerful chips. Compaq's innovation in technology was matched by its innovation in marketing. The company developed a strategy of selling its products exclusively through dealers (who became extremely loyal in the process) while IBM and several other computer makers alienated dealers by selling personal computers directly to large corporations at big discounts. In effect, Compaq exploited IBM's weakness to become a billion-dollar world leader in personal computers within its first four years of operation.

In the fiercely competitive personal computer market—a $70 billion market worldwide—Compaq has recently found that other, smaller companies have been trying to exploit its own weaknesses. Specifically, competitors have recognized that Compaq's prices are high and that its computers are not necessarily the technology leaders. Moreover, its dealer network strategy has often resulted in customers not getting quality after-sale service.

In reality, the so-called clones are gaining on Compaq. Compaq's market share was flat at approximately 4 percent during the late 1980s and has declined somewhat since then. Although its revenue increased by more than 20 percent in 1990, that was primarily due to a 50 percent increase in overseas sales; domestic sales increased by only 4 percent. At the same time, the makers of clones (Dell, AST Research, and Packard Bell, for example) have grown significantly. Packard Bell grew from less than a 1 percent market share in the United States in 1987 to nearly 4 percent in 1989. And, IBM, which lost ground in 1988, recaptured most of its 15 percent market share from 1987, as shown:

U.S. Personal Computer

	1987	1988	1989
IBM	15.0%	9.1%	14.0%
Apple	14.9	13.3	10.7
Tandy	7.1	5.6	4.8
Compaq	3.8	3.6	3.8
Packard Bell	0.0	1.7	3.7
Epson	2.3	2.2	2.7
NEC	1.3	1.6	1.9
AST	0.9	1.3	1.9

Source: Business Week, November 19, 1990, p. 132.

Compaq's competitive advantage over IBM was its technical leadership and its dealer network. Moreover, since IBM's prices were certainly far from the low end, Compaq did not consider it necessary to establish a low-price strategy. In fact, Compaq's strategy was to charge IBM-type prices for computers with more features and superior quality to IBM's. Eventually, Compaq began to charge higher prices than even IBM.

Although Michael S. Swavely, president of Compaq North America, was quoted in 1990 as saying "You can charge a premium price if you build the best machines,"[1] price has since become a major factor in this industry. At the same time, consumers are recognizing that there is little technological advantage to purchasing a Compaq over a clone costing almost half as much. One clone maker has even created a series of ads mocking Compaq's high prices. In comparing products, Dell Computer referred to its own lines with such quotes as "unbelievable prices," "top of the mark," and the "lap [as in laptop computer] of luxury" and to Compaq's as "unbelievable," "top of the mark-ups," and the "lap of lunacy."

As a result Compaq, which lost market share until 1991 but has since regained some, has slashed costs, prices, and margins. In

May 1992, for example, consumers paid a 67 percent premium for a Compaq over a comparable Gateway 2000 system. Six months later that premium was only 25 percent, with Compaq's gross margins reduced by one-third to 28 percent. Compaq, which had been a victim of price wars, has become the aggressor.

Traditionally Compaq would add "bells and whistles" to its machines and would price them at or above IBM's models. Rivals, though, would match those features at much lower prices (often 60 percent lower). So Compaq engaged in a strategy of cost cutting while retaining its basic standards of quality. Compared to its Deskpro 386/25M model, Compaq's newer Prolinea 3/25ZS is simpler, has a lower-cost motherboard, has fewer expansion slots, has a lighter membrane keyboard, uses a lower-level power supply, has no audio board, uses a slightly slower chip, and has a smaller disk drive. None of these changes have a tremendously detrimental effect on quality, thus allowing Compaq to offer the same basic technology at a 60 percent reduction in price.

Aside from problems due to price and cost, it is becoming more difficult for computer makers to sustain a technology advantage for an extended period of time. In 1986 Compaq introduced the first personal computer to use Intel's 80386 chip. For months, Compaq had the market to itself. Two years later, however, when Compaq was the first to use the 80386SX chip, the clone makers quickly entered the market. Moreover, both Hewlett-Packard and IBM, who are not necessarily regarded as technology leaders, introduced computers using the 80486 chip *prior* to Compaq.

Compaq recognized that it had lost its competitive advantage and has attempted to increase market share by a more aggressive pricing strategy, with prices just 10 to 15 percent higher than the leading clone makers. Although that strategy has increased sales, it has hurt gross margins (which, as noted above, have recently fallen to below 30 percent).

Innovative Companies Keep Bouncing Back

Apple Computer had a competitive advantage throughout the early 1980s, but faced turmoil in 1985 after the forced resignation of Steven Jobs, the company's founder. Yet it bounced back, introducing several new successful product lines and making the Macintosh model a strong seller for businesses, thereby regaining the competitive edge that it had been losing.

Apple soon beefed up its models, resulting in higher prices for the units. Although that was tolerable for large businesses, it was not for individuals and schools, which were Apple's earlier target markets. So between late 1989 and early 1990 the company again began to lose its competitive edge, with higher prices resulting in stagnant sales. The company then introduced several new product lines, including the Macintosh Classic (a $1,000 stripped-down version of the Macintosh), of which two hundred thousand models were sold in its first year. To keep the momentum going, Apple added several new models of the Macintosh, such as a six-pound notebook computer.

As was the case with Compaq, sales increased with the low-priced units but at the expense of gross margins, which dropped from 50 percent to 48 percent in two years. Thus, despite a nearly 20 percent increase in sales, earnings grew by less than 10 percent. Nonetheless the company has been well on the way to a second "recovery," as reflected by a steady climb in the price of its stock.

Innovative Pharmaceutical Companies

In the pharmaceutical industry, Marion Laboratories is generally regarded as a leader in innovation. Marion, which was started forty years ago by Ewing M. Kauffman (who was formerly a wholesale drug salesman), was capitalized by a $7,000 investment from an outside investor. Despite its dramatic growth, it is still a relatively small pharmaceutical company today, with its revenues equal to the total R & D budgets of some of its larger competitors. Yet it is a leader in corporate productivity, operating income per employee, and EPS.

Marion's strategy is quite unique. In an industry where a product introduction can take more than five years and cost more than $50 million (but can sometimes result in revenue streams in the hundreds of millions of dollars at gross margins in excess of 70 percent), Marion has played the role of copycat. The company does not perform primary research; rather, it licenses from other companies such successful products as Carafate, an antiulcer agent, and Cardizem, which is used to treat angina. Marion uses a "search and development" strategy in which it conducts worldwide research for pharmaceutical technologies that have been proven safe and effective. Marion then usually negotiates a royalty arrangement by which it can bring the products to market much more rapidly than typical pharmaceutical products.

Low-Tech Competitive Advantages

Of course, low-tech companies can also gain a competitive advantage by providing value to their customers. Membership warehouse chain Costco, for example, was successful in achieving rapid inventory turnover and high sales volumes by offering a limited assortment of nationally branded merchandise in a wide variety of product categories at discount prices. Its competitive strategy has been to enter new markets early and to become the dominant warehouse club in those areas by maintaining low prices, building a membership base of high-volume customers, and establishing multiple locations in larger cities. Based on its success over the years, the strategy seems to have worked exceedingly well. Costco's stock nearly quadrupled in a four-year period after it went public in 1985. Other low tech companies, including Nike, La Quinta, and McDonald's have successfully used other competitive advantages.

Production Efficiency

High-Tech Production

T. J. Rodgers founded Cypress Semiconductor in 1983. Since that time the company has grown at a 40 percent annual rate to become a $250 million business. Cypress is perhaps the leading manufacturer of high-performance memory chips known as static RAMs, which are used in workstations. In the 1990s the company has gotten into newer (and higher-margin) chips that have such names as PROMs, RISC, and ECL.

Cypress has a tremendous advantage in terms of production efficiency. The company's sales per employee are equal to those for Japanese manufacturers and are twice the levels of such outstanding companies as Advanced Micro Devices (where Rodgers used to work) and National Semiconductor, which had previously set the standards for the industry. Cypress has succeeded because it has been able to balance the demands of R & D and marketing. As noted by William Tai (of Alex Brown & Sons), Cypress's competitive advantage is that it is skillful in "Product development, marketing, and execution. Most semiconductor companies get one, maybe two, right. Rodgers is a genius at all three."[2]

Low-Tech Production

Among companies that have low-tech products, Nucor has demonstrated the importance of production efficiency. Although it was significantly smaller than such major steel processors as U.S. Steel and LTV, Nucor became a major competitor in the steel industry in the late 1970s due to its low-cost minimills. The minimills are much more cost-efficient than the processing used by the large integrated producers in that they use electric furnaces to turn scrap metal into steel, rather than beginning by scratch with coal and iron ore.

Nucor is still perceived as a small, efficient company among the steel makers, although it is now a $2 billion company that is growing at a remarkable 20 percent per year rate in a low-growth industry. Its efficient steel processing—primarily in its minimills—has made Nucor highly competitive with its larger counterparts. In fact, as noted by John Jacobson, a steel analyst at AUS Consultants, "Nucor is the model for steel companies of the future."[3]

Another low-tech success story, Crown Cork & Seal Company, has also shown a high level of production efficiency. The company has shut down its older plants and has opened newer, more automated, higher-capacity factories. Its efficiency derives largely from its U-shaped production lines, which, for example, allow persons working on the can seamer to have a clear view of the labeling operation.

Cost Control

It is vitally important for fast-growth companies to control costs. Contrast Bonneville Pacific Corporation to Catalyst Energy, two independent power companies that enjoyed fast growth throughout the 1980s. The two companies grew up under the 1978 Public Regulatory Policies Act (PURPA), which enabled entrepreneurs to build power generating plants and sell electricity to regulated utilities.

Bonneville was started in Salt Lake City when its founders invested $160,000 in the company. The founders were careful in locating appropriate energy sites, hiring builders, and contracting to sell the power. The company built its equity base through an IPO, which enabled it to take on larger projects. Nonetheless, the company still kept its cost-conscious business practices intact.

Catalyst, though, based its operations in an expensive high-rise office building in New York City. The officers/founders, who were formerly investment bankers with Salomon Brothers, are better known as deal makers than hands-on managers. Catalyst was well-capitalized from the start, with $2 million of paid-in capital. Unlike Bonneville, however, Catalyst was involved in the financing of deals rather than the development of plants. Although Catalyst has twice the revenues of Bonneville, the earnings of the two companies have been comparable.

Using Distribution

Retailing

The Limited's inventory system is unmatched in the retail industry. The company has the largest and most automated distribution center in the world. Located in Columbus, Ohio, it brings orders from more than three hundred factories throughout the world on a daily basis and provides instantaneous data linkages among the retail stores, the distribution centers, and the overseas factories. Consequently, The Limited can bring out a line of clothing to its retail stores at a pace that is ten times faster than its competitors, a decided competitive advantage in the retail apparel industry.

Overnight Success

Federal Express has also used its distribution system to gain a competitive advantage. In the 1970s, Emery and the other air freight companies were actually freight forwarders. They did not own airplanes; rather, they put packages on commercial airplanes to their proper destination. Thus they were dependent upon the airline industry for timely delivery. Federal Express, in contrast, owned and operated its own fleet and was therefore able to develop an integrated air/ground delivery network. It became the first company in history to surpass the billion-dollar mark in sales in its first decade of existence.

Establishing Linkages

One reason fledgling companies have difficulty surviving is that they lack the resources to compete effectively against larger and better-capitalized companies. A successful competitive strategy to overcome this problem is to form linkages or alliances with larger companies, suppliers, and customers. These linkages could be joint ventures, equity purchases, financing arrangements, or other connections. By forming such linkages, the smaller company gains access to additional financial, technical, or marketing resources. Customers and suppliers will generally be quite aware of these linkages. In addition, such business relationships are often spelled out in a company's prospectus (when it is in the process of going public), in its 10-K (its annual report), or its 10-Q (its quarterly report).

Sharing Technologies

Forming alliances with strong, established companies often gives early-stage ventures both greater financial muscle and technical assistance to overcome persistent problems and challenges during the early years. In the 1980s Genentech entered into a number of long-term commercial arrangements with major pharmaceutical companies, which Genentech believed would eventually be its likely competitors. Hence it developed a strategy of working with several of them (including Lilly and Hoffman La-Roche) on product development and commercialization. Such alliances benefit both the emerging venture in its immediate financial needs and the more established company, which gains a "window on technology." In the case of Genentech, one of its partners (and early investors) Lubrizol Corporation, also gained as a result of its 20 percent ownership position in Genentech.

Developing a Link with Customers

Compaq believed that one of the keys to success in the personal computer industry was to develop strong relationships with retail computer dealers. Competition for dealer shelf space was intense. As was clearly stated in the company's prospectus, however, Compaq was successful in developing important business relationships, so even before it went public in November 1983 its products were carried in more than eight hundred dealer sales locations, including those affiliated with several national and regional chains such as Businessland, Computerland, Sears and Entre Computer.

Growing with the Customer

In a somewhat similar but more extreme situation, Jan Bell Marketing announced in its prospectus that it was aligning its fortunes with the growth of its two main customers, Sam's Wholesale Warehouse (owned by Wal-Mart) and the Price Club, from whom it was generating more than half its sales. Consequently Jan Bell's business increased as those firms continued their remarkable growth—as did Jan Bell's stock price, which increased by 700 percent between 1986 and 1989.

Of course, should retail sales for key customers fall off, or should the company's financial position deteriorate, then a supplier such as Jan Bell would suffer. In fact it would be harder hit, since Jan Bell is not nearly as strong a household name as Price Club or Wal-Mart. Such was just the case for Jan Bell, whose stock price eventually declined dramatically between 1989 and 1990.

The Problem of Depending on a Few Large Customers

While establishing close ties with customers and other companies is important, overdependence on one or two large customers or suppliers could make a company quite vulnerable if that relationship should end. If half of a company's sales come from a single client, then the company would lose half its business if the client should no longer need its services.

Doing business almost exclusively with the government, for example, has its advantages and disadvantages. The government always pays its bills, albeit very slowly. One risk in doing business with the government is that as administrations, priorities, and programs change, so does government funding, which may hurt a company with substantial government contracts.

Overdependence on one or two large customers or suppliers makes a company very vulnerable.

An extreme case of overdependence was carpet cleaner ZZZZ Best, which relied on a single client for virtually all its revenues. In the year immediately prior to its IPO, it generated 86 percent of its revenue and 85 percent of its gross profit from its insurance restoration business—and all from one source, Interstate Appraisal Services. To make matters worse, it was uncertain that this relationship would continue. According to ZZZZ Best's prospectus:

> The company has no written or oral agreements with Interstate with respect to future restoration work and there can be no assurance that it will continue to direct business to ZZZZ Best. Moreover, the amount of business which Interstate can direct to the Company is dependent upon the number, nature and extent of claims resulting from damage to commercial facilities insured by companies represented by Interstate, over which the company has no control.

Of course, this was just one of the many problems which led to the decline and fall of ZZZZ Best.

In stark contrast, fast-growth retailer Home Depot has not been dependent on any single customer or vendor; it buys its merchandise from hundreds of vendors, and no single vendor accounts for as much as 10 percent of its purchases. This factor alone was not responsible for the company's more than seventyfold increase in stock price in the 1980s, but it was characteristic of Home Depot's carefully laid out long-term strategy.

Price

One of the most difficult strategies for emerging fast-growth businesses is to compete on price. It can be done, but it must be done carefully. First, the business must have a consistent strategy; that means being a price leader *every* day. As the large auto makers have learned, you cannot get around the issue by giving rebates or holding sales; this merely conditions people to wait for the price breaks before shopping. Second, the business must be incredibly attentive to cost control. Inventory must move quickly; efficiency is vital. Finally, price must govern every decision that is made by the company. That means buying in bulk, buying directly from the source without a middleman's markup, selling to retailers who operate on low margins themselves, taking advantage of manufacuters' discounts through cash purchases, keeping overhead low, and so forth.

Selling to Warehouse Clubs

It is just such a strategy that has propelled the growth of Jan Bell Marketing, which sells private label jewelry to warehouse clubs. Jan Bell's prices for gold chains, tennis bracelets, rings, and the like are about one-third of those of other manufacturers. Incredibly, however, by following the strategy outlined above, its net profit margin has been around 9 percent, or almost twice that of other jewelry manufacturers. Because the company has had an ample supply of cash (as a result of a recent public offering), it has been able to get cash-purchase discounts from its suppliers of

3 percent to 5 percent. Moreover, the company can get other discounts of 10 percent to 15 percent by selling year round, rather than just during the holiday season. The result is that Jan Bell has had compounded annual sales and earnings growth rates of 50 percent since 1984.

Home Fix-Ups

Home Depot has a strategy of being the leader in any item that it sells. If it does not have a competitive advantage in terms of price and selection, then it will drop the product line. For example, Home Depot was one of the largest sellers of unfinished wood furniture in this country, with sales in just this one product line hitting $80 million a year. Yet, the company dropped the line when it saw that it could not be the "power retailer" in this area. IKEA, the Swedish retailer, devotes most of its two-hundred-thousand-square-foot stores to furniture, as compared to Home Depot's two thousand to seven thousand square feet per store devoted to furniture. Consequently IKEA was able to beat Home Depot on both price and selection, thereby prompting Home Depot to abandon that relatively small part of its business as IKEA expanded.

Huge Success for Minimills

Nucor (of Charlotte, NC), another fast-growth business that is regarded as a price leader, is a steel company that has had earnings on par with many high-tech companies. Despite its small size, it has become one of the low-cost producers in its industry by using the latest steel-making technology as well as by offering attractive incentives to its employees.

Nucor's basic strategy involves the use of minimills—smaller plants that produce certain types of steel products more efficiently, with less people, and at lower costs than its competitors. The minimills are far different from the integrated mills at Bethlehem Steel and U.S. Steel, for example, that convert raw ore into complex products. Minimills are now considered the state of the art. In the 1970s 10 percent of U.S. steel production was by minimills. In the 1990s 25 percent to 30 percent is, and by the turn of the century, minimills will account for 35 percent to 40 percent of production. The minimills are smaller in size and produce less than 1 million tons per year. They are cost efficient because they use electric arc furnaces to melt scrap into molten steel, avoiding the need for coal, iron, ore, and massive blast furnaces. On a per ton basis, the costs are one-third to one-half of those of integrated mills.

In the 1970s 10 percent of U.S. steel production was by minimills. In the 1990s 25 to 30 percent is, and by the turn of the century, minimills will account for 35 to 40 percent of production.

Nucor has combined the efficiency of the minimill with an attractive incentive program in which the company's nonunion workers are paid for their productivity. There are bonuses paid weekly for superior performance, with attractive incentives for groups.

Nucor's neighbor, Unifi (Greensboro, NC), is also a low-cost producer in an industry that many people would consider even less glamorous than steel—texturized polyester yarn. Unifi has overtaken the major players in this industry, most of which have left the market.

More Bang for the Buck

La Quinta's Carefully Constructed Strategy

La Quinta Motor Inns is one of the fastest-growing and most successful hotel/motel chains in this country. Its occupancy rates are 10 percent to 15 percent above the industry average. Its strategy is fairly simple: it offers its guests quality accommodations (the same quality and size of Holiday Inn) and essential services in convenient locations (near business districts, airports, and universities) at reasonable rates (at approximately 30 percent lower prices than Holiday Inn). Since it does not provide banquet facilities, meeting rooms, and the like, it can keep costs low and be price competitive.

La Quinta has installed twenty-four-hour restaurants (similar to Denny's) next door to each of its motels; these serve the same purpose as typical hotel restaurants. La Quinta reduced its own costs and risks, however, by not owning the restaurants. The rationale was that people did not come to Holiday Inn because of its restaurants, so La Quinta was not giving up anything by not having them. As it turns out, most hotels and motels actually lose money on their restaurants; moreover, the restaurants cause 95 percent of the complaints. So it was not a bad strategy for La Quinta to follow.

Most hotels and motels actually lose money on their restaurants; moreover, the restaurants cause 95 percent of the complaints.

Another competitive advantage that La Quinta has demonstrated relates to its cost structure. Typically hotel and motel customers pay 0.1 percent of the value of a room for each night's lodging. (In other words, it takes the hotel one thousand days of occupancy to pay for the cost of one room.) For a three-hundred-room luxury hotel in Los Angeles that costs $120 million to build, the cost per room would be $400,000, and one night's stay there would generally run around $400. Similarly, a small forty-room motel in the middle of Pennsylvania might cost $1 million to build, which translates into $25,000 per room; customers would be expected to pay around $25 per night for a stay there. Since La Quinta supervises the construction of its facilities itself, it costs the company 30 percent less than Holiday Inn to build its motels. So if it offers a 30 percent discount relative to Holiday Inn on its rooms, it could still make the same profit.

La Quinta has a defined niche—the economical business traveler who does not want to stay in a budget motel and would prefer to pay less for the same quality offered by Holiday Inn. La Quinta provides the same luxury at a lower price, and in fact it has done better than Holiday Inn by providing more convenient locations. Whereas Holiday Inn—which has tried to cater to vacationers (who are less predictable) as well as business travelers—often built locations just off the access ramps of major turnpikes, La Quinta built its hotels near business districts, hospitals, universities, and industrial complexes. Moreover, it has kept costs low by doing the following:

- Building 120-room hotels (half the size of typical competitors)
- Supervising construction in-house, using a standard blueprint
- Reducing overhead by having its hotels managed by live-in retired couples
- Receiving favorable financing from insurance companies who share in hotel profits

Competing on Value Rather Than Price

In the competitive marketplace, customers generally understand what constitutes value. For that reason, successful fast-growth companies generally compete on value rather than price, even if it means charging a premium price for a premium product.

High-Tech Value

Low price is certainly not the strategy employed by Cray Research. In fact, Cray charges a premium for its supercomputers. Nonetheless, its customers will still buy the equipment because it is generally regarded as the best available in the world.

Lo-Tech Value

Among low-tech companies, Loctite makes anaerobic adhesives that hold metal assemblies together better than fasteners. This has brought significant savings to its customers in terms of maintenance expense and repair costs. Customers are quite willing to pay the premium price (it costs more per ounce than fine wine or perfume) because of the benefits that it provides them.

Customers will also pay premium prices for financial printer Pandick's services because it is one of the few companies that can meet their time-sensitive demands. The company prints prospectuses and other documents that are subject to numerous last-minute changes. In a business where speed and accuracy are critical, Pandick has emerged as a leader. Pandick pioneered the computerization of the entire typesetting process nearly twenty years ago, thereby giving it a significant competitive advantage that it has yet to relinquish.

Seizing an Opportunity

Just Do It

Nike has been called the success story of the 1970s. It grew from a $2 million company in 1972 to a $700 million company a decade later by taking advantage of its competitive position. Phil Knight, a collegiate runner at the University of Oregon, actually proposed the idea in an MBA paper at Stanford (in much the same way as Frederick Smith proposed the idea for Federal Express in an undergraduate paper at Yale—perhaps we professors ought to pay closer attention to our students). As Knight later recalled, he wrote of a tremendous opportunity in this industry:

> Adidas shoes were beginning to dominate the U.S. market and that didn't make any sense, because Germany was not the place to put shoe machinery. I thought it might be possible to take over the market with low priced but high quality and smartly merchandised products from Japan, as had already happened with cameras and optical equipment.[4]

Initially Knight began importing athletic shoes from Japan. Ten years later Nike became a shoe company in its own right, carving out a niche in the performance athletic shoes market. Its heavy emphasis on R & D resulted in shoes with high-quality soles and better support and comfort. As the fitness boom continued through the 1970s, Nike became the dominant footware supplier in the U.S. market.

Great Chicken and More

L. D. Stewart has demonstrated how a company in one of the most competitive of industries can gain a key advantage by seizing an opportunity. In 1982 Stewart got together with five of his friends and, with a $139,000 investment, opened up a restaurant in a dilapidated shack in Clearwater, Florida. The restaurant, known as Hooters, was located at the previous site of The World's Worst Pizza, Redeye Rock 'n' Roll, and a muffler shop. Hooters had a limited advertising budget but made up for it with an atmosphere that its customers did not forget: there is always plenty of beer and chicken wings and plenty of sexy women to serve them. It did not take long for Hooters to develop a loyal repeat clientele.

Hooters soon opened up a few more locations in nearby Tampa and in other cities in the state. The standard formula of beer, chicken, and atmosphere became an instant success. Of course, it means that patrons must be prepared to wait if they are visiting Hooters on a Friday or Saturday evening or after a football game.

Hooters gained national recognition when one of its waitresses, Lynne Austin, became Playboy's Miss July in 1986. This certainly did not hurt Stewart's expansion efforts. In 1993 there are about fifty locations in the Southeast that generate about $100 million per year in revenues. The company has been profitable—with net margins currently at 16 percent in this highly competitive industry—ever since it opened its first location in Clearwater. Moreover, as a long time Tampa Bay Buccaneers season ticket holder, I can honestly say that Hooters has far surpassed the Bucs in generating consistency, excitement, and customer loyalty.

Opening Up Industries

It is particularly attractive when companies have the ability to open up whole new industries, as was the case of McDonald's in fast food, Federal Express in overnight delivery, Head in ski equipment, Apple in personal computers, and Digital Equipment in minicomputers. This provides greater support for the earlier contention that investors and others interested in a particular company or industry be aware of technological, social, and other trends that are developing. An excellent example of an entrepreneur opening up new markets is the case of Thomas Bata, who grew up in Czechoslovakia where his father was the owner of a shoe company. After his father's death in 1932, the younger Bata assumed control of the company. When it became apparent that his country might fall to Hitler, Bata fled and opened up a factory in Canada. Sixty years later the Bata Shoe Company sells 250 million pairs of shoes a year. A famous story told by Thomas Bata summarizes his philosophy of opening up new markets: "Two shoe salesmen were sent to a poverty-stricken country. One wired back, 'Returning home immediately. No one wears shoes here.' The other cabled, 'Unlimited possibilities. Millions still without shoes.'"[5]

Failure to Sustain a Competitive Advantage

Consider the following examples of companies that failed to sustain a competitive advantage:

- Vector Graphic was a profitable $36 million fast-growth computer maker in 1982. Yet it was eventually crushed by the IBM PC. Vector filed for bankruptcy in 1985.
- In 1983 Psych Systems was a successful fast-growth $6 million company that built minicomputer systems for psychologists and psychiatrists. The product, however, was too expensive for the company's clientele, who purchased less expensive systems. The following year, Psych Systems filed for bankruptcy.
- Xonics generated $87 million in 1982 with its technology for early detection of life-threatening illnesses. Yet the company did not correctly forecast the emergence of medical imagining and consequently filed for bankruptcy in 1984.

Thus, as suggested several times throughout this book, fast growth is not enough to guarantee success; it is vital for a company to maintain a competitive advantage in its industry.

The Bleak Side of the Computer Industry

Several of the fast-growth companies have had ups and downs throughout their existence. Consider Tandon Corporation, founded by Jugi Tandon, who was formerly a project engineer at Memorex. Memorex was essentially responsible for the growth of the disk drive industry, having had its alumni start more than two dozen companies, including Shugart Associates, Seagate Technology, Conner Peripherals, Metaphor Computer Systems, Data Measurement Labs, Miniscribe Corporation, and Quantum Corporation. In 1975 Tandon was formed to manufacture magnetic heads for floppy disk drives. Tandon purchased the components for $12 apiece and sold the magnetic heads for $18, as compared to the competition's $50 price. Within eight years Tandon's product line consisted of all types of disk drives, and its sales reached $300 million. The Tandon drives had the competitive advantage of such innovations as double-sided recording, which appealed to such major customers as Radio Shack and IBM. Moreover, Tandon was able to keep costs low by manufacturing the disk drives cheaply overseas. Tandon's strategy was quite basic: reliability and low costs.

Tandon Corporation went public in 1981, bringing considerable wealth to Jugi Tandon. That suited his lavish life-style (which included a collection of more than thirty automobiles) rather well. Unfortunately, competition grew from American and Japanese companies who were able to offer even lower prices. In addition, IBM, which had accounted for half of Tandon's revenues, started developing secondary sources of supply. Moreover, a new generation of disk drives with more advanced technology began to replace the existing drives; consequently Tandon was forced to write off $137 million of obsolete inventory in 1984. As if that was not enough, several foreign suppliers were draining large amounts of cash from the company. In 1987 Tandon became the target of a class action suit for mismanagement, and its stock price declined dramatically.

A Grounded Airline

People Express Airlines had its ups and downs in more ways than one. People Express began operating in 1980, prompted by the provisions of the 1978 Airline Deregulation Act. Its management team was led by Donald Burr, who had previously been president of Texas International. People Express's strategy was to expand the size of the air travel market by attracting passengers who were traditionally either auto drivers, bus riders, or nontravelers. Even as an upstart company, it had attained several competitive advantages:

- Low fares, beginning with a $19 one-way fare from Newark to Pittsburgh (as compared to $123 for US Air) and typically 40 percent to 75 percent below its competitors, which was possible due to the company's low cost structure (low salaries, efficient operations, and so forth)
- Frequent flights from its hub of Newark to other cities on the East Coast
- Strength as a regional carrier, a sharply focused niche
- An advertising strategy that presented People Express the smart travel choice for the thrifty, busy traveler
- A strong orientation toward people, both its customers and its employees

The company grew dramatically. In four years, Donald Burr built People Express into a billion-dollar company, thereby making it the fifth largest airline company in the country. Along with the growth, however, People Express lost its competitive advantages. Competitors reduced their overhead significantly, thereby closing the cost gap. In addition, they continued to offer the usual amenities that were not offered by People Express, while People Express continued to operate out of a congested terminal at Newark International Airport and to provide a primitive reservation system that angered travel agents and their customers. The company also lost its status as a niche carrier by attempting to become a direct competitor with the larger national carriers. The crowded larger airports People Express now served and long waits at the terminal in Newark were hardly seen as the appropriate choice for the "smart" traveler. Although People Express eventually poured hundreds of millions of dollars into building a new terminal and in developing a more adequate reservation system, these changes came too late. By 1986, just six short years after its start, this high-flying fast-growth company was heading downward. Eventually it was sold to Texas Air for $200 million or about $4 per share, one-sixth of its value in 1983.

People Express had made several serious strategic mistakes. The company had established a strategy early on to serve (profitable) markets that were underserviced by the major carriers, yet it expanded to other markets. The opportunity and temptation were there, but this was a step against the airline's original successful strategy. It was also a dangerous move since People Express did not have a computerized reservation system tied in to travel agents as American and United did. But the company was concentrating so heavily on growing that it did not take the time to develop the tools to sustain a competitive advantage.

In addition, People Express attempted to be a price leader. That was reasonable since the company took steps to keep its costs much lower than the industry average by flying into secondary airports, paying low wages, providing no-frills services, and so forth. When some of the major carriers sought to regain market share by lowering prices, however, People Express had lost its major competitive advantage.

Why did the company fail? Interestingly, some of the same things that prompted its success may have contributed to its demise. Despite its meteoric growth, the company had only three layers of management, with a policy of filling job vacancies from within. Thus, as the company grew, its entire work force—most of whom were in their twenties and thirties and lacking in experience; Donald Burr, the "elder statesman," was only thirty-nine— was expected to take on additional responsibilities in a rather unstructured environment. This proved to be far more than the company could handle.

Ups and Downs in Telecommunications

At around the same time that People Express rode the deregulation wave to stratospheric heights, MCI Communications took advantage of deregulation to battle AT & T directly. By offering discounts on no-frills long-distance telephone service, MCI became a fast-growth success story. As with People Express, however, other discounters entered the picture, and the price gap with AT & T began to close. Service became a more distinguishing competitive factor than price alone, thereby taking away one of

MCI's most powerful competitive advantages. Since that time, however, MCI has built a strategy that stresses far more than price. Thus, unlike People Express, MCI has bounced back to become a powerful force in the telecommunications industry.

Toys Are Not Always Fun

Perhaps more dramatic than the failure of People Express was the demise of Worlds of Wonder (WOW), which was launched in 1985 with an initial investment from Donald Kingsborough and a $9 million letter of credit from Texas heiress Josephine Abercrombie. The company was an initial success, thanks to its Teddy Ruxpin doll. It raised more than $100 million in an initial public offering after it had been in business for just one year; by its second year, profits hit $18 million on sales of $327 million.

Shortly thereafter WOW learned that the toy business is not always fun and games, as it was unable to duplicate the Teddy Ruxpin's success when it introduced Lazer Tag in 1987. Toy stores started to sell lower-priced clones, which cut into WOW's market share. In addition, the company erred when it spent an exorbitant $38 million on advertising. By the end of 1987 WOW, which owed creditors $300 million at the time, filed for Chapter 11 bankruptcy. By that time its stock, which had traded at $29 on the day of its IPO, was virtually worthless.

Retailing Woes

On a much smaller level, consider Pak Melwani, an Indian-born entrepreneur who got his start in 1978 when he placed an ad in *Cosmopolitan* magazine selling silk blouses priced at $22. He received three thousand orders; within a decade he had built Royal Silk Ltd. into a $42 million mail-order business.

During that time, however, there were indications that the company was beginning to lose its competitive advantage. When Melwani started a chain of retail stores in 1982, he soon came to realize that the retail and catalog businesses are very different: in retail, fashions change constantly, unlike the less volatile mail-order business. As the company put more attention into the retail part of the business, the company not only experienced problems with customer service in its catalog business (where orders would sometimes take sixty days to be filled), but it never actually mastered the retail end. Thus it lost out in *both* of its businesses. In 1988, with the catalog business losing more than $500,000, the company filed for Chapter 11 bankruptcy.

When the Party Stops, It's Time to Change Strategy

Fast-growing companies must be prepared to shift strategy. They can have a competitive advantage at one point, but what do they do when they begin to lose that advantage? How can they develop another purposeful strategy? These are questions that certainly were not addressed adequately by People Express, nor by Worlds of Wonder. Fortunately, some companies have been quite successful in altering their strategy in order to recapture a competitive advantage.

Ups and Downs in the Computer Industry

From its inception, Apple's Macintosh line of computers had the advantage of being easy-to-use machines. Moreover, unlike IBM, Apple did not have to worry about clone manufacturers. Recently, however, IBM and the clones have come close to Apple in terms of ease of use, primarily by using a "mouse" and Microsoft Windows software. (I love to tell my wife, a loyal IBM employee for twelve years, that our IBM computer is finally as good as an Apple.) Thus it has become difficult for customers to justify paying 30 to 40 percent more for a Macintosh when there are far fewer competitive advantages. For Apple, those higher prices were accompanied by more than 50 percent gross margins, 25 percent greater than those for other computer makers. Eventually market share for Apple in the United States began to decline, dropping from 15 percent in 1987 to 9 percent in 1990. (As with Compaq and several other competitors, although domestic sales dried up during that time, total revenues climbed primarily as a result of foreign sales.) Apple responded by introducing new models with lower price tags and with more advanced software, accounting in part for its 70 percent increase in earnings in 1992.

A Large Retailer Alters Its Strategy

It is certainly possible to alter a strategy, but it takes work that will often involve changing the image and changing the product line. Apple did this fairly successfully. More dramatic was the case of JC Penney, a much larger and more established company—in a much slower-growing industry—that refocused its business definition to become a "national department store" rather than a "mass merchandiser." JC Penney had always been mentioned in the same breath as its two major competitors, Sears and Montgomery Ward. In the 1980s JC Penney attempted to change that image by concentrating on apparel and home furnishings and, in the process, by upscaling its image. The company dropped $1.5 billion worth of products (such as appliances and home electronics) and expanded its apparel departments. The clearance racks were replaced by wooden shelves and the stores took on a boutique-like appearance, in much the same manner as the upscale fashion-oriented department stores. As a result, JC Penney's average ROE has been 50 percent higher than Sears since the late 1980s.

The Lessons Learned From Failure

In the late 1980s and early 1990s corporate America has given us some classic cases of large corporations being unable to sustain a competitive advantage. Part of the problem has to do with an inability to move fast enough in the right direction. Large corporations, like any other large objects, obey the principles of physics as they pertain to force, mass, and acceleration.

The problem is aggravated when these large corporations lose touch with their customers. For example, Digital Equipment and IBM became megacorporations in mainframes and minicomputers largely as a result of huge spending on R&D and marketing. But those days are gone now that the industry is driven by low-margin microcomputers. For Digital Equipment (where as recently as the 1980s, 90 percent of its sales came from minicomputers), this change proved to be disastrous as the minicomputer market began to dry up.

When momentum is going in the wrong direction, the only solution frequently is to dismantle the old organization—often with the help of outsiders, as has been the case with Digital Equipment's new CEO, Robert Palmer. It is often a long, slow, and painful but necessary process. Following more than $3 billion in losses over a two-year period, Palmer cut thirteen thousand jobs, fired a dozen vice presidents, closed plants, and reorganized the company into nine business units that focus on specific product markets.

Like Digital Equipment, IBM lost touch and got fat and slow. Interestingly, IBM's problems of 1992 and 1993 were evident in 1986, yet most people ignored them. In 1986 revenue growth was negligible, earnings growth was nonexistent, and the stock price was at $125 a share after losing one-fourth of its market value (from a peak of nearly $100 billion seven months earlier). But chairman John Akers was confident enough at that time to suggest that four or five years from then, people would see how superlative the company's performance was.

Over the next four and a half years, as revenue growth failed to keep up with the industry and as worldwide market share dropped from 30 percent to 21 percent (with each percentage point representing $3 billion in annual sales in the data processing industry, which doubled in size to $300 billion), the stock price dropped to below $100, prompting IBM to be removed from anybody's list of the most-admired corporations. Finally, Akers told his managers that IBM was "in a crisis," which was followed by the stock losing an additional 50 percent of its value over the next year and a half.

IBM and Digital Equipment failed to sustain their competitive advantages as their industry changed. Interestingly, some of the smaller businesses in this industry, including Apple and Compaq, have managed to bounce back despite periodic setbacks to sustain their competitive edges.

Competitive Advantage: Important Summary Points

1. Successful growth companies usually display a strong competitive advantage in terms of such factors as proprietary

technology (for example, Apple, Autodesk, Microsoft, Genentech, Sun Microsystems), innovativeness (for example, Compaq, Marion Laboratories), price (for example, Costco, Home Depot, Nucor, La Quinta), value (for example, Cray, Loctite, Pandick), production efficiency (for example, Cypress Semiconductor), distribution, or linkages.

2. The competitive advantage should be sustainable even if the company must adapt to new market conditions.

3. Fast-growth companies that have not been able to sustain a competitive advantage have often failed (for example, Vector Graphic, People Express, Worlds of Wonder).

Superior Product/Service Quality

Product Quality

Quality Standards

American industry—and American consumers—as a whole should thank the Germans and Japanese for an increased awareness of quality. The United States has lost some of its competitive edge in terms of quality over the last two decades. This is evident in the case of the American automobile industry, where American cars have been ranked (according to the well-respected J. D. Power survey) consistently behind Japanese and German models.

The United States has gotten better. This is partially because *quality* and *reliability* have recently become buzzwords for companies, especially in the automotive and electronics industries. This was a notion developed by the likes of W. Edwards Deming, Joseph M. Juran, and Peter Drucker and advanced by such experts as Tom Peters and Bob Waterman (authors of *In Search of Excellence*), and William Ouchi (author of *Theory Z*), who described how the most successful American companies provided high-quality products and services to their customers. The notion has further been enhanced by the pressure placed on American companies to compete for such lofty targets as the Baldrige Award and other quality commendations. As noted in the mid-1980s by Robert Cole of the University of Michigan in talking about the improvement in the quality of American automobiles as compared to Japanese automobiles, "The best of ours are [now] about as good as the worst of theirs, and that is a tremendous achievement."[1]

Top 10 Quality Cars

1990	1991	1992	Model
1	1	1	Lexus [Toyota] (Japan)
4	1	2	Infiniti [Nissan] (Japan)
*	*	3	Saturn [GM] (USA)
8	4	4	Acura [Honda] (Japan)
2	3	5	Mercedes-Benz (Germany)
3	6	6	Toyota (Japan)
**	7	7	Audi [VW] (Germany)
**	8	8	Cadillac [GM] (USA)
6	4	9	Honda (Japan)
**	**	10	Jaguar [Ford] (Britain)

*not available; **not ranked in top 10.
Source: J. D. Power survey of owner-reported problems.

Since that time, however, American quality standards have steadily improved, and many American companies—for example, Motorola, Intel, Cray Research, Gillette, Coca Cola, Maytag, and A.T. Cross—have become the recognized leaders in the world in terms of quality. Just as the Japanese used American companies as benchmarks for performance during the 1950s and 1960s, successful American companies have attempted to use Japanese standards as benchmarks for their own performance (Xerox, for example, has recently done to Canon what Canon did to it years earlier).

The quality improvements have been especially pronounced among smaller, often high-growth companies. In some cases, larger companies have provided the impetus. For example, Motorola has given its suppliers until 1994 to apply for the Baldrige Award or risk being dropped. Perhaps thanks to Motorola and other similar outstanding companies, the percentage of Baldrige entrants that are small companies has risen from 18 percent in 1988 to about 50 percent today. Moreover, in 1991 all three of the Baldrige winners were small companies, as were two of the Baldrige winners in 1992.

The Best-Built American Car

Quality has begun to be used more and more—sometimes wrongly, of course—by American companies in their advertising efforts. In fact, sad as it may seem, in 1990 Buick actually advertised that it was "the only American car to rank in the top 10 in quality" (even though it ranked fifth among all cars that year and fell off the list by 1992) and that its LeSabre was the "best-built American car" (even though it ranked sixth among all models that year, after having fallen from second place the previous year). It does not seem right to brag about being fifth or sixth; apparently, Buick felt that being best of a poor group was an accomplishment.

Fortunately, the successful fast-growth companies have often been better at demonstrating superior quality standards. Cisco Systems, which has gone public, is one of the world's quality leaders in computer network connectors. MIPS, also a public company, is a leader in RISC microprocessor chip design. And, Sun Microsystems (in technical workstations), Convex Computer (in mini-supercomputers), and Cray Research (in supercomputers) are quality leaders in their respective niches.

How Important is Product Quality?

According to the PIMS data base, developed by the Strategic Planning Institute, high market share results in profitability; however, *sustainable* market share is a direct result of "relative [that is, versus the competition] perceived [by the customer, rather than by the provider] product or service quality." The data suggest that relative quality is the single most important factor affecting the performance of a business.[2] Moreover, businesses rated in the top third in terms of perceived quality are, on average, more than twice as profitable as those rated in the bottom third. This relationship holds regardless of sector, geography, or growth.

Quality is the single most important factor determining the success of a business.

A follow-up study to Michael Porter's model of market share and profitability (cited in Chapter 5) further emphasizes the importance of product quality, especially as it relates quality to price. The study found that businesses classified as "high relative quality, high relative price" and "high relative quality, low relative price" (that is, differentiated businesses) were most profitable, with returns on investment of 36 percent and 34 percent, respectively.[3] Businesses classified as "low relative quality, low relative price" (the low-cost, low-price businesses) were also profitable, with returns on investment of 15 percent. In other words, companies can get away with marginal-quality products if they charge low prices for them. Companies classified as "middle relative quality, middle relative price" (those "stuck in the middle" of the curve) however, were by far the *least* profitable, with returns on investment of only 2 percent.

Although it is amazing how many companies refuse to recognize this, in a recent Gallup survey it was reported that consumers would pay 21 percent more for a better-quality car (an increase from a 10 percent premium for quality in a 1985 Gallup poll); 42 percent more for a better-quality dishwasher (versus 3 percent more in 1985); 67 percent more for a better-quality television (versus 6 percent more in 1985); and 72 percent more for a better-quality piece of furniture (versus 4 percent more in 1985).[4] Furthermore, the survey found that Americans were generally dissatisfied with the quality of products available and that people from the West Coast and individuals with higher incomes—two "leading indicator" consumer groups—were by far the most *dissatisfied* with the quality of products made in the United States.

Customers will pay significantly more for a higher quality product.

Fortunately, as noted earlier, the successful fast-growth companies—such as Cisco Systems, MIPS, Sun Microsystems, and Convex—have done a superb job of providing superior products for their customers. Couple that with service quality and you have the makings of an outstanding company. For example, although Dell was known as a leader in terms of price during its early years, it later added features to its product line and became a leader in customer satisfaction, as evidenced by its receiving a J. D. Power customer satisfaction award.

Often companies undertake programs geared to enhance quality through "total quality management" (TQM), "zero defects," "statistical quality control," "benchmarking," or some other catchphrase. More important however, is that such a program be accepted and reinforced throughout a company—in other words, everyone employed by the company should share an intense love for the product or service. You can often assess the success of a quality effort by asking the following questions:

- What quality standards are set?
- How do people feel about the quality of the product or service?
- How are these feelings conveyed to the employees and customers?
- How are these feelings reinforced?

Obviously one can monitor Baldrige or J. D. Power award recipients or can read *Consumer Reports* if you want to assess quality. But it may be more appropriate to simply touch or feel or use the product. Using these methods, product quality becomes exceedingly apparent for low-tech products, since consumers come into contact with them often on a daily basis. The following examples demonstrate how basic food products and other commodity items can be differentiated in such a way as to be perceived as outstanding in terms of product quality.

Eating Quality

MAN CANNOT LIVE BY BREAD ALONE. Quality becomes apparent in our daily eating habits. Consider Margaret Rudkin's start as a successful entrepreneur in the late 1930s. Ms. Rudkin's son, Mark, suffered from asthma, which his doctor thought was a result of an allergic reaction to chemical additives in his food. Seeking to provide a natural diet for her son, Rudkin began to bake whole grain bread (from a recipe of her grandmother's) at her country estate in Connecticut, which was known as Pepperidge Farm. When the doctor tasted the bread, he asked her to bake some for his other patients. Soon her friends began to ask her to bake some loaves for them. She sold some bread to a local market in Connecticut, with great results. Within a short time her husband, who was a stockbroker in New York City, tried to sell some of the loaves to the department stores in the city; soon he was carrying all the loaves that he could handle on each trip.

Within a year, Rudkin was selling about four thousand loaves per week. Not long after that, she was selling four thousand loaves per day. Her "recipe" for success was, quite simply, *quality*. She would discard anything that was less than perfect. Her company, named Pepperidge Farm after the estate, grew so large in the early 1960s that she sold out to Campbell's, the soup company.

LET THEM EAT CAKES. Dunkin' Donuts, which prides itself on serving the "best coffee in the world," has also demonstrated a commitment to quality. Even during a period when coffee consumption in America declined by 10 percent, a typical Dunkin' Donuts shop increased its sales of cups of coffee by 20 percent. The company has a twenty-page set of specifications on what is required in a coffee bean. They also guarantee that the coffee that they serve their customers is fresh: beans must be used within ten days of their delivery, and coffee not served within eighteen minutes of being brewed is thrown out. To top it off, Dunkin' Donuts is one of the few places left that uses real cream rather than milk, half and half, or powder.

Quality Commodities

CHICKEN. Most people think of chicken as a commodity. Yet Frank Perdue has found a way of differentiating his chickens from the countless other brands that are available. Despite a ten-centsa-pound price premium over the other brands, Perdue chickens generally have a commanding lead in market share over the competition in most of the company's East Coast locations. This is attributable to the higher perceived quality of Perdue chicken, which is largely a result of the breeding techniques and quality control. In essence, Perdue has made a commodity product into a non-commodity.

HOME AND OFFICE PRODUCTS. In a similar manner, several companies have demonstrated how typical items found around the office or home can be differentiated from commodity items. For example, Sealed Air Corporation pioneered the bubble wrap that comes stuffed in boxes that are used for shipping or moving fragile contents. At a sales meeting, CEO Dermot Dunphy told his people, "The lesson to be learned is that no matter how commonplace a product may appear, it does not have to become a commodity. Every product can be differentiated."[5]

Like bubble wrap, writing pens are considered commodity items. Yet those made by A. T. Cross (Lincoln, RI) were recently included in *Fortune* magazine's list of the nine best products in the world. That should not be startling, since there is emphasis on quality in every phase of production. *Every* fountain pen, rather than one in each hundred or thousand, is hand tested at the factory to make sure it meets the standards of the company. In addition, every employee is a quality control inspector: anyone can reject an imperfect part, no matter what the reason. Not surprisingly, although Cross pens are guaranteed for life, fewer than 2 percent of all units made have been returned.

Equally impressive is Herman Miller, Inc. (of Zeeland, MI), which, aside from producing some of the finest-quality products in the United States, is often considered one of the best corporations to work for in the country.[6] It is one of the few corporations in which 100 percent of the employees own stock. Over the company's sixty-year history it has established a reputation for making high-quality office furniture, thereby differentiating it from the scores of other companies that manufacture furniture. Since

1974, annual sales for this extremely profitable company have grown from $40 million to nearly $1 billion.

STEEL. It is difficult to think of the products of some industries—for example, steel and tires—as anything but commodities. Some companies in these industries, however, have done just that. For example, Worthington Industries, which was founded in 1955 by John McConnell, is now a billion-dollar steel company. The company is known for its quality, with standards that are considered *five times* higher than the industry average. Yet there are no quality control inspectors; rather, each employee takes on that role. Quality has resulted from the same two key factors evident in the other high-quality producers just discussed: a strong customer orientation and a strong employee orientation.

Service Quality

A Role Model?

Once upon a time IBM was regarded as one of the best-managed and most-admired corporations in the world. IBM's early success can be attributed to its commitment to customer service. That focus was established by Thomas J. Watson, Sr., and then reinforced by his successor, Thomas J. Watson, Jr. The senior Watson was one of the most successful industrialists in the United States during the 1920s and 1930s, building IBM into a dominant player in its industry. Interestingly, though, he was uncomfortable with computers. He spent his whole life with punch cards, which were used with machines that processed census data and payrolls. In fact, in 1943 he suggested, "I think there is a world market for about five computers."[7]

It was, of course, Watson, Jr., that pushed IBM into the computer field that precipitated its growth. In the process, IBM overtook rivals like General Electric, RCA, Honeywell, and Remington Rand. Over the younger Watson's fifteen-year tenure as CEO (from 1956 to 1971), IBM grew at a 16 percent annual rate, and the company's stock increased in value by $36 billion. This would certainly suggest that IBM followed the pattern of successful fast-growth companies, at least during this time.

The key to IBM's growth was marketing to customers. Watson, Jr., recognized that IBM often came in second when it came to product innovation. Yet IBM was unmatched when it came to marketing, sales, and distribution—in short, the art of attracting and retaining customers. IBM offered more than machines; it offered service—particularly the continued assistance of IBM's staff. (This is what prompted the slogan "IBM Means Service.") Of course, there was a profit motive behind IBM's strategy: the company would receive enormous revenues year after year from leasing computers to satisfied customers.

Although IBM can certainly be faulted for its recent failures, its first seventy years were splendid. It should not be surprising that there is research suggesting that "the IBM way" makes sense from a profitability standpoint. In a sample of better performers versus worse performers in terms of perceived customer service, it was found that the better service providers gained market share at the rate of 6 percent per year and had a 12 percent return on sales, while the worse performers lost market share at the rate of 2 percent per year and had only a 1 percent return on sales.[8]

Better service providers surpass competitors by gaining market share at the rate of 6 percent per year and raising return on sales by 12 percent.

Again, notwithstanding IBM's recent demise, we should be cognizant of the lessons learned from IBM's commitment to service. This is clearly seen in its effective magazine advertising campaign during the late 1980s and early 1990s. At the top of the ad it states, "If your failure rate is one in a million, what do you tell that one customer?" Successful companies recognize that they must strive for a 100 percent success rate (that is, zero defects).

After all, a 99.9 percent success rate, although it sounds pretty good, would still translate into the following:

- Two unsafe landings at O'Hare Airport per day
- Sixteen thousand pieces of mail lost per hour
- Five hundred incorrect surgical operations per week
- Twenty-two thousand checks deducted from the wrong bank account per hour

How Fast-Growth Companies Provide Quality Service

What about service quality for smaller, faster-growing companies? Consider Intuit, a computer software company that is best known for its Quicken program, which enables individuals and small business owners to write checks and keep track of their finances on a computer. Quicken, which has a sixty percent market share, is one of the most successful personal finance programs ever developed. This was certainly the primary reason why Intuit was ranked among the top fifteen companies in the 1990 *Inc.* 500 listing with revenues of $33 million. Since that time, Intuit's revenues and earnings have more than tripled.

What makes Intuit successful is its intense commitment to its customers. As noted by Scott Cook, the company's founder and president, "We have hundreds of thousands of salespeople. They're our customers. . . . [Intuit's mission is to] make the customer feel so good about the product they'll go and tell five friends to buy it."[9] The reason the customers are so enthused that they will tell their friends about the product is because Intuit offers a faster, less expensive (the retail price of less than $50), easy-to-use (Intuit claims that it takes less than six minutes to learn) program that is supported by excellent postpurchase service.

Perhaps it is Cook's Harvard Business School background, or maybe his Procter & Gamble experience, that has made Intuit such a market-driven company. For example, Intuit has an annual customer survey to find out which features its customers use or do not use and like or dislike; it runs focus groups for people who are *not* users of Quicken; it compiles information from customer call-ins and letters to be used by product development teams; it continuously tests its programs; and it launched a "follow me home" campaign in which Quicken customers are asked to let an Intuit representative observe them when they first use the program. The idea is that Quicken should be so easy to use that anybody who purchases it will use it. After all, if they do not use it, they will not tell their friends and associates to use it.

But the real test of customer service is what happens when the customer has a question or a problem about the software. This is why Intuit's technical support representatives make up almost one-fourth of the company's work force. They routinely take work home with them at night or over the weekend to do whatever is necessary to satisfy a customer. Almost every Intuit employee—including Cook—spends at least a few hours each month working the customer service telephone lines, demonstrating how much emphasis Intuit places on customer support. The company tracks daily and weekly statistics on customer support performance (for example, how many customers wait longer than one minute). These statistics are discussed at weekly meetings that create peer pressure to improve customer service.

During a time when computer software companies are charging their customers for after-purchase service, Intuit does it for free. Moreover, Intuit recently installed a $500,000 telephone system so that customers would not have to wait as long when they call. Of course, Intuit recognizes that it costs nearly $5 million per year (or about 15 percent of revenues) to provide these services. That is why they get it right the first time—a form of customer service that is more important than money-back guarantees, 800 numbers, or customer complaint forms.

Product Features and Service Quality

HIGH-TECH QUALITY. As important as product quality is for technology products, service quality if equally is not more important on occasion. High-tech people brag about "specmanship" (the superior technical specifications of a product), but often the deciding factor in purchasing these products is something as intangible as service or reliability. Consider Regis McKenna's assessment of Intel Corporation:

The power of intangible positioning became clear to me a few years ago when I was doing a market survey for Intel. As part of the survey, I talked to a number of engineers about a certain memory chip. I remember asking one engineer why he selected the Intel chip. The chip was a fairly technical product, and you might have expected the engineer to answer in technical argot: "The memory had an access time of so many nanoseconds," or "Its power dissipation is only such-and-such." That didn't happen. Instead, the engineer told me his company buys almost all its chips from Intel, so it was natural to buy the new chip from Intel too. Had he evaluated the new product? Not really. "We just tend to buy from Intel because we have a business relationship there," he explained. "We know where they are going and we trust the company.". . . Most buying decisions are made the same way. Product managers spend days, if not weeks, drawing up charts and graphs that compare products on the basis of specifications and price. But buying decisions are rarely based on these objective standards. The important product comparisons come from the minds of those in the marketplace. And in people's minds, it's intangible factors that count.[10]

LOW-TECH QUALITY. Liz Claiborne's success was enhanced by the company's decision *not* to build its own manufacturing plants, thereby giving the company less control over clothing designs (that is, product features). Although that decision resulted in increased per unit costs, it gave the company greater flexibility than its competitors. In addition, Liz Claiborne did not maintain a traveling sales force. This forced the company to concentrate on obtaining orders from large department stores and specialty retailers whose buyers routinely traveled to New York City, where the company had its showroom. What resulted was an intense customer orientation and an ability to act quickly to meet customer needs.

Traditional Service Organizations Provide Excellence in Service

Like IBM's "IBM Means Service," there are other reminders—often found in such company slogans as "When it absolutely, positively has to get there overnight" (Federal Express) and "No problem at Nordstrom" (Nordstrom)—that stress the importance of customer service. We see that clearly in some traditional service companies.

AIRLINES. Jan Carlzon, the architect behind the turnaround at Scandinavian Airlines Systems (SAS), referred to the millions of fifteen-second encounters between his people and their customers as "moments of truth"; these are the moments when the company must prove to customers that SAS is the best airline around.[11] For Carlzon, that means that a ticket agent, flight attendant, baggage handler, or anyone else working for SAS has just fifteen seconds in which to gain or lose a loyal customer.

RETAILING. Tom Peters tells an interesting story of service excellence at Nordstrom, the extremely successful chain of department stores located on the West Coast. It involves a seminar participant who was an executive with a company based in Portland, Oregon.

> His two daughters and his wife are Nordstrom fans. They constantly bubble about it and pester him to shop there. He was frankly fed up with all the talk. Moreover, despite their comments to the contrary, he secretly suspected that Nordstrom charged an arm and a leg. (Nordstrom's policy is to match anyone's price for a garment, if asked to do so.)
>
> But he did need a suit badly. And a major sale was going on. At worst, he figured, he didn't have too much to lose, especially with the sale. Reluctantly, he went to Nordstrom.
>
> The service in the store was good, he had to admit. And he did find a fine suit on sale, although he also picked up a second suit—at full price. Nordstrom promises same-day alterations. He noted, however, that there was a little asterisk next to the promise—next-day alteration was promised during sales. He chortled at this small chink in the armor.
>
> He came back at 5:45 P.M. the next day to pick up his suits. It was fifteen minutes before closing. He needed the suits for a trip that night.

To his surprise, though he'd only been there once, his salesperson greeted him by name! The fellow then trotted upstairs to pick up the suits. Five minutes passed. The salesperson reappeared—without the goods. They hadn't been finished.

Though he needed the suits, our friend admits to secret glee. Without the suits, he took off for a Monday appointment in Seattle, after which he proceeded to Dallas for the big meeting of the trip.

He checked into his hotel and went to his room. A message light informed him that a package had arrived for him. A bellman fetched it—Federal Express. Yes, it was from Nordstrom. In it were his two suits. On top of them were three $25 silk ties (which he hadn't ordered) thrown in gratis! There was also a note of apology from the salesperson, who had called his home and learned his travel arrangements from one of his daughters. With a smile of resignation, he admits that he is now a believer.[12]

There are countless stories about Nordstrom just like this one. The result is that Nordstrom has grown from a $250 million company in the late 1970s to a $3 billion company in the early 1990s, with its most significant growth coming in the highly competitive market of southern California. Moreover its sales per square foot (one of the most vital measures of success of any retailer) is not only the highest among department stores, it is three times the industry average.

Service for a Commodity

GROCERS. Stew Leonard's (of Norwalk, CT) is the world's largest dairy store and perhaps the most profitable grocery store in the nation. The company generates more than $100 million annually—or about $1,000 per square foot—from one store that carries only eight hundred items, which are often thought of as commodities. Its one hundred thousand square feet of store space (Stew Leonard's was started in 1969 and has since expanded twenty-seven times) includes an in-store bakery, a dairy, a fish market, and an ice cream store. The store's success starts with quality—it has the freshest milk and bread available—but equally important is its attention to customers. Stew Leonard's has a sign etched in a three-ton chunk of granite that says: *"Rule #1: The customer is always right. Rule #2: If the customer is wrong, see*

Rule #1." It is symbolic, of course, but it certainly serves as a great reminder in disciplining the organization in caring for their customers.

BANKING. Consumer banking is also often thought of as a commodity-type service. Yet Carl Schmitt, the founder and CEO of University National Bank (UNB) in Palo Alto, California—more of a constrained, focused-growth success story than a fast-growth company, but still worth discussing—has shown how his bank can be differentiated. The key to the success of UNB is its commitment to customer service. For example, the bank takes pride in having all bank statements close on the last day of every month; then everybody employed at the bank, including the CEO, gets together to mail out the statements to customers. (It sounds simple, but nobody else does this.) UNB also offers services for its customers that include vans to pick up deposits; no lines (if one starts to form, officers of the bank wait on the customers); newsletters; a free shoeshine; and calculators, pens (without chains), and scratch pads at the deposit table. All of these are reminders that customer service is the basic belief upon which the bank was founded.

TIRE DEALERS. An extreme example of a company that sells an atypical commodity is found in the tire industry. A couple of years ago I was commissioned by the National Tire Dealers and Retreaders Association (NTDRA) to examine the profitability (or lack of profitability, as is often the case) of independent tire dealers. During one of my trips I came across Direct Tire, located outside of Boston. Direct Tire, which is owned by Barry Steinberg, is a close to $5 million business whose 3 percent net margins are twice the industry average.

From the moment you arrive at Direct Tire, you see that it is not your typical tire dealer; it is packed with Mercedes-Benzes, Porsches, BMWs, Jaguars, and the like. If a customer is looking for a $2,000 set of wheels for a $60,000 car, there is clearly just one place in Boston to go to get the job done: Direct Tire. Steinberg realizes the importance of nichemanship.

Steinberg also recognizes the importance of satisfying his customers, which happens as a result of a substantial investment by the company. Appointments are scheduled at the customer's convenience, so that he or she can get in and out within an hour. Loaner cars are provided to customers (at a cost of about $29,000 per year to Direct Tire), and the dealer issues *lifetime* guarantees on tires and service. Customers are happy to pay a premium of 10 percent or so for these benefits.

If you have shopped for tires at a typical tire dealership, you will no doubt recall the sloppy, unkempt waiting and working areas that are, in some cases, bad enough to be health hazards. For Direct Tire, though, customer service starts from the moment you enter the store. The waiting area is spotless. There is fresh-brewed coffee (at a cost of $2,500 per year) and current magazines such as GQ and Vogue (at a cost of $900 per year) available for customers. The workers are all in uniform (at a cost of $21,000 per year) to enhance the professionalism surrounding this small business.

These small signals, however, are just part of Steinberg's strategy to make every customer a repeat customer. Everything is geared for that purpose. The company uses a headhunter—which is unheard of in this industry—to find experienced, qualified people, and it pays employees 15 to 25 percent above the industry average (at an additional cost of $17,000 per year). The company uses a customized computer software package (at a cost of $48,000) to track inventory, thereby cutting down on the waiting time for customers (while it maintains an optimal level of inventory). To make sure that it carries just about any tire that a customer might need, the company also stocks about $250,000 worth of inventory—or about 20 percent more than many of its competitors—including hard-to-find (and high-margin) tires for upper-end automobiles. Some business owners look at these added costs as expenses; Steinberg looks at them as *investments,* all of which enhance customer loyalty—not to mention sales and profits—for Direct Tire.

Customer Complaints: Turning a Problem into an Opportunity

Just how important is quality customer service? Perhaps that issue is best addressed by examining the impact of poor service. In a study by Technical Assistance Research Corporation, it was found that only 4 percent of the customers who have a bad experience actually report it, primarily because they feel that nothing will be done about it. What is alarming is that more than 90 percent of those that do not complain will not come back, regardless of the amount of the purchase. Moreover, not only will the average person who has had a bad experience go elsewhere for his or her next purchase, but he or she will tell nine to ten people about the episode.

Only 4 percent of the customers who have a bad experience actually report it and more than 90 percent of those that do not complain will not come back.

Fortunately, it was also found that if the complaint is resolved, about 90 percent of the customers will come back. Thus, even if there is a bad experience, loyalty can be regained. As Stew Leonard remarked on a PBS special featuring his grocery store, "The customer who complains is your friend. What worries me is the one who doesn't complain and never comes back."

No company will be able to sustain growth by being merely as good as its competitors. As successful high-tech and low-tech companies illustrate, it is essential to offer products and service of a recognizable superior quality.

Product/Service Quality: Important Summary Points

1. Research suggests that sustainable market share is a direct result of relative perceived product or service quality.
2. Successful fast-growth companies have generally adhered to a strategy that emphasizes superior product or service quality (for example, Cisco, MIPS, Sun Microsystem, Convex Computer, Cray Research).
3. Quality is quite apparent among fast-growth companies in the foods industry (for example, Dunkin' Donuts, Ben &

Jerry's Homemade), as well as among companies that provide commodity-type products or services (for example, Perdue Chicken, Sealed Air, A. T. Cross, Herman Miller, Worthington); these successful companies recognize the importance of differentiating their products from those of their competitors.

4. Service quality supports the quality of a company's products; successful growth companies have demonstrated a strong sense of commitment to the service that they provide (for example, Intuit, Intel, Nordstrom).

8

Innovativeness

When we think of innovation, we are often reminded of inventors such as Thomas Edison, who actually created an "invention factory." As the reader will soon see, however, scientific inventions are just a small part of innovation. Of course, successful fast-growth companies have often been the pioneers in such technologies as computers and office automation, as demonstrated by Cray Research (in supercomputers), Apollo Computer and Sun Microsystems (in workstations), Apple Computer (in personal computers), and Microsoft (in computer software). A careful examination of the relative R & D budgets of such companies provides some information on the innovative capabilities of high-tech businesses. Low-tech companies, however, have been responsible for changes in the more routine ways in which we work (for example, Federal Express in overnight delivery) and live (for example, Kinder-Care in day care centers, Liz Claiborne in women's fashion, and Nike in fitness). These businesses may be just as innovative as some of the high-tech successes I have identified.

Innovation involves creating new products or services, new markets, and/or new approaches to conducting business. Many successful fast-growth companies have followed such a strategy, of competing via intense innovation.

The ability to innovate is at the heart of success. Typically, innovative companies demonstrate a sense of *constant experimentation, action* (even if there is some duplication, sloppiness, or inefficiency), and *simplicity of structure* (to allow for the recognition of experimentation and action). To assess the extent of innovativeness, simply ask the following questions:

- Are innovations prevalent, or are people "stale"?
- What is the source of innovations?
- Does the structure allow for innovation?
- Is there experimentation? Is it rewarded?
- How much money is spent on R & D?
- What happens when an idea fails?

Proprietary Technology: A Classic Case of Innovativeness

A Star Is Born

The high-profile innovators have often been technology companies. And perhaps the highest profile fast-growth technology company of the 1980s and 1990s is Apple Computer. Apple's history goes back to the time when Steven Jobs was designing video games for Atari and Stephen Wozniak was working on pocket calculators for Hewlett-Packard. Wozniak had designed a home computer, but he could not convince his employer to produce and market it. In fact, Wozniak spent months trying to *give away* the schematics, with no intention of selling the completed machine. At the same time Jobs was unable to get Nolan Bushnell, the founder and CEO of Atari, to commit resources to the project. So they decided to go off on their own, and the two college dropouts set up shop in Jobs's garage.

The two whiz kids were boyhood friends who gained experience in electronic circuit design when they teamed up to build several "blue boxes," which were illegal devices used to make free long distance telephone calls. When they got together, their plan was to sell circuit boards to "hackers" who wanted to build their own computers. (Jobs was able to convince Wozniak that it would be more profitable to sell the circuit boards than to give away the schematics.) Their initial capital, which was obtained primarily from the sale of Jobs's Volkswagen and Wozniak's calculator, was $1,300.

They called on a friend, Paul Terrell, who had just opened up The Byte Shop, one of the first computer stores in Silicon Valley. Jobs and Wozniak hoped to sell one hundred boards, which would cost them about $25 apiece in parts, for $50 each. Terrell, however, was more interested in a fully assembled product made from the circuit boards; he placed an order with Jobs to buy fifty fully assembled computers that would sell for $500 to $600. In addition, The Byte Shop agreed to pay cash on delivery, provided that the computers worked.

Jobs was able to convince suppliers to give them the same terms (net thirty days) as much larger manufacturers. He and Wozniak ordered parts for one hundred computers and built the machines over the next few weeks. They then took fifty of the computers down to The Byte Shop and were able to pay their suppliers within twenty-nine days of receiving the deliveries. They still had fifty computers for the next order and not really expended any of their capital; any new orders would be sheer profit.

Although initial sales were not strong, the units eventually sold and paved the way for Apple's growth. It also became apparent that Jobs and Wozniak would need additional outside capital. They were put in touch with Don Valentine, a local venture capitalist, by Nolan Bushnell, Jobs's former boss at Atari. Valentine referred them to another venture capitalist, Mike Markkula, who assisted them with their business plan and invested $90,000 of his own money in the venture. They then recruited Michael Scott, director of manufacturing at National Semiconductor, to become president at a 50 percent cut in his pay. That, plus the initial venture capital funding (of less than $100,000) they received, enabled them to secure a $250,000 line of credit from the Bank of America.

The new entrepreneurial team then raised $600,000 from such notable venture capital sources as Arthur Rock, Hambrecht and Quist, Henry Singleton (a founder of Teledyne), and Venrock Associates. When Apple went public at $22 per share in 1980, the company raised $110 million, the largest initial public offering since Comsat raised $200 million fifteen years earlier. In the immediate after-market, Apple's stock traded at $34 per share; by June 1983 the stock had reached a high of $63 per share.

In the three years prior to Apple's IPO, earnings had grown by 700 percent. This allowed the underwriter, Morgan Stanley, to price the stock at a premium comparable to other high-growth technology companies such as ROLM, Paradyne, and Tandem, which were selling at approximately eighteen times their antici- pated 1981 earnings. Apple's total valuation at the time of the company's IPO was in excess of $1 billion, or eighty-five times its previous year's earnings of $11.7 million. When Apple went pub- lic, Steve Jobs's shares were worth $165 million. The early in- vestors did quite well, too; for example, Arthur Rock's $57,600 investment in 1977 grew to $14 million in three years.

Apple, primarily as a result of its innovative technology, has been largely responsible for changing the way people live and work. When Apple was incorporated in 1977, there were fifty thousand computers in the world. A decade later, fifty thousand computers were built and sold each day. It is ironic that in the same year that Apple was formed, Ken Olsen, chairman of Digital Equipment Corporation (the third-largest computer company in

---

When Apple was incorporated in 1977, there were fifty thousand computers in the world. A decade later, fifty thousand computers were built and sold each day.

---

the United States behind IBM and Hewlett-Packard, and a re- markable entrepreneurial success story in its own right), said, "There is no reason for any individual to have a computer in their home."[1]

Seizing an Opportunity

Personal Computers

Apple is often given credit for creating the first home computer. It would be more appropriate, however, to say that Apple *sold* the first home computer. Another company had the dubious distinc- tion of creating the first home computer—without reaping the sales benefits.

Xerox Palo Alto Reserach Corporation (PARC) is a research facility located near Stanford University that was designed and funded by Xerox. Its purpose has been to use available information and technology to create the "office of the future." Its prime location near first-rate universities and in the heart of Silicon Valley made it very easy to attract some brilliant minds in the area of information technology. By 1974, three years before the birth of Apple Computer, Xerox PARC had created the first personal computer, which was called the Alto. It had also created a computer with a graphic screen, overlapping pop-up windows, icons, fonts, and a mouse—very much like Apple's Macintosh models of the 1980s and 1990s.

When Steve Jobs toured the Xerox PARC facility in 1979, he became, to put it mildly, intrigued by the Alto. According to Larry Tesler of Xerox PARC, Jobs was *"leaping and jumping around the room and yelling things. He kept saying over and over, 'Why aren't you doing something with this?' The implication was, 'If you don't, we will.' "*[2] The staff at Xerox PARC also pleaded with corporate executives to produce such a personal computer for the general public. But the executives, fearing that the business market would not accept this new invention, felt that it was too risky a project.

Steve Jobs seized this opportunity to begin the development of Apple's Lisa model, which was far from a success, and ultimately the Macintosh. Unlike Xerox, which was focused on the corporate market, Jobs sought to develop a computer that would be fun to use by children and adults of all ages. Obviously, his vision was correct, as evidenced by the remarkable success of the Macintosh.

Supercomputers

Cray Research has been a pioneer in the field of supercomputers. The company, which was founded in 1972, was one of only a handful of companies to make the *Inc.* 100 list of small fast-growth publicly held corporations for five consecutive years (after which it was too large to qualify). Growth has continued over recent years: sales have grown from $11 million in 1977 to $1 billion in 1992.

Several years earlier Seymour Cray had earned a reputation as a technical whiz while working on the development of some of the early Univac models at Sperry. He and several of his colleagues later went along with Bill Norris to launch Control Data Corporation (CDC); while there, Cray was head of the design team for the CDC 7600, which was the first supercomputer. Yet CDC never considered supercomputers to be its primary thrust. Cray seized the opportunity in this market by forming his own company that would specialize in supercomputers. The company was founded on the principle of innovation and has consistently invested heavily in research and development. In fact, Cray Research has generally ranked at or near the top of the list of R & D dollars spent per employee and as a percentage of revenues.

Cray's overall success has been a direct result of its emphasis on new product innovation, which has enabled the company to develop state-of-the-art supercomputers, thereby making it a world leader in its industry. Its strategy of innovation was spearheaded initially by its founder, Seymour Cray, and more recently by its CEO, John Rollwagen. In essence, Cray attempts to make its previous line of supercomputers obsolete by pioneering new machines to replace its existing line.

Chips and Drives

Similar to Cray Research, several semiconductor companies—notably Analog Devices, LSI Logic, and Cypress Semiconductor—have used their innovative capabilities as the backbone of their competitive strategy. These three companies have all been successful by seizing opportunities in this highly competitive industry.

Analog Devices (of Norwood, MA), a $500 million semiconductor business, operates at the leading edge of technology in an industry that has been plagued by oversupply, price wars, foreign competition, and other problems since the 1980s. In Analog's market niche of high-performance scientific applications, quality and reliability are more important than price. It targets its efforts in markets in which Analog will be the market leader and, in many cases, the sole source of supply. Ray Stata, founder and CEO of Analog, is devoted to innovation and is coauthor of a book on the topic.[3] Yet with all his emphasis on innovative products, Stata has certainly not lost sight of the importance of creating an attractive environment in which employees can work. His company is always listed among the best-managed companies in the semiconductor industry.

LSI (which stands for "large-scale integration") Logic grew by an average of 45 percent per year over its first ten years of operation. The company went public in 1983, raising $160 million, which was at the time the largest IPO in history. LSI Logic's success is largely attributable to Wilfred Corrigan, former CEO of Fairchild Semiconductor, who left Fairchild in 1979 when it was taken over by Schlumberger. Corrigan has stressed product innovation, as evidenced by the success of the LSI's Application Specific Integrated Circuits (ASICs), (which have several standard chip functions but can easily be customized). LSI, which is among the fastest-growing companies in the United States and one of the largest semiconductor companies in the world, is in the early 1990s a nearly $750 million company. It has become the industry leader in circuit design software, which enables systems engineers to create their own custom chips in weeks rather than months or years; this is an extremely important advantage in the rapidly changing computer industry.

Like Analog and LSI, Cypress Semiconductor has been successful as a result of its emphasis on product innovation. As a niche player in the high-end market, Cypress is limited in its growth prospects for a given product line. Consequently, it has developed dozens of new product lines that have enabled the company to continue its successful fast-growth pattern.

An innovative company that has experienced even more significant growth in a somewhat different niche of the computer industry is Conner Peripherals (of San Jose, CA), a manufacturer of disk drives. The company, started in 1987 by executives from Seagate Technology, had $113 million in revenues in its first year. Conner grew to *Fortune* 500 status in its third year and reached the billion-dollar mark in sales in its fourth year; no other company has reached those milestones that quickly. The reason for its success is largely a result of its intense innovation, including the 3 1/2" disk drive and more recently the 2 1/2" high-capacity disk drive, which has applications in the notebook computer market. Ironically, Seagate, which gave rise to Conner Peripherals, had made a name for itself with its 5 1/4″ disk drive. Seagate overproduced the 5 1/4″ drives, however, and was slow to react when demand increased for the 3 1/2″ disk drives.

Pharmaceuticals and Health Care

Key Pharmaceuticals (of Miami, FL), is one of the few new pharmaceutical companies founded in the United States since the late 1930s. Generally, only the large established companies (like Johnson & Johnson, Bristol-Myers Squibb, Eli Lilly, and Merck) can afford to spend the necessary time and money in product development, wait five to ten years or so for FDA approval, and then market their products to the health professionals. In an industry dominated by multibillion-dollar giants with R & D budgets in the hundreds of millions of dollars, however, Key has found new ways to administer old medicine. The company innovates in the administration of drugs that the FDA had already accepted as safe and effective. Key's asthma treatment product, Theo-Dur, is a time-released drug made from theophylline, which has been used for decades. Similarly, Key's angina treatment product is a bandage treated with nitroglycerine that can be worn over a patient's chest, a significant improvement to the previously used nitroglycerin pill that would be taken orally. Such innovations have prompted the multibillion-dollar international pharmaceutical companies to enter into joint agreements with Key.

Marion Laboratories traditionally ranks as one of the most innovative companies in the pharmaceutical industry and as one of the most productive companies in the United States in terms of profitability per employee. Unlike other pharmaceutical companies, however, Marion's innovativeness is in its licensing arrangements with foreign companies, which eliminate the often billion-dollar developmental costs. Recently, Marion licensed Cardizem from Tanabe Seiyaku Ltd. (of Japan), which turned out to be an extremely profitable venture.

In the health care field, one of the innovation leaders is U.S. Surgical (of Norwalk, CT), a $500 million company that has been growing at nearly a 50 percent annual rate in the 1990s. U.S. Surgical produces 70 percent of the world's surgical stapling equipment. The company has recently "edged out" into the area of surgical sutures (stitches), battling Ethicon (a division of Johnson & Johnson), which has traditionally controlled 80 percent of the sutures market. Prior to entering this market niche, U.S. Surgical spent months asking doctors what they wanted in a suture, then invested heavily in R & D to satisfy the doctors' needs. Similarly, U.S. Surgical conducted extensive market research among physicians in developing instruments used in laparoscopic surgery, a technique that enables surgeons to remove a gallbladder through a tiny incision with the aid of a tubelike instrument and a miniature camera. Compared to traditional gallbladder surgery, this technique results in less complications, a speedier recovery, a much smaller scar, and a much smaller bill for patients.

Other Technology Products

There are several other companies known for their technological innovations in such diverse industries as telecommunications (MCI Communications) and filtration (Pall Corporation). MCI started out as a private telephone line service between Chicago and St. Louis that used microwave technology, rather than the embedded twisted copper wire lines that were used by AT & T during that time. In the late 1960s the company was in financial trouble, so it turned to William McGowan, a well-known turnaround expert. McGowan realized that the FCC routinely granted requests for private-line licenses between two cities if no one objected; in fact, thousands of such requests were granted each year by the FCC. So McGowan submitted several hundred requests for private-line service between major cities; these requests were not noticed until he had created an entire long distance telephone network that could compete with AT & T. After years of dealing with changes in FCC regulations, McGowan built MCI into a $10 billion company.

During the 1970s Pall Corporation, a manufacturer of filters used in industrial plants, hospitals, aircrafts, and numerous other applications, had the highest return on investment of any corporation listed in the *Fortune* 1000. Most new products during at least the first half of that period were developed by David Pall. As the company has grown and as technologies have changed, its R & D group has grown dramatically, as has its management approach. This has resulted in a much higher rate of product innovation.

After You Seize the Opportunity

Several companies that have been successful in seizing an opportunity fail to sustain their advantage. There are several good examples in the computer software industry, in which it is vital to act quickly and stay ahead of the competition. Consider Borland, for example, the fifth-largest computer software company, whose products include Quattro Pro, Paradox, and dBase. Borland's success has resulted from its having two-thirds of the $500 million market for data base software. Despite significant growth during the 1980s the company has been hurt in the early 1990s, particularly by Microsoft with its Access data base program. Microsoft took advantage of Borland's delays in production by shipping its Windows-based Access program before Borland could ship its own Windows-based program.

Lotus Development also learned that it can be crippling to let programming schedules slip, as was the case with a recent release of its popular 1-2-3 spreadsheet program. But it can be equally dangerous to ship a product too soon: Lotus did just that with a subsequent version of 1-2-3, which was rife with bugs and had to be replaced. As a result of these miscues and the success of Microsoft's Excel spreadsheet, Lotus's market share of spreadsheet software has dropped from around 75 percent to about 50 percent in the early 1990s. Considering that 70 percent of Lotus's revenues are in spreadsheets, that loss in market share is dramatic.

Similar troubles have plagued Mentor Graphics, who in 1989 was the world leader in software used to simplify the task of designing advanced computer chips. Mentor's customer list at the time included Apple, Boeing, and Samsung, and there were expectations that the company sales would rise from about $400 million in 1988 to more than $1 billion by 1991. Like Lotus, however, Mentor experienced delays in development, followed by a shipment of software that was plagued with bugs. Sales for 1992 were $355 million, about 17 percent less than in 1989; furthermore, Mentor lost about $115 million between 1991 and 1992.

Mentor, like so many high-tech companies, learned that leaders of one technology generation often fail to catch the next one.

High-Tech Innovators Must Continue Growing

Technological advancements have had a profound impact on technology companies, especially those in the computer industry. One outcome has been that technology (as well as competition) has driven down the costs of computing power and, therefore, the price of computers to the ultimate end user. Computer companies

---

Falling prices force companies to sell a larger quantity of the same model just to stay even from the previous year's sales.

---

must sell a larger quantity of the same model of a machine (now at a discounted price) just to stay even from the previous year's sales. As noted by Jim Treybig, founder and CEO of Tandem Computer, "The economies of our business are frightening. We can deliver a lot more power for a lot less money each year, but the industry isn't growing as fast as it once did. The bottom line is, if your company doesn't have big growth, you have a horrible problem."[4]

High-Tech Innovations in Service Companies

Generally we think of the high-tech manufacturing companies (such as Digital Equipment, Apple Computer, and Sun Microsystems) as the leaders in technological innovation. Yet some service companies have been on the cutting edge of technology as well. Although the end uses of a technology may be low tech, its development might have involved a high degree of technological innovation. For example, there was mail delivery before Federal Express. But Frederick Smith, founder of Federal Express, used technology and innovation to create a new market—guaranteed overnight delivery. (Interestingly, Smith's father was founder of Dixie Greyhound Bus Lines, and his grandfather was a steamboat captain on the Mississippi River. So, in three generations, the family mastered the water, highway, and air transportation business.)

Smith's idea for Federal Express called for developing a network in which packages from all over the country could be flown to a central location and then sorted, redistributed, and flown to their destination cities for truck delivery. The idea would involve flying the packages at night while the air lanes were virtually empty. Smith called his company Federal Express because he planned to sell his concept to the Federal Reserve as a means of shipping cancelled checks to cut down on the float time. Although it turned down his proposal, the Federal Reserve has a very similar type of system in effect today.

Smith started with $4 million from an inheritance and soon raised $72 million in debt and equity. The company started shipping in April 1973, handling only 18 packages on its first night in business. In 1993 the company handles 1.5 million packages each night and generates $8 billion in sales, having grown by an average rate of nearly 40 percent over the past decade.

Federal Express has earned a reputation as a leader in technological innovation largely due to its Cosmos II Tracking System, which enables the company to track all the packages it handles daily. The system, which utilizes a pocket-size, full-function computer linked to central data bases, enabled the company to receive several awards for excellence in technology, including the coveted Computerworld Smithsonian Award.

Of course, not all of Federal Express's innovations have been successful. Its Zapmail same-day data transmission service, which was perhaps ahead of its time, took a $190 million write-off in 1986, two years after it was started.

Low-Tech Innovations Can Also Result in Success

During the Depression, an unemployed worker named Charles Darrow invented a game called Monopoly while reminiscing about his happier days in Atlantic City, walking along the boardwalk and shopping on Park Place. The game was a fantasy game for poor people who wanted to become rich. Darrow started to produce two sets a day. Soon, he went to Parker Bros. to see if they had any interest in manufacturing the game. They were not interested, however, since they felt the game was too complicated and took too long to play.

After Darrow sold two hundred sets in a department store in New Jersey, the company reconsidered. Orders took off. Within a few months, twenty thousand sets were sold in a week. In 1935 eighty thousand sets were sold. As of 1993, more than 250 million people have played the game, and more than 100 million sets have been sold worldwide.

Creating New Markets

Successful entrepreneurs like Charles Darrow often create new markets. Lenox China revolutionized the fine china industry by promoting bridal registry, in which the prospective bride and groom choose a pattern of china and their friends and relatives purchase parts of that set as wedding gifts. The same concept has since been used for baby showers and other occasions.

On a much larger scale, such companies as McDonald's, Home Depot, and Costco have created markets for products that had previously been sold in a far different manner. Walt Disney Productions created a separate film company, Touchstone Pictures, so that it could make films that catered to a more adult audience without sacrificing Disney's profitable family image. These companies have used innovative marketing to generate billions of dollars of sales.

Low-Tech Innovations for High-Tech Products

There are also low-tech innovations in high-tech companies. Even for a company as technology oriented as Cray Research, one of its greatest innovations has been in financing for its customers. Cray has been a leader in finding leases for customers on a limited budget, such as nonprofit and governmental institutions, who are major users of Cray's equipment.

Innovative Marketing

More Food for Thought

We have seen numerous innovative marketing practices over the years. Wally Amos took a recipe that had been around since the early 1920s, but added his skills as a promoter, to launch Famous Amos Cookies. He started the company in 1975 while working as a theatrical agent, using every show-biz antic to create a grand opening for his retail cookie store when it opened in Hollywood. The chocolate chip cookie was the star, complete with the red carpet treatment. Amos currently sells his delicious cookies throughout the world.

More extreme—and far less successful—is another entertaining food company, Pizza Time Theatre, creator of the high-tech Chuck E. Cheese restaurants and founded by Atari's founder, Nolan Bushnell. The company, which was certainly innovative in its marketing efforts, generated $166 million in 1983 by selling pizza in a carnival-like atmosphere. Nonetheless it filed for bankruptcy the following year, largely a result of problems in product quality; the food it was serving was far less enjoyable than the entertainment.

Cable Stars

Innovation has been quite prevalent in the cable television industry. Consider MTV. The idea of marrying music and television was innovative in itself, but the real innovation was in *marketing* the idea. Robert Pittman (the son of a Methodist minister, from Brookhaven, Mississippi) came up with the idea of a twenty-four-hour music network for Warner Amex. Pittman needed the support of the music industry as well as cable viewers for his idea to get off the ground. Thanks to a major ad campaign in which viewers were encouraged to call cable companies to tell them "I want my MTV," demand exploded. The venture has turned out to be a huge success.

Another illustration of innovative marketing in the cable television industry is Home Shopping Network (HSN), which was the brainchild of Lowell "Bud" Paxson, an owner of radio stations in the Northeast and in Florida. Interestingly, the idea for HSN came by chance when Paxson found that he could make more money selling merchandise directly over the airwaves than he could by selling advertising time. This happened accidentally in 1977 when one of Paxson's radio stations was forced to accept some electric can openers from a client that was otherwise unable to pay for its advertisements. Paxson sold the can openers over the air to listeners, who would then pick them up at the radio station. He then began selling items from distressed or overstocked merchants and eventually created a full program day revolving around direct sales.

In 1982 Paxson brought his idea to cable television. He was able to capitalize the venture with the help of an investment of $500,000 by Roy Speer (for 60 percent of the equity in the company). By the following year sales had topped $3 million, and by 1984 sales had tripled. The company went national the following year, and shortly thereafter it went public in one of the most publicized IPOs of the 1980s. Although HSN was a tremendous initial success for its investors, it has since hit on rough times. Plagued by problems such as declines in earnings, problems with management, litigation, and questionable related-party transactions, HSN's stock price lost more than 90 percent of its value from 1987 to 1988 before rebounding somewhat in the early 1990s.

Innovative Management

Management by Walking Away

Innovative management often supports other innovations. For example, Harry Quadracci, founder of Quad/Graphics (of Pewaukee, WI), a very successful high-tech printing company, has come up with an innovative management variant on MBWA known as management by walking away.[5] Every year, the company holds a "spring fling" in which the entire management team takes off for one day and leaves the workers to run the company. The workers are responsible for all management decisions during that day. Importantly, this activity is symbolic of the autonomous environment provided to the workers every day. There are other innovative management practices, including a three-day, 36-hour workweek (where employees work three 12-hour shifts and then are off for three or four days); employee stock ownership and profit sharing plans; employee education programs; and a multimillion-dollar employee sports center. All of these have supported the growth of this extremely well-regarded company.

Encouraging Innovation

It is not enough to have an innovative idea from time to time. Managers of successful fast-growth companies recognize that they must provide an atmosphere that encourages innovation from all employees. For example, Stu Buchalter of Standard Brands Paint promotes experimentation and creativity at his stores by having store managers set aside store space to be used for "experiments" in new products and merchandise displays. If a store manager wanted to set up an "odd color paints" section in one of the stores, such an idea would be strongly encouraged.

Thus innovation by itself is just a starting point. Companies must give their risk takers an opportunity to experiment and, if necessary, to fail. That becomes a primary task of management. As noted by Jim McManus, founder and CEO of Marketing Corporation of America, a high-growth company known for its ability to experiment, "Most big companies fire or demote their risk-takers who fail. The consequence is that the company loses its ability to learn from failure and to generate better new ideas. Since MCA was founded, we've launched twenty new businesses. Ten were successes and ten were losers—and no one has been fired or demoted as a result of the losers."[6] This is reinforced by author George Gilder: "[Breakthrough] projects the entrepreneurs initiated and carried through had one essential quality. All had been thoroughly contemplated by the relevant experts and the dominant companies, with their large research staffs and financial resources, and had been judged too difficult, untimely, risky, expensive, and unprofitable."[7]

You Don't Have to Be First, But You Have to Be Innovative

Just how important is the idea? Consider the following cases in the computer industry. It was UNIVAC, and not IBM, that had the technology advantage in the mainframe computer industry. It was Adam Osborne of Osborne Computer, and not Compaq Computer, who was the innovator in developing a portable computer and in bundling the software with the hardware. And it was Dan Bricklin, founder of VisiCorp (which made VisiCalc), and not Lotus Development, that created the first spreadsheet software package. In the 1990s, IBM is the world leader in the computer industry while Univac, which has since been acquired by Sperry Corporation, has always been playing catch-up. And Osborne Computer and VisiCorp have both gone out of business, while Compaq and Lotus have both thrived.

Certainly you do not have to be first with a product, but you have to be innovative enough to differentiate yourself from the

---

Innovating technology is not enough to be successful, as Univac, Osborne, and Visicorp have shown.

---

others. For example, Compaq Computer was one of dozens of companies in the early 1980s to manufacture IBM-compatible computers, but one of the few to have survived the decade. The company differentiated itself by introducing a portable computer and, perhaps more importantly, by developing strong linkages with computer retailers. Compaq recognized that the retailers dictated how much shelf space the manufacturers would get, and that shelf space would soon be scarce. So, unlike the others (including IBM and Apple), Compaq never competed with retailers by selling its computers directly to the end users; rather, retailers were offered exclusive franchises. Of course, since its early days, Compaq has also taken on the role of innovative product developer, introducing new models faster than its competitors.

Like Compaq, Sun Microsystems entered an industry when an established leader already existed. The pioneer in workstations—desktop computers connected to a powerful central unit and to one another—was Apollo Computer (which was later purchased by Hewlett-Packard). Sun, however, developed a strategy of building powerful yet inexpensive machines that were compatible to those of its competitors. Thus customers could fit Sun's computers into their existing system without any risk.

Sun was able to turn a weakness into a tremendous opportunity. As a young company, it could not afford to design the special customized electronic circuitry needed in high-performance workstations. So, recognizing that custom parts became obsolete in a matter of months, Sun used off-the-shelf state-of-the-art components, which enabled it to take advantage of the technological breakthroughs of other companies as they occurred. In essence, the company contracted out for the technology that its larger competitors would develop in-house more expensively, but it could bring the product to market just as fast as its competitors. As of 1993 Sun is a very successful $4 billion company.

. . . And You Have to Act Quickly

Just Do It

Innovation often means simply developing new products more effectively and more quickly than the competition. As Karl Weick once remarked, "Chaotic action is preferable to orderly inaction." After all, it has been said that the Edsel was the most market-researched car in American history.

Successful fast-growth companies often develop new products with lightning-like speed. For Nike, the world's leading designer and marketer of sports shoes with annual sales of about $4 billion (and with a higher than 10 percent net income after taxes), its greatest competitive advantage is its new models. Specifically, Nike sells more than eight hundred models of its shoes for use in more than two dozen sports.

Nike has pioneered the notion of "subsegments" in its industry. For example, it has three lines of basketball shoes, each selling for more than $100 a pair retail and expressing a different "attitude"—the Air Jordan, for those who want to be like Michael Jordan; the Flight, which is a lightweight shoe; and the Force, which has a customized-fit air bladder similar to the Reebok Pump. Furthermore, Nike updates each shoe at least every six months, tempting its fashion-conscious customers to buy new Nikes long before their old Nikes have run their last mile. One downside to this strategy has been that from time to time, Nike has been laden with excess inventory, which they have been forced to sell at significant discounts.

Unlimited Success

The Limited, with its more than three-thousand stores, takes one month to do what its competitors take nine months to do. In the world of fashion, where styles change dramatically from month to month, this serves as a significant advantage. The Limited controls hundreds of factories in Asia and throughout the world. So when one of its many buyers spot a fashion trend in Italy, France, or elsewhere, the company can act quickly to get the style to its retail stores, which are fully computerized to hook up with its headquarters in Columbus, Ohio. A few years ago, Verna Gibson spotted scores of teenagers buying bulky sweaters in a small shop in Florence, Italy. The Limited copied the design, then named it "Forenza" to sound like an Italian designer. The company sold more than 3 million of the sweaters, making it one of the most successful apparel product introductions in history. As a result Gibson became president of The Limited's stores division, making her one of the leading female executives in the United States.

As noted by 1992 presidential candidate H. Ross Perot (founder of Electronic Data Systems, which was purchased by General Motors) about the importance of acting quickly, "It takes five years to develop a new car in this country. Heck, we won World War II in four years."[8] Perot elaborated on the difference between his own company and the megacorporation that purchased it: "The first EDSer to see a snake kills it. At GM, the first thing you do is organize a committee on snakes. Then you bring in a consultant who knows a lot about snakes. Third thing you do is talk about it for a year."[9] From Thomas Edison to Liz Claiborne to Steven Jobs, history proves that innovators who act quickly are more often than not responsible for the success of fast-growth businesses.

Innovation: Important Summary Points

1. Successful fast-growth companies have often been leaders in terms of innovativeness (for example, Apple, Cray Research, Microsoft, Federal Express, Liz Claiborne, Nike).
2. Innovativeness is readily seen among high-tech companies that have seized an opportunity as a result of their proprietary technology. This is evident among computer makers (for example, Apple, Cray), computer products manufacturers (for example, Analog Devices, LSI Logic, Cypress Semiconductor, Conner Peripherals), pharmaceutical and health care companies (for example, Key Pharmaceuticals, Marion Laboratories, U.S. Surgical), and other technology companies (for example, MCI, Pall, Kollmorgen).

3. Companies that provide seemingly low-tech products and services can utilize high-tech innovations (for example, Federal Express).
4. Low-tech growth companies have been innovative in creating new markets (for example, McDonald's, Home Depot, Costco, A. T. Cross, Lenox China).
5. Successful fast-growth companies have often utilized innovative marketing (for example, MTV) and innovative management practices (for example, Quad/Graphics, Standard Brands Paint, MCA).
6. It is more important to be the innovator than to be the product developer (for example, IBM, Compaq, Lotus).
7. Successful fast-growth companies often act with lightning-like speed (for example, Nike, The Limited).

Strong Cultural Foundation

Ben & Jerry's: A Wild and Crazy Culture

On a recent trip to New England I had the pleasure of visiting an ice cream factory started by two very bizarre characters—Ben Cohen and Jerry Greenfield—that produces some pretty bizarre (but delicious) flavors of ice cream. The company's start was equally unusual: Ben was a potter in the Adirondacks who was getting allergic to clay dust but not selling much pottery. Jerry was studying to go to medical school. They pooled their resources to give them $8,000, then got a $4,000 bank loan after their SBA loan was turned down. The two entrepreneurs started operating out of an abandoned gas station. Business was fine in Vermont during the summer months, but certainly not during the winter. So they began packaging and distributing it, with Ben serving as the driver. In a PBS special highlighting the company, Ben described the two founders and the mission to which they adhere: "We're two slightly crazy guys next door living up in Vermont, home of milk and green fields, making some world-class ice cream in some pretty unusual flavors."

Everything about Ben & Jerry's reinforces the "homemade" image. Their ads look homemade. Even their corporate annual report (Ben & Jerry's Homemade, Inc. is a publicly held corporation) looks homemade. All of this is to emphasize that their ice cream is homemade. Ben and Jerry attempt to reinforce the image (or value system, or culture) that they are "two real guys," just as it says on the container of their ice cream. One may contrast this to Haagen-Dazs, which, although the ice cream tastes great, is marketed to appear like it is an imported specialty item. The name sounds Scandinavian, but it is a made-up name; it has *no* meaning. The company prints a map of Scandinavia on its cartons of ice cream, even though the product is made in New Jersey. (When I met the president of Haagen-Dazs at a conference at which we were both speaking, I jokingly asked him if the ice cream made in Oslo has a map of the New Jersey Turnpike on the carton.)

Everything about Ben & Jerry's reinforces the "homemade" image.

The culture at Ben & Jerry's is certainly characterized by informality. Moreover, the culture promotes a sense of community, globally and within the local Ben & Jerry's "family." Yet there is a "wacky' quality that exists with Ben & Jerry's. For example, the company once sponsored a contest where the grand prize included a day at Disney World with Ben's uncle. Even the company's annual meeting of stockholders is more like a carnival—complete with singing, dancing, and refreshments—than a corporate meeting.

As might be expected, product innovations result from this off corporate culture. In the 1980s Ben received an anonymous postcard from a couple of followers of the rock group the Grateful Dead who thought that "Cherry Garcia" (named after Jerry Garcia, the band's bearded leader—who, incidentally, bears a striking resemblance to Ben Cohen) would be a great name for a flavor. After some experimentation Ben & Jerry's introduced its new flavor, made of bing cherry ice cream with chocolate chips.

The culture at Ben & Jerry's is reinforced with *every* activity. As a result of this obsessiveness with culture, everyone at Ben & Jerry's knows what is expected of them. Its stockholder's report is quite appropriately named "a report to shareholders, customers, community members, suppliers, and employees." In fact, throughout the corporate annual report are reminders of the cultural foundation of the company. On the cover of a recent report were reminders that the company earmarks 1 percent of its profits to support world peace and that it is committed to recycling, saving the tropical rainforests, and so forth. Inside the report is the company's clearly stated three-part mission: its product mission, its social mission, and its economic mission. Certainly the company recognizes that its purpose of being goes well beyond a single goal. As noted by Reynold M. Sachs, who played a key role in the growth of Digital Switch, which generated tremendous returns for its investors, "Ironically, individuals whose primary or only goal is financial gain end up failing to make the money that they dreamed about. . . . If that is your primary goal, you're more likely to fail than to succeed, perhaps because it's shortsighted and it gives you incentives to make wrong decisions."[1]

With the company's growth has come a very genuine commitment to serve as a leader in promoting social change. Fun, charity, and goodwill are vital to the company's mission. In 1985 the company started the Ben & Jerry's Foundation, which receives 7.5 percent of the company's annual pretax income to be used for numerous social causes.

Unlike those of most corporations, Ben & Jerry's corporate reports include a social report describing such activities of the Ben & Jerry's Foundation as summer camps for youths, programs for the handicapped, and antipoverty projects. In addition, there is a report of the independent social auditor to assess the social activities of the company. In 1989 the social auditor was William C. Norris, founder and chairman emeritus of Control Data Corporation and a role model for social activity in Control Data's hometown of Minneapolis.

Leaders Establish and Maintain the Culture

Millipore Corporation develops some rather complex technologies, such as liquid chromatography and separation. In the early 1970s the company had a single product line and a single direct sales force. Two decades later the company is edging out into related products at an increasingly rapid rate; it has entered more than one hundred distinct market niches and sells its products throughout the world.

The catalyst behind Millipore's growth and success has been Dee d'Arbeloff, who was born in Paris and received an MBA from

Harvard. He joined Millipore in 1962, when sales were $2 million, with the intent of gaining the necessary manufacturing experience to launch a company of his own. Fortunately for Millipore, that never happened. Five years later, with Millipore's sales reaching $11 million, he became executive vice president. In 1971 he became president, and nine years later he became chairman of the company. In 1993 Millipore is a $750 million company, with its ROE having grown by 16 percent per year over the preceding decade.

As the company has grown, so have the demands on management. Moreover, as much as the leader may resist it, the complexity that accompanies growth poses a genuine threat to the cultural foundation of the enterprise. As Dee d'Arbeloff notes:

> Suddenly, you find yourself facing the need to change everything about the way you run the business except the basic values. You have a fundamental dilemma: The company has become complex and you've got to hire specialists and create divisions to keep it together. But the very process of imposing formality on an organization tends to create bureaucracy and parochialism. These forces in turn can cause people to lose their business judgment and to focus on the more particular needs and agendas of their own division, department or function. At that very time, you yourself are no longer as close to the details of the business as you once were. I used to run customer seminars and I used to be out there selling, so I knew firsthand what was going on. I can't do as much of these things anymore. And you have to adapt, or else the vitality of the business— the innovativeness, the responsiveness to changing external events—will fall between the cracks. The CEO simply can't have his finger any longer on the day-to-day pulse of the organization to the extent he used to—there are just too many pulses. The job becomes one of somehow helping each employee think like and behave like a founding owner-entrepreneur. But there's one thing you can't delegate, and that's the job of maintaining the critical balance between innovation and control.[2]

Clearly Millipore's CEO has shaped the innovative and entrepreneur of culture of the company, just as Ben Cohen and Jerry Greenfield have shaped the culture of their smaller enterprise. These leaders are different in management style, yet their influence in their own particular company has been pervasive.

Examples of Culture in Action

Loose and Strict Controls

Obviously, Ben & Jerry's is an extreme case. As noted earlier, its loose culture is reinforced by every action that the company takes, from product introduction to annual meetings to business conferences. In contrast, Automatic Data Processing (ADP) has established a culture that appears rather paradoxical. Its culture, which was shaped in turn by Henry Taub, Frank Lautenberg, and Josh Weston, is both loose *and* strict. There is no executive dining room, nor are there reserved parking spaces. There is a heavy emphasis on decentralization and open communications. The atmosphere is so conducive to enhanced morale and commitment that more than 60 percent of the employees are shareholders of the company. Nonetheless, the culture is also rather rigid. The company expects to excel in both short-term and long-term performance; there are no trade-offs. These high standards promote intensity and have resulted in superior performance, as evidenced by the company's phenomenal success since its founding.

Discipline is vital for ADP, which must carry out the same discipline of error-free accounting services for its clientele; there is no room for error. ADP reinforces this value system in many ways so that ADPers are well aware of what is expected of them. For example, there are Tuesday night sales meetings held throughout the country, which are referred to as "roll call," in which salespeople report their sales for the previous week. The effect is that the peer pressure is as motivational (or as embarrassing) as a Weight Watchers meeting in terms of producing positive results for the sales force. Sales goals are established weekly rather than monthly, and bonuses are tied directly to achieving sales, service, and profit goals. This has resulted in incredible long-term growth in sales and profitability.

Innovation and Entrepreneurship

In the last chapter I discussed the importance of innovation as it relates to product development. Yet innovation can be a vital component of a company's culture if it is reinforced throughout the company. Consider Kollmorgen, which in the early part of the twentieth century was a small, single-product, single-customer company supplying periscopes to the U.S. Navy. Although growth and profitability have been disappointing in the early 1990s, during the 1980s Kollmorgen was a very successful high-growth diversified technology company, generating more than $500 million per year in revenues. The major growth for Kollmorgen came after World War II when the company began to broaden its product line. Despite its growth, however, the company maintains an entrepreneurial atmosphere, with innovation being the key to success. The company has several small divisions, each run like entrepreneurial companies. There are attractive financial incentives based on profits generated by each division, thereby further reinforcing the importance of innovation and entrepreneurship at Kollmorgen. In addition, the company has a very small corporate staff, whose basic purpose is to protect Kollmorgen's entrepreneurial culture.

Innovation and Customer Service

Like Kollmorgen, Cray Research under Seymour Cray and John Rollwagen has developed a culture that revolves around its commitment to innovation. Yet the company does more than innovate; its value system is one that advocates a strong people orientation and a closeness to its customers. People enjoy more autonomy at Cray than they do at larger corporations. Moreover, its engineers are expected to serve as vital linkages with Cray's customers.

Competitive Orientation

Internal competition often leads to external competition. W. J. Sanders, chairman of Advanced Micro Devices (AMD), has instilled such an attitude among his people. In 1989, at an executive retreat for AMD in Hawaii, Sanders was asked to enter a ten-kilometer race that was intended as a morale builder for the company. Although Sanders was quite fit, he refused to go up against his staff. As he said, "I'm not putting myself in a position where I can't win."[3]

Internal competition has prepared AMD quite well for the extreme external competition that it faces in the semiconductor industry. AMD, a manufacturer of Intel microprocessors, did quite well as a result of Intel's success with its 80286 chip, with more than 10 percent of its revenues in 1988 coming from chips designed by Intel. More recently, however, AMD has been hurt by Intel's refusal to license the manufacturing rights to its 80386 chip.

Customer Orientation

Even a company whose workforce is primarily composed of hourly workers selling such mundane products as home improvement items can exhibit a strong culture. When Home Depot began operating in the Northeast, it took on the expense of relocating dozens of its employees to head the various departments in those stores. The reason is that the company wants all of its stores to be run by employees who are acclimated to Home Depot's culture. In its own words, it wants people who "bleed orange," a term of prestige derived from the orange aprons worn by the workers.

Home Depot's culture, which is largely a product of founders Bernard Marcus and Arthur Blank, is based on intense awareness of customer service. In fact, Home Depot has so much clout among manufacturers due to its volume purchases that it has *forced* several suppliers to rewrite instructions to meet its own customer needs better. The most striking feature of Home Depot's culture is that it has successfully managed to marry a low-cost, low-price strategy with one that is based on customer service. Very few retailers can juggle both of those demands.

The result is that Home Depot's sales have been approximately $300 per square foot, a higher figure than Sears, K-mart, or Wal-Mart can claim. This has fared well for the company's stock, which has been the best-performing issue to have gone public during the 1980s, gaining 7,000 percent from Home Depot's IPO in 1981 through the end of the decade.

Antibureaucracy and Informality

Certainly, Ben & Jerry's epitomizes informality in a corporate culture. There are, however, other companies that thrive on a loose, antibureaucratic culture. Tandem and Genentech, for example, are known for their weekly "beer busts." Similarly, ASK Computer Systems, founded by Sandra Kurtzig (and her husband, who left the company prior to its meteoric growth) has reinforced its tradition of informality with its "Friday bashes." Yet despite the fact that running shoes and other casual clothing are commonly seen around the office, the work ethic is intense. ASK's employees are well known for working around the clock to develop new manufacturing software applications for their clientele.

In 1985 Sandra Kurtzig resigned as CEO of the company to spend more time traveling and to be with her family. Following her resignation, although earnings continued the climb, it soon became clear that the company was missing something—its entrepreneurial philosophy. New managers had distanced themselves from the operations, and the focus on new product development declined. ASK's board was successful in luring Kurtzig back after a four-year absence to the company that she founded. In addition to making several personnel changes, she has been extremely successful in bringing the old ways back to ASK. The employees even feel that the food and beer at the "Friday bashes" have improved since she rejoined the company. As of 1993 ASK is the largest technology company founded and run by a woman; it employs over one thousand persons and has more than fifty offices worldwide.

APRIL FOOL'S AT SUN. There is also a strong sense of informality at Sun Microsystems, one of the great fast-growth success stories of the 1980s and 1990s. Some engineers at Sun once played an April Fool's Day prank on CEO Scott McNealy: McNealy, a golf enthusiast, came to work and found his office transformed into a twelve-yard, par-three golf course, complete with sandtraps and a birdbath. (McNealy bogeyed the hole.) Such behavior is consistent with the loose culture at Sun, which includes monthly beer bashes and weekly dress-down days. As noted by McNealy, "We're trying hard to be different from the other companies. One of our goals is to provide an environment that people have a blast working in. We like to think of Sun as a $2 billion start-up."[4]

TRANSITION TO FORMALITY. An interesting development occurs with high-growth companies. In their earliest stages, these companies are driven by an individual *entrepreneur* who clearly establishes the corporate culture. Large companies, in contrast, are driven by the *company* and its institutional strengths and weaknesses. In between, as the company is growing, it is often in a cultural transition state that entails more complexity of structure, greater barriers in communication and information processing, and increased formality.

Managers often have difficulty in dealing with this transition. For example, when MCI was going through such a transition, CEO Bill McGowan found out that somebody was developing a personnel practices manual. His reaction was "Find out who's doing this and fire him!"[5] Although nobody was fired, the message was as clear as the MCI telecommunications lines: the company would not tolerate bureaucratic rules, policies, and manuals. For a manager to fit in at MCI, he or she must adhere to a culture that is based on the use of solid business judgment and common sense, rather than on strict procedures and regulations.

BUREAUCRACY AND MEMOS. Often bureaucracy is measured by the volume of memos sent. Tom Peters and Bob Waterman, in their best-selling book *In Search of Excellence* demonstrated the complete antithesis of bureaucracy in highlighting Procter & Gamble's one-page memo policy. Yet many successful smaller, fast-growth companies have outdone Procter & Gamble. Pall Corporation, for example, has shyed away from memos. As one of its executives said, "I rarely see a memorandum from Abe Krasnoff, our chief executive. Sometimes he sends me a handwritten note, but his notes are always hard to read. Fundamentally, I don't think Abe is happy with the written word because he thinks he should be there in person."[6]

Reading a Culture

The culture—the set of shared values or beliefs—of a company is what ties the purpose of the organization to its customers, to society, and to its higher-order values. Nothing is too trivial when it comes to reinforcing that culture, including the seating arrangements in meetings, the office furnishings, the company picnic, or the retirement parties. Interestingly, very few people fail in their jobs due to the work requirements, which would indicate a weakness in the company's recruitment or training practices. Rather, people fail because they cannot read a culture or cannot adjust their own personal value system to match the company's.

For that reason, to be successful with a business, it is vitally important to decipher its value system. It is crucial to ask the following questions:

- What is the background of the founder, or the person who laid the groundwork for the culture?
- How does the company respond to crises (when its true values often are most tested and more pronounced)?
- Who are considered deviant, and how does their status define the boundaries of the value system?

Obviously, it is difficult for an outsider to read a culture; you simply have to see it, feel it, and experience it. But when you find a company with a strong, positive value system that is shared by its employees, you have one of the most basic elements of a successful business.

Culture: Important Summary Points

1. The chief architect in establishing and maintaining a strong culture is the CEO.
2. There are numerous kinds of cultures, any of which could favorably influence the success of a growing company. These include loose and strict controls (for example, ADP), innovation (for example, Kollmorgen, Cray), customer orientation (for example, Home Depot), informality (for example, Tandem, Genentech, ASK Computer Systems, Sun Microsystems, MCI, Pall, Standard Brands Paint), and community service (for example, Ben & Jerry's).

Valued Customers,
Valued Employees

A characteristic of the better-performing fast-growth companies has been their concern for customers as well as for their own employees. These two often go hand in hand.

Valued Customers

Customer service starts with having a clear sense of the target market. As the late Senator George Aiken of Vermont once noted, "Get into the community and find out what their problems are. That's the best politics." Certainly, the same could be said about providing customer service: it is vital to get into the field or into the store and see what the customers want. This involves more than simply gathering consumer research; close contact with customers is vital. As Stanley Marcus, of Neiman-Marcus once said, "Consumers are statistics. Customers are people."

Consumers are statistics. Customers are people.

Thus a company that values its customers is actually driven by its customers; meetings and informal contact with key customers are a must. The signals that a company is doing it right include the following:

- It routinely keeps in touch with customers
- It calls its customers and follows up
- It assesses performance with customer focus groups or some other customer feedback
- It tests itself by calling on itself and its competitors with typical customer requests
- It deals effectively with customer complaints

Selling: It's Not a Kroc

In the late 1930s Ray Kroc became the executive sales agent for the Multi-Mixer, a milkshake machine that had the capability of mixing six shakes simultaneously. He did quite well with this business, but he had his mind set on loftier goals. In 1954 he received an order from a restaurant for eight Multi-Mixers. Kroc wondered what kind of business this was: why would any restaurant need to mix forty-eight milkshakes at the same time? So he went to the restaurant in San Bernardino, California, to see for himself. Kroc was amazed when he saw the huge crowds around the hamburger stand under the two bright arches, a stand owned by two brothers named McDonald.

The McDonald brothers had already sold six franchises, but they were not interested in expanding the company much further themselves. Kroc offered to expand the business further in return for 1.4 percent of the gross sales, while the McDonald brothers would retain their original business. Within five years Kroc had one hundred stores running from coast to coast, with average sales in excess of $200,000 per store. Soon after, Kroc purchased the company—including trademarks, copyrights, formula, systems, and everything else—from the McDonald brothers for $14 million. McDonald's, which in the 1990s is a $7 billion company, has since gone on to become the clear leader in the fast foods industry, largely due to its intense product and customer orientation. After all, it was Kroc himself who once said, "You've got to see the beauty in a hamburger bun." Since the early 1980s McDonald's average ROE has been over 20 percent, well above that of any other large restaurant chain.

Closeness to the Customer Pays Off

HOSPITAL INFORMATION SYSTEMS. Often smaller, growing companies have a competitive advantage over larger companies when it comes to caring for customers, since they are able to be much closer to the customer. As noted by Jim Macaleer, CEO of Shared Medical Systems, a leading supplier of computer-based information systems to hospitals, "Our top priority is caring more. This is our only business. We don't have anywhere else to go. We have to care about our customers more than anybody else cares about them. And we do."[1]

STEEL. That closeness with customers is often a result of meeting with customers to assist in providing new product ideas. At Worthington Industries, for example, *all* employees—from the machine operators to upper management—meet with customers to assess better how the latter can use the company's steel products.

COSMETICS. Closeness with the customer is very pronounced in companies with a strong direct sales force. This is quite evident at Mary Kay Cosmetics. Mary Kay Ash, after having worked for two other companies that used pyramid selling (Stanley Home Products and World Gift), founded Mary Kay Cosmetics in Dallas in 1963. She recruited and trained women to be "beauty consultants" who would give home demonstrations of the products and who would, in turn, recruit other women to do the same. The consultants would receive commissions on their sales as well as on sales by women they recruited. The key competitive factor, therefore, was in Ash's ability to recruit and motivate salespeople through commissions. Within ten years of its founding the company was generating over $30 million in revenues; another ten years later, revenues had reached $384 million.

COOKIES. Like Mary Kay Ash, Debbie Fields started selling in a storefront. Her product was cookies, however, and her sales were direct to the customer; during slow times, she would go outside to give out samples. Within the first week, the original Mrs. Fields' Cookies was profitable. Eight months later Debbie Fields opened a second store, and sales continued to grow rapidly. Within ten years the company had hit the $50 million mark in revenues (a lot of cookies!). Throughout the company's history, quality products and customer service have been the underlying factors in generating sales.

Listening to the Customer Has Its Benefits

RETAILING. Successful fast-growth companies recognize how important it is to listen to their customers. Retailers have an opportunity to listen to customer input on a daily basis, yet very few take advantage of that opportunity. One company that does is Stew Leonard's, the nation's largest single grocery store.

There's a big sign at Stew Leonard's that says, "Our mission is to create happy customers." One of the ways the company makes them happy is by listening to them. The customers serve as advisers/consultants to the business: they make suggestions, and the company will generally try them out. That is how the fish and salad bars, which have provided tremendous revenues for the store, got their start. One customer suggested that Stew Leonard's start selling pistachio nuts; it now sells literally a ton a week.

MANUFACTURING. Manufacturing companies typically do not have nearly as great an opportunity to listen to customers on a daily basis. Nonetheless, it is often more critical for manufacturers to get such feedback. Two very successful fast-growth companies whose business revolves around manufacturing—and whose growth is largely attributable to their desire to listen to their customers—are Pall Corporation and Loctite.

Over the decade of the 1980s, Pall Corporation increased its sales annually by an average of 16 percent while its ROE averaged 25 percent, one of the highest levels in its industry. A large part of that achievement has to do with the company's intense focus on the customer. Pall has grown from a small company manufacturing filters and related equipment into a much larger operation by carefully edging out into numerous other market niches. From where do the ideas come to enter new markets? The customers. Pall's senior managers meet directly with customers in order to learn about their needs. This philosophy has trickled down the entire corporation, as customer service representatives as well as engineers are expected to work with customers to design filtration systems that meet the latter's needs. As noted by CEO Abe Krasnoff in describing the corporate structure, which is designed to maintain a closeness with its customers, "This multi-faceted organization is expensive, but well worth it. It enables us to address customer problems from every conceivable angle. I am intent on giving better service than anyone in the world—I really am—and this organization enables us to do it."[2]

Loctite has a similarly strong emphasis on its customers. As CEO Bob Krieble notes:

> From the start, we have had a sales force with missionary zeal. They get their kicks out of helping customers make better machinery and lower their maintenance costs. We are far and away the leader in this market, but we have only realized ten percent of our potential. And so our salespeople spend most of their working hours in customer plants looking for new applications that will save the customer money or increase performance.[3]

Failing to Listen to the Customer

Steve Hui cofounded Everex Systems in 1983 and built the clone marker into a $400 million business. While prices were falling and customers were demanding value at lower prices, Everex was engaged in a research project designed to add features (and higher prices) to its product line. Dell Computer, meanwhile, worked on efficiency, and its phone lines were ringing off the hook. Although the two companies were comparable in size during the last half of the 1980s, Everex was forced into bankruptcy, with its shares worth just pennies, while Dell's market capitalization in the early 1990s is around $2 billion.

Going the Extra Yard for the Customer Gives a Company a Competitive Advantage

The notion of "going the extra yard" in terms of customer service is characteristic of the better-performing growth-oriented companies.

PRINTING. Pandick Press has established a successful niche strategy of printing such time-sensitive financial documents as offering statements, prospectuses, and shareholder notices. This is a business where speed, accuracy, quality, and predictability have enabled Pandick to differentiate itself from countless other printers.

Pandick's competitive advantage is clearly seen in its emphasis on the customer. The company has gone several steps beyond merely providing speed and accuracy. For example, it has more than a dozen conference rooms in its New York office to enable its clients (who are investment bankers) to make last-minute changes in financial deals, sometimes during the graveyard shift. In addition, Pandick's customer representatives will work with clients on a twenty-four hour basis. This enables the client to complete a prospectus and have it in the office of the SEC within hours. In so doing, the company has emerged as the nation's leading printer of these quick-turnaround documents due to its superior quality and its willingness to go out of its way for customers.

RETAILING AND BANKING. Among service companies, Patagonia (despite some turbulent times in the late 1980s, as described in Chapter 4) and University National Bank (UNB) stand out in terms of going the extra yard for customers. Patagonia, a retailer of outdoors equipment, offers a "guide line" where customers can get answers to any questions related to sporting goods, regardless of whether the company sells that kind of equipment. At UNB (which, as noted earlier, has more of a constrained growth pattern than many of the other companies mentioned in this book), every year on the anniversary of a customer's first transaction, he or she is sent a gift with a note that says thanks for spending another year with the bank. These examples are just a few of the ways that the better-performing companies differentiate themselves from their competition in terms of customer service.

Valued Employees

Valued employees are often just as important as valued customers. Dave Packard once responded as follows when he was asked for his formula for success: "People."

Listening to Employees

Successful fast-growth companies recognize the importance of listening to their people and making sure that the latter feel they are

---

"People"—the formula for Dave Packard's success.

---

an important part of the business. This may involve training employees to reach their potential, or it may involve opening up channels of communication to ensure that people are heard. Whatever is done, it is important to reinforce the positive signals continually and, if possible, to eliminate *any* negative signal that may get in the way of such an effort. Slogans such as "family feeling," "our people," "our team," and "our associates" work fine, but *all* policies and actions must demonstrate that the company does in fact treat its people as family. Otherwise, employees will feel that the slogan is mere lip service. The following are a few guiding questions to determine if the company is taking the right steps:

- How are employees shown that they count? How is that reinforced?
- How are customers made aware that they are important?
- What provisions are made to develop the skills of employees?
- How does the company get its people involved?
- How does the company communicate with its people?

RETAILING AND CONSUMER PRODUCTS. According to the late Sam Walton, founder of Wal-Mart, a company that has grown from a small-town discount store into the nation's largest, most profitable, and most highly regarded retailer, "The key is to get into the store and listen to what the associates [Wal-Mart employees] have to say. It's terribly important for everyone to get involved. Our best ideas come from clerks and stockboys."[4]

There are countless stories to show how Walton listened to his associates. The *Wall Street Journal* once reported that "Mr. Walton couldn't sleep a few weeks back. He got up and bought four dozen donuts at an all night bakery. At 2:30 a.m., he took them to the distribution center and chatted for a while with workers from the shipping docks. As a result he discovered that two more shower stalls were needed at that location."[5] The same story reported the following: "Not long ago he flew his aircraft to Mt. Pleasant, Texas, and parked the plane with instructions to the co-pilot to meet him 100 or so miles down the road. He then flagged a Wal-Mart truck and rode the rest of the way to 'Chat with the driver—it seemed like so much fun.' "[6]

Since Sam Walton's death, American industry has begun to appreciate the impact of his successor, David Glass. Although Glass is clearly not as charismatic as Walton was, he certainly is comparable in terms of his persistence and vision. Glass was named the most-admired leader among the most-admired companies in a 1993 *Fortune* magazine survey.[7]

Victor Kiam, CEO of Remington Products, has adhered to a similar philosophy of listening to his people. Regular all-hands meetings of employees have resulted in several new product developments. For example, the Remington shaver used in surgical preps (through a joint venture with 3M) was a direct response to an employee suggestion.

TECHNOLOGY PRODUCTS. Millipore, a leader in high-tech applications of materials separation, has attempted to maintain a closeness with its people despite the increasing complexity of its product line. Clearly, a formalized matrix structure was not the solution. As noted by the company's chairman, Dee d'Arbeloff, "Every high tech company has an informal matrix structure. It's formalizing it that causes trouble. People don't know how to serve several 'bosses' simultaneously and equally without getting into squabbles that slow down decision making and action."[8]

Millipore is certainly a far different company than either Wal-Mart or Remington Products. Yet despite the informational demands placed on it Millipore has been equally successful by maintaining a closeness with its employees, which it achieves by promoting open communication and fostering an entrepreneurial culture. All of these companies certainly reinforce Dave Packard's view that people are the formula for success.

The Value of People

In 1978 Tom Melohn, a twenty-four-year veteran of such large food companies as C & H Sugar, Swift & Company, and Pet, bought North American Tool and Die (NATD), then a $2 million manufacturer of precision metal stampings and subassemblies, with the help of a partner. Apparently Melohn learned some good lessons as a food executive that enabled him to build employee morale at NATD. These lessons all revolve around a common theme: the value of people. Fifteen years after Melohn took over NATD, sales have grown dramatically, while turnover (which had been at 27 percent) and absenteeism have been virtually eliminated. Melohn's success has made him a bit of a celebrity, as he has appeared on national television and has been highlighted in Tom Peters's books on excellence in management.

Melohn refers to his people at NATD as his "gang" or his "family." There are no separate executive and employee washrooms, and no special executive parking spaces. The work environment, including the washroom and shop floor, is kept neat, clean, and organized. Special employees are recognized as "superperson of the month." Furthermore, employees are *given* shares of stock in NATD each year.

When Melohn and his partner purchased NATD, they established three goals: increase sales and profits, share the wealth, and instill job satisfaction and fun on the job. The way to accomplish these goals was by creating an atmosphere of *complete* trust between the owners and all the employees. Most important, this is not something that the management can do once in a while or once a month at meetings. Rather, as suggested by Melohn, "You've got to really mean it when you say you want such an atmosphere. You truly have to believe in it. Then, you've got to work at improving relations every day in every situation. Otherwise, your employees will sense the hypocrisy and it will be for naught."[9]

Attracting People

BALANCED PRIORITIES. Not surprisingly, such successful fast-growth companies as Millipore, Standard Brands Paint, Sealed Air, Quad

Graphics, Cray Research, Analog Devices, and Teradyne have all devoted great attention to attracting and maintaining quality personnel. A distinguishing feature of Analog Devices, a high-tech company that manufactures devices that enable computers to communicate to us as well as to one another, is its well-balanced orientation to technology, the market, and its people. Clearly the company is a technology leader—in fact most of us would be hard-pressed to understand this technology—that has achieved that position due to its constant innovation and new product development. This technological superiority is used as a basis for attracting and retaining high-caliber people. Analog devotes about 20 percent of its strategic plan specifically to ways of attracting, developing, motivating, and rewarding the necessary people to ensure its innovative and technological advantage. Training, development, and educational benefits are all vital parts of this plan.

Retaining People

STOCK INCENTIVES. One of the ways to attract and retain good people is to make people feel like they are a part of the organization. What better way to do so than to give people an opportunity to become owners of the company, be it through stock options or through some other type of employee incentive program? This is where smaller growth-oriented companies have clearly distinguished themselves from the larger, stable corporations. Whereas employees (including top management) own less than 5 percent of

---

Whereas employees own less than 5 percent of the stock of the largest 100 companies in this country, employees own one-third of the stock of medium-sized high-growth companies, and own more than half of the stock of smaller, growth companies.

---

the stock of the largest one hundred companies in the United States, employees will typically own around one-third of the stock of medium-sized high-growth companies, and often more than half of the stock of smaller fast-growth companies.

STEEL SUPERSTARS. There are two shining stars in the steel industry: Worthington Industries, which grew at an average annual rate of 16 percent over the past decade (ten times the industry average) while reporting an industry-leading average ROE of 20 percent, and Nucor, whose 18 percent average ROE was second-best in the industry over the same decade. At Worthington Industries, there are no time clocks; all employees are on salary. There is an attractive profit-sharing plan in which the average bonus is 40 percent of an employee's annual salary. In the company's first thirty-five-years it has never laid off a full-time workers; rather, employees are reassigned to other areas as needed. There are such attractive perks for workers as the company's $2 barbershop, which they can visit during the company's time. The company respects its people, providing them with flexibility and the responsibility of managing their own time. In return, the employees have demonstrated a strong sense of commitment to the company, as evidenced by the fact that more than 80 percent of the employees own stock in the company.

Nucor has found a way to keep costs low while providing attractive incentives for its people. Base wages are approximately $8 per hour, but during good times the workers generally earn twice that amount as a result of bonuses. When demand falls, workers are not laid off, since Nucor does not have an unusually high payroll. In fact, with a no-layoff policy for the company's more than five thousand nonunion employees, Nucor is able to go to a three-day or four-day workweek if the need arises. In addition, rather than paying pensions, Nucor gives retirees a profit-sharing payout of up to $150,000. The result has been that Nucor's labor costs are $60 per ton, or about half of that of the large steel companies.

EQUITABLE COMPENSATION. Nucor has what may be considered a fair and equitable system of compensation. CEO Ken Iverson and the other top executives receive bonuses, but the bonuses are based on the profits of the company. Furthermore, the company does not have such perks as company cars or executive dining rooms, **so**

the executives all share in the risks and rewards. Since Iverson took over the presidency in 1965, Nucor has not had a losing quarter (as of 1993), despite the industry as a whole being one of the most severely hurt in the 1980s and 1990s.

Other high-performing fast-growth companies acknowledge the importance placed on their people by the salary structure of the company. For example, at Herman Miller, Inc., the directors recently decided that the CEO cannot earn more than twenty times the average factory worker's salary (which is about $25,000 per year). Although this is not as dramatic as the Ben & Jerry's policy of the chairman earning only five times the salary of factory workers, it is quite unusual among large corporations to cap the CEO's salary at $500,000. (Contrast that to the more than $10 million compensation packages received by Lee Iacocca of Chrysler, Mike Eisner of Disney, Jim Manzi of Lotus, Paul Fireman of Reebok, and Jack Welch of General Electric, in the 1990s.) Moreover, it is a symbolic gesture to show the people that their relative worth is high.

INNOVATIVE REWARDS. There are several companies that utilize innovative rewards to ensure the proper working climate. At University National Bank, employees get a $50 check on their birthday, champagne for New Years, a ham for Christmas, and roses for Valentine's Day. These are signals that reinforce the feeling that the bank cares about its people. The company also has a very flat structure (that is, fewer levels of management). Consequently there is lower overhead at the top levels, which has resulted in premium salaries for its employees. Marion Labs, which refers to its employees as "associates," rewards people for productivity. If productivity exceeds the plan, the company declares an "uncommon summer," whereby employees get Friday afternoon off. If there is extraordinarily strong productivity, Marion declares an "uncommon winter," which results in time off between Christmas and New Year's.

At Mary Kay Cosmetics selling is the key, it is fitting that the successful salespeople are well rewarded. At the annual sales awards meeting, high achievers are given such awards as mink coats, diamonds, vacations, and the famous yearlong use of a pink Cadillac. At Ben & Jerry's, employees are rewarded for reducing costs or improving profits with a "Fred-of-the-month award," complete with a "Fred's Famous" T-shirt. The award is named after Fred Lager, chief operating officer of the company, who has been largely responsible for improving the company's profitability in the early 1990s.

It is important to recognize that the perks and rewards are secondary, especially if management loses touch with the customer and with the bottom line. At Esprit, for example, employees received such lavish perks as raft trips to Africa and backpacking trips to the Grand Canyon. Yet amidst the troubled marriage of founders Doug and Susie Tompkins and a turbulent economic environment, Espirt lost sight of the customer and failed to catch early financial warning signs, resulting in stagnation, layoffs, and disappointing earnings.

Extraordinary Treatment of Ordinary People

CEO Yvon Chouinard of Patagonia, the outdoors goods company, once remarked, "We're all basically average. The key is to get average people to do above average work." Chouinard has accomplished this with the outstanding amenities that he provides for his people. These include subsidizing a top-notch day care center, which has resulted in reduced turnover, and a company cafeteria. Although such programs appear to lose memory, they are great long-term investments for keeping good people and for strengthening commitment.

Harry Quadracci, founder of Quad/Graphics, shares Chouinard's philosophy. In twenty years, he led a company that was started with a $35,000 loan to his home to become a $500 million leader in high-tech graphics printing. During that time he continually demonstrated an intense effort to provide the ideal climate for his people, who own a sizable amount of stock in the company (one of the characteristics of successful fast-growth companies). There are execise classes, day care, food service, and educational opportunities, all of which makes people feel "quadricized"—they live, eat, and sleep Quad/Graphics. Quadracci gets the most out of his people because people feel like they are truly a part of the business.

Valued Customers and Employees: Important Summary Points

1. Successful fast-growth companies generally recognize the importance of having high regard for their customers and for their employees; the two go hand in hand.
2. Smaller companies are often in a position to be much closer to their customers (for example, Shared Medical Systems, Mary Kay Cosmetics, Mrs. Fields' Cookies); this provides them with a distinct competitive advantage.
3. Successful fast-growth companies realize the importance of listening to the customer (for example, Stew Leonard's, Pall Corporation, Loctite) as well as going the extra yard for the customer (for example, Pandick Press, Patagonia).
4. Listening to employees, like listening to customers, is often a sign of success for growing companies (for example, Wal-Mart, Remington Products, Millipore, Kollmorgen, NATD).
5. Successful fast-growth companies often use innovative management practices and incentives for attracting and maintaining high-quality personnel (for example, Analog Devices, Teradyne, Worthington, Nucor, UNB, Marion Laboratories, Mary Kay Cosmetics, Ben & Jerry's, Patagonia, Quad/Graphics).

Quality Management

The Management Team: The Most Vital Component of Success

A prerequisite for the success of fast-growth ventures is the presence of a high-quality management team. As suggested by Jeffry Timmons, one of the leading academic experts in the area of entrepreneurship, the five most important factors considered by professionals when investing in emerging businesses are as follows.

- The kind of entrepreneur and the quality of the team.
- The kind of entrepreneur and the quality of the team.
- The kind of entrepreneur and the quality of the team.
- The kind of entrepreneur and the quality of the team.
- Market potential.[1]

The management team ideally is composed of bright, capable, trustworthy people with successful records of relevant experience. They should have a mix of backgrounds, with experience in the technical, financial, operations and marketing areas. Furthermore, a talented board of directors should *augment* management and should provide the management team with leadership, experience, and guidance.

Computer Stars

For anybody examining the background and capability of members of the management team, that information is often readily available. For privately held companies it will usually be contained in a business plan; for publicly held companies it will be contained in a prospectus or a proxy statement, either of which will be publicly available. In fact, many of the examples on the following pages are drawn from company prospectuses.

In 1982 Sevin Rosen Management, a venture capital firm in Dallas, invested $2.5 million in a start-up company that was then called Gateway Technology. Gateway's plan was to manufacture an IBM-compatible computer. Ben Rosen, general partner of Sevin Rosen and a seasoned venture capitalist, had trouble believing Gateway's sales projections of $35 million in its first year and $198 million in the second year. Nonetheless, Rosen saw a capable management team in which to invest. Gateway later changed its name to Compaq Computer and sold $111 million in its first year—a record, at that time, for a start-up—and $329 million in its second year. Sevin Rosen's investment grew more than fifteen-fold to $38 million at the time of Compaq's IPO. Since that time Compaq, which in 1992 generated $4 billion per year in revenues, has been a leading stock on Wall Street.

THE IMPACT OF COMPAQ. Another important point related to Compaq is that although it is a fairly new venture itself, it has been largely responsible for the growth of several other ventures that supply products to it. One, for example, is Conner Peripherals, a company started by Finis Conner, who had earlier been with Alan Shugart at Shugart Associates and Seagate Technology, where he pioneered a line of 5 1/4" disk drives, a significant improvement over the previously used 8" drives. Conner Peripherals supplies the more compact and more durable 3 1/2" disk drives to Compaq as well as to other computer manufacturers. Conner Peripherals, which amassed first-year sales of $113 million in 1986—topping Compaq's previous record—actually received $12 million in seed funding from Compaq itself in exchange for 40 percent of the ownership of the start-up. Conner Peripherals went public in 1988 and is now a billion-dollar company, having attained Fortune 500 status in a remarkable four years. (Not surprisingly, the only other company to have matched this feat was Compaq). Perhaps half of Conner's sales go to its investor/customer Compaq.

It should be noted that in Compaq's successful attempts at cost cutting in the early 1990s, it has put pressure on its suppliers for more favorable pricing. So when Conner Peripherals' disk drives were costing Compaq more than those of Quantum Corporation, Compaq made Quantum its primary disk drive supplier. Subsequently Compaq sold its stake in Conner for an $86 million gain.

AVOIDING THE ONE-MAN SHOW. Effective management teams which are commonly found in most established companies, are becoming very evident in fast-growth companies in the 1990s. In addition to Compaq, companies such as Linear Technology, AST Research, and Quantum have each avoided the "one-man show" and have assembled top management teams that are able to look beyond the narrow confines of specific functional areas to the broad concerns of the company as a whole. Their position in the corporation shows the importance placed on the controller or vice president of finance, who speaks the language of the investor, as well as the vice president or director of marketing, who bears the responsibility for sales growth.

Turning on the Investor

Investors invest in management teams. Perhaps the most attractive arrangement for an investor is to fund a venture managed by a previously successful entrepreneurial team: if they have succeeded before, then they are likely to succeed again. For example, Tandem Computer was founded in 1974 by Jim Treybig, along with a dozen other experienced managers, primarily from Hewlett-Packard. It is not surprising that Kleiner Perkins Caufield & Byers, the Mayfield Fund, and some of the other leading venture capital firms in the country invested in this start-up firm. Over the next ten years, Tandem returned nearly forty times the original investment in the company. Tandem has already had some of its managers leave to form their own ventures; perhaps the best known is Stratus Computer.

Apple Computer presents another illustration of how a management team should be assembled. The demand for the original Apple computer was too great for young entrepreneurs Steven Jobs and Stephen Wozniak to handle alone, so they sought the help of two experienced managers with backgrounds in marketing and manufacturing: A. C. (Mike) Markkula, formerly vice president of marketing at Intel, and Michael M. Scott, formerly head of production at National Semiconductor. Scott took a 50 percent cut in salary to join the upstart company, while Markkula invested nearly $100,000 of his own money in the venture.

Apple recognized the importance of having a management team with a broad range of experience. As such, the company beautifully combined eager young entrepreneurs with experienced professional managers from established companies. The management team also had a good mix of experience in marketing, manufacturing/operations, and finance.

Armed with experienced managers, Apple was then able to raise $600,000 from such established venture capital sources as Henry Singleton (who founded Teledyne), Arthur Rock (who earlier had invested in Teledyne, Fairchild Semiconductor, and Intel), Hambrecht & Quist, and Venrock Associates. As a result of the company's early success in attracting venture capital, Apple was seen as an attractive enough investment opportunity to raise $110 million at the time of its IPO, representing the largest IPO since Comsat had raised $200 million fifteen years earlier. Since that time Apple's stock price has appreciated fivefold.

A Future Success?

One of the more interesting management teams formed in the early 1990s is that of Echelon, Inc., of Los Gatos, California. The founders include M. Kenneth Oshman, formerly CEO of ROLM (the "O" in ROLM is for Oshman) and A. C. Markkula, former chairman of Apple. Echelon has been quite successful in raising venture capital, largely as a result of its prominent management team. The company is developing an integrated home control system, based on a neuron chip, whereby all electrically powered devices of a home, business, or automobile are operated through a central controller that can be accessed through a phone line or a remote controller. The founders raised $30 million in early-stage funding after a few phone calls.

Management Is More Important Than the Technology

The success stories of technology companies like the ones just described have often seduced us into believing that it is solely technology that is responsible for the company's success. Although there is a tremendous competitive advantage in having a proprietary technology in an emerging growth market—which was clearly the case of Apple Computer, Cray Research, Autodesk, and Microsoft—we should not overlook the fact that those same companies have also had superior management teams.

High-tech lovers often fail to recognize that technology can only get a company so far; investors who lost money on Wedtech, Psych Systems, Vector Graphic, and Columbia Data Products can attest to that. (Similarly, as noted earlier, such companies as The Limited, Wal-Mart, and The Gap brought phenomenal returns for investors even though they could hardly be referred to as high-tech companies.) Over the long term, it will be the quality of the management team that will enable a company to use its technological capabilities to its fullest potential.

A strong argument can be made that venture capitalists who invest in smaller, privately held businesses are among the most astute investors. After all, they invest in companies in the risky early years, when there is the least information available about those companies. There is an important adage in venture capital circles: it is better to invest in a first-rate management team with a second-rate product than a first-rate product with a second-rate management team. Thus it stands to reason that public investors would do well by following the advice of the venture capitalists and investing in management.

It is better to invest in a first-rate management team with a second-rate product than a first-rate product with a second-rate management team.

Consider, for example, Aryeh Finegold, who is credited with Daisy Systems Corporation's early success. Finegold joined Ready Systems (of Palo Alto, CA), a developer of real-time operating system software. Finegold was largely responsible for the ability of the company, which was then generating about $6 million in sales, to raise $7 million in second-round financing from several major venture capital companies, including Accel Partners, Adler &

Company, Venrock Associates, and Warburg, Pincus & Company. According to Jim Swartz, managing partner of Accel Partners, "There's one major reason why we did the deal and that's Aryeh Finegold."[2] Consistent with Swartz's view, Ramon V. Reyes of Nazem & Company, a venture capital firm in New York, recently suggested that "more than ever, the name of the game is management. If you find a company with the right horses, you back it to the hilt. Otherwise, you think twice."[3]

Most investors feel that management is more important than the product or service itself. As noted by Arthur Rock, a venture capitalist whose company has funded such firms as Fairchild Semiconductor, Scientific Data Systems, Teledyne, Intel, Diasonics, and Apple Computer:

> Over the past 30 years, I estimate that I've looked at an average of one business plan per day, or about 300 per year. . . . Of the 300 likely plans, I may invest in only one or two a year, and even among those carefully chosen few, I'd say that a good half fail to perform up to expectations. The problem with those companies is rarely one of strategy. Good ideas and good products are a dime a dozen. Good execution and good management—in a word, good *people*—are rare. . . . If you can find good people, they can always change the product. Nearly every mistake I've made has been I picked the wrong people, not the wrong idea.[4]

Does Leadership Matter?

Different Leaders at Different Stages

There are different kinds of leaders, depending on the stage of development of a business. At the early stages, there are the founders/entrepreneurs. A good example would be Steven Jobs and Stephen Wozniak, the visionary founders of Apple. As the company grows there are the enterprise builders, who put together the management team and pave the company's long-term direction. John Sculley, who left Pepsi to become CEO of Apple, fits this mold. Finally, there are the corporate leaders who reinforce the direction of a company in its mature stage. An example of this is Jack Welch (as well as his support group of top executives) at General Electric.

Generally, a leader will require different skills in the different kinds of situations. Thus it is quite common for leaders to play a role in only one of three stages described above. Steve Jobs (Apple Computer), Mitchell Kapor (Lotus Development), and Seymour Cray (Cray Research) were instrumental in launching their very successful companies; however, after a few years they all left the companies they founded.

Multifaceted Leaders

Although it is quite uncommon, one will occasionally find some successful entrepreneurs who have played critical roles in all three stages; Bill Hewlett and Dave Packard (of the company bearing their names) are good examples. In fact, it should not be surprising that large companies that keep on growing—such as Wal-Mart, Humana, and Steelcase,—are still run by the founders or their families. Of course, some entrepreneurial leaders have gone one step beyond by taking on the role of "turnaround leader" as well as enterprise builder. Victor Kiam of Remington Products has played such a multifaceted leadership role as architect of the tremendously successful LBO of Remington.

Although it may be too early to tell in 1993, it is quite possible that Bill Gates, founder of Microsoft, will also play a multifaceted role in the building of his corporation. He has been sensational in the first stage, and he certainly has the intellectual capability and the skills to excel (pardon the pun) in the subsequent stages.

Trimming the Fat at Nutri/System

Nutri/System provides a vivid example of how important leadership is in the long-term success of a company. In 1981, the year in which it went public, Nutri/System under Harold Katz (who founded the company in 1971) was a high-growth $50 million franchisor of weight loss centers. The centers, which offered weekly group therapy sessions, required customers to buy pre-packaged calorie-controlled entrees at high markups. By 1983 there were 680 centers across all fifty states, with revenues of $167 million. During that time Katz, who owned 65 percent of the stock in the company (then worth an estimated $300 million), enjoyed a lavish life-style and had an office to match, complete with marble walls and an indoor fountain. When Katz began to diversify his business interests, Nutri/System began to fall apart. Several lawsuits were filed by the franchisees. By 1984 the stock had lost 90 percent of its value, and revenues declined to about $100 million by the following year.

With Nutri/System at a low point, A. Donald McCulloch, a marketing expert with experience at General Foods and Pepsi, entered the picture. McCulloch became CEO with the stipulation that he could buy the company from Katz if he turned it around. McCulloch did just that by introducing programs of cost control and innovative marketing while establishing a strong relationship with the franchisees. He sold the corporate jet and the lavish headquarters and leased less expensive offices. He sold off unrelated businesses. He began to employ innovative advertising, such as using radio disk jockeys to provide firsthand testimonies of the value of Nutri/System. (This may seem rather bizarre, since the radio audience cannot see the results on these radio personalities; but it has worked.) Despite the high cost of Nutri/Systems' services (clients pay based on the amount of weight they want to lose—for example, it could cost about $700 for clients who want to lose thirty pounds) and products (food costs will be approximately $50 to $70), Nutri/System advertised effectively (using such lines as "The only thing you gain with Nutri/System is self-esteem" or "What price can you put on happiness?") to enhance sales and profits considerably. After the buyout by McCulloch and his partners, average revenues per company owned center quadrupled to more than $1 million. The average revenues per franchisee doubled to more than $500,000, thanks in part to incentives for the franchisees and to the sales training efforts that enhanced their selling skills. As of 1992 Nutri/System was expanding at the rate of one new center per day, approximately 750,000 people signed up per year, total revenues were about $1 billion per year.

Up until recently it appeared McCulloch would be the one to benefit the most from his successful turnaround of Nutri/System. He (and his partners) took the company private in 1986 in a $70 million transaction, putting up only $10,000 in cash and taking out $2 million in home equity loans. For that he received 65 percent of the company, and the shareholders were paid $7 per share for their stock (a 40 percent premium over the stock price at the time, but well below its stock price from 1983). As recently as 1992 a public offering of Nutri/Systems would have resulted in a $3/4 billion valuation for the company and over $500 million for McCulloch's stake. Once again, however, the tide of events changed. Amid several lawsuits and $100 million of cumulative losses, McCulloch's and Nutri/System's fortunes disappeared faster than a dieter's weight.

The Impact of Knowledge and Education

Obviously, knowledge and education have played a key role in fostering entrepreneurship and ultimately in the success of fast-growth companies. This is especially true in such high-tech businesses as computers, telecommunications, health care, and biotechnology. Consequently scientists from such prestigious universities as MIT, Harvard, Stanford, Caltech, the University of California, and the University of Texas have been major forces in the development of U.S. high-tech industries. Thus it should not be surprising that the high-tech centers in this nation—such as Boston, San Francisco, and Austin—are also the locations where these prominent universities are situated. MIT alone has been responsible for the success of more than fifty start-ups in the 1980s and 1990s. These include Matritech (Cambridge, MA), which is involved with new ways to detect cancer; Oculon (Seattle, WA), which has developed a technique to inhibit cataract formation in the eye; and Cirrus Logic (Milpitas, CA), a manufacturer of high-performance chips. Such ventures have often brought attractive returns to the investors. For example, an early-stage investment of $2.5 million in Cirrus Logic in 1986 by Fred Nazem, a venture capitalist based in New York City, increased in value by nearly twelvefold in three years.

With all the emphasis placed on college degrees, though, it is ironic that perhaps the most brilliant leader of a fast-growth company does not even have one. Fifteen years after Bill Gates left Harvard without a diploma, he is chairman (as well as technological champion, supreme manager, and organizational visionary) at

Microsoft, the largest and most innovative personal computer software company in the world. The company has grown more than a hundredfold since 1982 without any significant problems. Every plaudit applied to Microsoft in terms of innovation, competence, persistence, and effectiveness should be applied to the thirty-seven-year old Gates as well.

Rarely does the magic of a high-tech company last so long under the same leadership. For example, Apple, Lotus, Cray Research, and Ashton-Tate have all realized that founders do not hold permanent positions with the companies that they have launched. Yet Gates has demonstrated that a founder can be superb as a manager, negotiator, and leader. He has set an excellent example in adhering to a hard work ethic in which managers are expected to put in seventy-five-hour weeks. Yet there has been very low turnover, largely because of Microsoft's intense sense of loyalty for its people. Although salaries are low (even Gates earns only about $200,000 in base pay, which is quite a bit lower than the multimillion dollar salaries of some of his counterparts), people have received ample rewards in the form of stock (Gates's equity stake in Microsoft is worth about $6 billion). Before the company went public in 1986, all of the programmers received management-like stock options, ultimately making many of them millionaires following Microsoft's eightfold increase in value over the next four years.

Microsoft's initial success came from the dominance of its version of the disk operating system (DOS) used in IBM's first PC. As IBM and the clones have become more widely used, Microsoft has prospered; the company has sold more than 40 million copies of its DOS. Yet unlike other software companies—for example, Lotus, Ashton-Tate, and WordPerfect—that derive a vast percentage of their revenues from just one product, Microsoft has come up with one superhit after another. Microsoft's Word, Excel, and Windows are often regarded as the best products of their kind available.

Microsoft (or, more correctly, Gates) has also changed the way many of us live and work. The result of Gates's efforts has been a remarkably innovative business that has brought unheard-of profits—after-tax margins in excess of 20 percent—to the company and incredible returns to investors. Microsoft's market valuation is higher than companies that are ten times its size in terms of revenues.

Similar in many regards to Gates is Michael Dell, founder and chairman of Dell Computer, a $500 million computer maker based in Austin, Texas. It is no surprise that Dell, although only in his mid-twenties, is such a success. At age eight, he applied for a high school equivalency diploma by mail. At age thirteen, he launched a mail-order stamp trading company. Three years later, while working as a telemarketing representative for the *Houston Post,* he became salesman of the month. At age seventeen, he was earning $18,000 a year managing a group of his high school friends who were selling newspaper subscriptions.

Dell took an early leave from his college studies to launch his fast-growth success story. While a freshman at the University of Texas, Dell began selling computer parts by mail; he would buy components from manufacturers and assemble high-powered systems that outperformed the existing models. Dell had attained sales of nearly $200,000 in his first three months of business and $6 million by the end of his first full year. So he left college in order to devote a full-time commitment to his small, growing enterprise. As Dell noted, "I was having more fun selling computers than going to school. I realized that if I put any effort into my company, it could definitely become a multi-million dollar business."[5]

Dell began manufacturing and selling IBM clones with prices beginning at less than $1,000. He soon hired a team of seasoned executives to help manage the business and took the company public within a few years. Over its first eight years in operation, Dell achieved a competitive advantage over the larger, more established computer companies in its choice of distribution channels. Dell has been able to sell directly to the user at a lower price and with as good or better features than IBM and Compaq. Moreover, the company has provided customer support that is generally far superior to that of the computer retailers.

The Impact of Experience

A study conducted by Arnold Cooper and his colleagues of nearly three thousand start-ups found that companies that survived were more likely to have been started by full-time workers who had previous related experience in the same industry (although not necessarily in management), who had been graduated from college, and who were accompanied by full-time partners. In another study that examined the predictors of success of technically oriented ventures, it was found that senior management experience in prior venture start-ups was the single greatest influence on the performance of the company.[6] These studies support some of the findings of an earlier study of computer software firms, which found that the best predictor of success of a venture was prior experience in the software business.[7]

Successful companies are more likely to have been started by college graduates who had previous experience in the same industry and who were accompanied by full-time partners.

Thus prior experience plays an important role in the success of growth-oriented businesses. Consider Mary Kay Ash, who founded the company sporting her name with a $5,000 investment in 1963. Many years earlier, as a single parent of three children, Ash began working part-time to support her family. She took a job with Stanley Home Products in Houston selling household products at home parties. She left to work for World Gifts Company in Dallas, selling decorative accessories; eventually she became national training director. She then left to start Mary Kay Cosmetics. The company had nine original sales reps, with first-year sales of about $200,000. Four years later the company went public, and it has since grown to a company that has a quarter of a million sales representatives.

Successful Track Records Heighten the Chance of Success

In the 1980s and 1990s numerous experienced managers with excellent track records at established companies (such as Digital

Equipment, General Electric, Honeywell, IBM, and Hewlett-Packard) have become very successful in starting their own businesses. Ed De Castro, who was unable to get Digital Equipment Corporation (DEC) to back his revolutionary new computer, left to form Data General, which became one of DEC's leading competitors; Richard Blackmer founded Oxygen Enrichment Company after spending twenty-five years as an engineer with General Electric; and Dean Scheff started CPT Corporation after having worked for Univac and Honeywell. Interestingly, Apollo Computer, itself a relatively new company, has given birth to approximately one dozen companies, most of which operate quite similarly to Apollo and are located in close proximity to it in the Route 128 area near Boston.

True-Blue Offshoots

Although many outsiders view IBM as a bureaucratic organization where employees typically spend their entire career, it is interesting to note that "Big Blue" has one of the best track records of turning out entrepreneurs. Former IBMers have become part of the management teams of such companies as Computerland (Edward Faber), Data Switch (Richard Greene), and Tandon (Don Wilkie), to name just a few.

For example, Gene Amdahl left IBM to launch the computer company sporting his name. He was the leader of the technical team that designed the IBM Model 360, the most widely used computer in the world at the time. In addition he was an IBM fellow, an honor that enabled him to pursue his own interests at IBM's expense. In 1970 he became disenchanted with IBM and resigned to launch a company that would compete with it in the design and manufacturing of mainframe computers. Despite the fact that this was far from an ideal time to raise venture capital, Amdahl's standing in the industry enabled him to raise more than $27 million from Heizer Corporation, Nixdorf, and Fujitsu, among others. Although no sales were made until 1975, he had back orders for $35 million in computers two years earlier. By 1976 the company realized its first profit; it went public in the fall of that year at a total market value of $165 million, with Amdahl's stake being worth $3 million.

Of course, a career path through IBM will not guarantee success for an entrepreneur. For example, Edward Esber, who left IBM to run Ashton-Tate (the developer of the dBase software package), resigned his position as chairman and CEO of the software company amid slumping sales. A more extreme example is that of Jesse Aweida, who left IBM to launch Storage Technology, one of the fast-growth companies of the early 1980s. Revenues increased steadily to almost $1 billion by 1983; however, earnings had declined at a faster rate than sales growth, forcing the company to file for bankruptcy in 1984.

Questionable Experience

The failure of several fast-growth companies has been attributable to the lack of relevant experience among members of the management team. This was evident at two fast-growth pioneers in the personal computer industry: Vector Graphic and Osborne Computer.

Vector Graphic was started by Bob and Lore Harp along with a friend, Carol Ely. Bob, who was senior staff scientist at Hughes, had designed a microcomputer memory board in his spare time and suggested that Lore and Carol try to sell it. Although the two women knew virtually nothing about computers, they became convinced of their company's market potential after visiting a computer show. They sold computer-related products, and eventually introduced their own model of computer. In 1981, five years after the company had been established, its sales had reached $30 million, and the founders began planning for an initial public offering. Bob still worked full-time at Hughes and designed new products in his spare time for a 5 percent royalty on sales. Unfortunately for the trio, when IBM introduced its personal computer, the market for Vector collapsed. Lore left Vector in 1983 following her divorce from Bob and amid a struggle with the board of directors. Three years later she began another venture, this time to produce and sell feminine hygiene products.

During roughly the same time period Adam Osborne, who was trained as a chemical engineer and had developed some expertise in the area of technical writing, started a small business in Berkeley, California, that published books on microcomputers. As the microcomputer industry began to develop during the last half of the 1970s, Osborne felt that there would be tremendous opportunities for him as a manufacturer of computers, even though he had no experience in manufacturing. An opportunity arose when McGraw-Hill purchased his publishing company.

Osborne's idea was to manufacture a low-priced personal computer. Its competitive features were that it would (1) have the disk drives and screen combined in the same box, rather than have them as separate components connected by wires; (2) be compact enough to be considered portable and to fit under an airplane seat; and (3) have software—including an operating system, a word processing program (Wordstar), and a spreadsheet program (Supercalc)—bundled with the computer. Osborne was able to get his costs for the software down to less than $10 per computer due to quantity purchases and special supplier arrangements. Unfortunately, there were a few drawbacks to the computer, such as the limited size screen of the computer.

At the early stages of the venture Osborne invested $100,000 personally and raised another $40,000 from Jack Melchor, a well-known venture capitalist. In 1981 Osborne raised another $900,000 from personal sources and from venture capitalists. Everything looked very attractive for the company, especially when the first prototypes were displayed at a trade show in March 1981 at a retail price of $1,795, approximately half of what other microcomputers cost at that time. The trade show proved very effective, as did publicity from the *Wall Street Journal*. Shipment of computers began by the end of June; by the end of that year, the company had sold more than seven thousand computers. The following year was even more prosperous, with revenues reaching $100 million.

Almost as quickly as the company prospered, however, it floundered. Osborne's lack of experience in managing such a venture caught up with him, and the company went bankrupt.

Star Managers in Low-Tech Industries

With technology companies like the ones just described, a typical strong management team would include three or four highly educated (from the likes of Harvard, Stanford, MIT, Caltech, North-western, or Columbia), young (often in their thirties) managers with engineering and/or sales experience who were previously in fast-track positions at outstanding companies (such as Hewlett-Packard, Intel, Advanced Micro Devices, or Microsoft). (And although it is not stated specifically in the prospectus, you can imagine that they are probably also the clean-cut all-American types who have a three-handicap in golf while playing only twice a year, and who run marathons in less than three hours without working up a sweat.)

APPAREL. Companies operating in typically low-tech, low-growth industries, however, often need a far different type of management team. One of the top-performing companies of the 1980s and 1990s has been Liz Claiborne, a designer of women's clothing. In this industry, an engineering degree from Caltech will not substitute for twenty-five years of apparel experience. Management of Liz Claiborne during its early years included Elisabeth Claiborne Ortenberg, Arthur Ottenberg, Leonard Boxer, and Jerome A. Chazen, all of whom had rich and extensive experience in the apparel industry.

RETAILING. Two of the most successful fast-growth retailers over the past decade have been Costco, a membership warehouse chain, and Home Depot, a home improvement chain. It is not surprising that the management at both companies was strong. Costco's managers had extensive experience in retailing and apparel, having held positions at such respected companies as the Price Company, Builder's Emporium, and Fed-Mart Corporation. Home Depot had put together an equally impressive management team with executives from Handy Dan, National Lumber and Supply, and Homeco. As noted earlier, Home Depot was the most successful IPO (in terms of subsequent stock price appreciation) of the 1980s.

Gaps in the Management Team May Spell Disaster

Not surprisingly, some of the major disappointments in retailing in recent years occurred at companies with major question marks in management. For example, the original officers and directors at Home Shopping Network (HSN) included primarily lawyers, real estate developers, and investment bankers with little or no experience in retailing or in running a fast-growth $100 million-a-year company. There was no evidence that HSN had anything to resemble a management team with a broad range of experience in operations, marketing, and finance at that time.

Similarly, the top executives of Silk Greenhouse were lacking in management experience in merchandising and retailing, as well as in managing a multimillion-dollar national retailing chain. It was not surprising to see that although Silk Greenhouse was an immediate hit despite a depressed stock market (it went public shortly after the market crash of 1987), the company's stock later came crashing down itself, losing 90 percent of its value in about a year.

Expertise in management is derived from training, years of experience, and maturity. A close look at the management of ZZZZ Best during its early high-growth days revealed that these three elements were sorely lacking. Specifically, according to the company's prospectus, founder Barry Minkow (who was later sent to prison), was twenty years old at the time of the company's initial public offering. Although Minkow was an experienced salesman, it would be safe to conclude that someone his age would lack the maturity and management training to operate as a CEO of a publicly held corporation.

Moreover, there was no substantive management background or experience for *any* top executives of the company. In describing the upper-level managers working with Minkow, the prospectus filed at the time of ZZZZ Best's IPO left the experience of the managers up to the reader's imagination, using statements like the following:

" . . . he was employed by various carpet cleaning establishments prior to joining the company . . ."

" . . . she was employed in the telemarketing departments of various carpet cleaning companies . . ."

" . . . owned and operated his own telemarketing consulting firm . . ."

" . . . owned and operated . . . an independent advertising firm . . ."

Such nebulous statements about the key executives of a soon-to-go-public company certainly raised a red flag to some investors; those who missed them lost a lot of money when ZZZZ Best went bankrupt.

Never Too Young, Never Too Old

It seems like there is never a right time nor a wrong time to start a business venture. There are typical career paths of successful entrepreneurs, yet the atypical paths of those who have turned their businesses into successful fast-growth companies are often far more interesting.

YOUNG. Although a survey of *Inc.* 500 CEOs revealed that nearly half had started at least one business prior to their current business, it does not always take vast experience and huge sums of capital to start a successful enterprise. Consider Dave Packard and Bill Hewlett, who were engineering students at Stanford in the early 1930s. They parted for a few years, during which Hewlett went to MIT and Packard went to work at General Electric. In 1939 the pair raised $538 and set up shop in a one-car garage behind Packard's house in Palo Alto.

Their first product was far from a success; it was an automatic foul-line indicator for bowling alleys, which had virtually no market. Fortunately, however, their next product was an audio oscillator that measured the intensity of recorded sound, which was based on a design developed by Hewlett for his master's thesis. Walt Disney, who was working on the movie Fantasia at the time, bought eight of the oscillators, and Hewlett-Packard was launched.

Interestingly, although Hewlett-Packard has been a leader in product technology, it is probably best known over its 50-year history for its management philosophy. The company's approach, which has included an informal, open-door practice strengthened by its now-famous MBWA ("managing by walking around") style, has made the company one of the most-admired corporations in the world.

YOUNG AT HEART. But just as Bill Hewlett, Dave Packard, Steven Jobs, Bill Gates, and Michael Dell have demonstrated that there are successful young entrepreneurs, so are there successful older entrepreneurs. Ray Kroc, who built McDonald's into the most successful fast food company in the world, began his successful entrepreneurial effort at the age of fifty-two.

The Impact of Persistence

When He Absolutely, Positively Must Meet Payroll

Persistence is another important quality of effective leaders who have been responsible for the success of fast-growth companies. Consider the story of Fred Smith, founder of Federal Express. It has been said that in the early 1970s, when Smith had difficulty meeting payroll for his then-small company, he flew to Las Vegas and won enough money paying blackjack to meet his payroll.

Headstrong

Perhaps even more extreme was Howard Head's attempt to develop an improved ski. Up until the mid-1940s, skis were made out of wood. Head, an engineer by training, set out to revolutionize the industry with the development of a metal ski—actually, a "metal sandwich," consisting of a layer of honeycombed plastic in between two layers of aluminum. The process of producing the skiis was long and tedious, but Head was persistent enough to produce six pairs to be tested in Stowe, Vermont. One by one, the skiis failed the "flex test" and broke.

Undaunted, Head quit his job at Martin in 1948 and, with $6,000 in poker earnings that he had stashed away, sought to perfect his metal ski. Every week he would send a new pair to be tested by a ski instructor in Bromley, Vermont, with the same result: they would be sent back broken. Apparently Head's thinking was quite similar to that of Robert Wood Johnson (founder of Johnson & Johnson), who once remarked, "If I wasn't making mistakes, I wasn't making decisions." Yet it was more than an ability to learn from failure that motivated Head; it was an amazingly strong sense of persistence. As he noted, "If I had known then that it would take 40 versions before the ski was any good, I might have given up. But, fortunately, you get trapped into thinking the next design will be it."[8]

Persistence paid off. It took three winters and several dozen adjustments, but eventually Head watched as instructor Cliff Taylor tested the skis. As Taylor finished his run, he said, " 'They're great, Mr. Head, just great.'. . . At that moment, Head says, 'I knew deep inside I had it.' "[9]

As noted by management guru Peter Drucker, "Whenever anything is being accomplished, it is being done by a monomaniac with a mission."[10] Howard Head's persistence was an underlying value surrounding decisions made at Head Ski Company and was largely responsible for the company's early success.

Persistence and Intensity

A different kind of persistence is found in the leadership at Automatic Data Processing (ADP). Even as a teenager, Henry Taub, founder of ADP, was the epitome of efficiency. While in high school the young Taub took on an evening job at Associated Transport. He found ways to improve the efficiency of his administrative position at Associated, primarily because he had to get home early enough to do his homework. After graduating from high school he enrolled at New York University, taking on a job with a small accounting firm at the same time in order to pay his tuition. His job basically involved bookkeeping, payroll, and billing, so when Taub graduated from NYU (at the ripe old age of nineteen) he had some excellent experience in administrative efficiency.

Taub then went to work at a larger accounting firm. He soon got fed up with the bureaucracy, however, and left to become an office manager at a small lingerie company. While there, he found out firsthand how disastrous it could be if payroll was late, in this case due to the unexpected illness of one of the payroll clerks. So Taub got together with a friend and, with a $6,000 investment put up by a third partner, started a company that would manage the payrolls of other companies, guaranteeing that they would never miss a payroll. And so ADP was formed; Taub was twenty-one at the time. Over the years, largely as a result of Taub's persistence and his intense work ethic, ADP has become one of the classic success stories in this country.

Taub not only spearheaded the early growth of ADP but developed a clear enough vision for the company to have two successful CEO transitions while he served as chairman of the board. The first was in 1976, when Frank Lautenberg, then a twenty-two year veteran with ADP, became CEO. Earlier Lautenberg had been responsible for several successful acquisitions that broadened the company's mission into several related niches, and as the company grew via those acquisitions, Lautenberg hired key people from such companies as IBM, Burroughs, and Digital Equipment to create a professional team of management to oversee the company's growth. The second CEO transition was in 1982, when Lautenberg left the company after being elected U.S. senator from New Jersey. Lautenberg was replaced by Josh Weston, who had been hired by Lautenberg in 1970 and groomed for the presidency for several years prior to taking on that position.

Since its early days, ADP has placed major importance on the role of the leader. Taub was the entrepreneur who led the company through its early days. It took more than a dozen years before the company reached the half-million mark in sales; fifteen years later, however, thanks largely to the leadership of Lautenberg, ADP was generating nearly $200 million per year. During Josh Weston's tenure as CEO, ADP's average annual ROE has exceeded 20 percent.

Once Is Not Enough

"Repeat entrepreneurs" such as Nolan Bushnell (Atari & Pizza Time Theatre), Steven Jobs (Apple and NeXT), William Poduska (Prime Computer and Apollo Computer), Alan Shugart (Shugart Associates and Seagate Technology), Phillipe Villers (Computervision and Automatix), Mitchell Kapor (Lotus Development and ON Technology) and Irwin Selinger (Surgicot and Patient Technology, Inc.) demonstrate the essence of persistence. Not only that, these entrepreneurs have found that securing funding from investors becomes increasingly easy with experience, thereby heightening the chance of success with their later ventures. As suggested earlier in this chapter, venture capitalists generally invest more in the experience of the entrepreneur or the entrepreneurial team than in the growth potential of a given product or service idea. So persistence pays off in more ways than one.

It's OK to Fail

Even failure counts as valuable experience, thereby further supporting the importance of persistence. From an investment standpoint, early investors generally prefer investing in repeat entrepreneurs who have launched businesses that eventually did not materialize than investing in unknown entities. For example, although Osborne Computer went bankrupt in 1984, its founder, Adam Osborne started a new software company within a year with $2.2 million in funding from venture investors. Similarly, after Robert McNulty's failed attempt with SportsClub, a discount sports retailer, he was able to raise funds for HQ Office Supplies Warehouse (Long Beach, CA), a chain of discount office products, and AG Automotive Warehouses, a chain of warehouse stores selling automotive parts. Of course, McNulty's earlier successful venture—HomeClub (of Fullerton, CA), which quadrupled its investors' money when it was sold to Zayre for $151 million in 1986, three years after it was founded—gave him the credibility to raise capital for these more recent ventures.

Bouncing Back

One of the real success stories of an entrepreneur bouncing back is of Wilfred Corrigan, who left Fairchild Camera and Instrument after the company had tumbled to a state of technological mediocrity following its acquisition by Schlumberger in 1979. Thanks in part to a $6 million infusion from Sequoia Capital, Corrigan took LSI Logic (of Milpitas, CA) from start-up to its initial public offering in 1982; at that time, semiconductor company was valued at $500 million.

We tend to see this notion of an entrepreneur bouncing back from failure quite often in high-tech companies, especially in Silicon Valley, where there seems to be more freedom to fail than in other parts of the country. As noted by Jean Deleage, managing partner of the noted San Francisco–based venture capital firm Burr, Egan, Deleage & Company, "It is as if there had been a 27th amendment to the American Constitution in Silicon Valley—one saying that to have failed is not an ineradicable black mark against you."[11] Such failure can even be very positive for U.S. economic development. As recently noted by Robert D. Hormats, vice chairman of Goldman Sachs International, "An entrepreneur who has gone bankrupt with one idea can come back and get the venture capitalist to start another idea. In a period of low savings rates, high government spending, and other economic problems, this stands out as a big advantage."[12]

The Impact of Integrity of Management

The integrity of management is a vital component of success for fast-growth companies. This quality can be assessed by examining such factors as the nature of transactions among key executives, the makeup of the management team, and compensation packages for top managers.

When executives engage in questionable related-party transactions that benefit themselves, their family members, or friends at the expense of other shareholders, it raises concerns about management's integrity. At the time of an IPO, the SEC requires that such related transactions be disclosed in a company's prospectus. Thus such transactions are easily identifiable for any investor searching for "red flags" in companies that have recently gone public.

When executives engage in questionable related-party transactions, it raises concerns about management's integrity.

One type of related-party transaction occurs when managers or directors use a company's resources for personal purposes, including loans to managers and other employees at below-market interest rates, loans to employees for nonbusiness purposes, and special business relationships with family members. A company should not be in the business of providing loans or other advances to employees or directors. If they need a loan, they should do what most people do—go to a bank. Consider such poor-performing fast-growth companies as TIE/Communications, which made interest-free loans to its executive officers; Silk Greenhouse, whose two top executives had taken out non-interest-bearing loans from their company totaling nearly $200,000; and Genex, where several officers and directors received interest-free loans. These transactions, which all occurred shortly before these companies went public and were clearly delineated in the prospectuses of these companies, raised serious concerns about the integrity of management.

An Extreme Case of Related Transactions

When it comes to related transactions among fast-growing companies, Home Shopping Network (HSN) and its CEO, Roy Speer, deserve special mention. Here are some examples taken from the company's prospectus at the time of its IPO:

1. HSN leased equipment from Speer's family trust.
2. HSN entered into two agreements with Interphase, Inc. (a company in which Roy M. Speer was the sole shareholder), paying monthly rentals totaling $40,000 for certain computer and communication equipment.
3. HSN had an agreement with Pioneer Data, Inc. (whose president and sole shareholder was Roy Speer's son, Richard), which provided computer advice, software programs, and personnel in return for 1 percent of the company's gross profit. In addition, Pioneer agreed to lease certain computer equipment to HSN at a rental of nearly $13,000 per month.
4. Interphase was retained by the company to construct a television studio for nearly $100,000.
5. HSN borrowed nearly $400,000 from Interphase at 2 percent above prime.
6. HSN (through its predecessor) assumed the lease of Home Shopping Medical Center (whose name was subsequently

changed to Western Hemisphere Sales, Inc.), which was owned by the Speer family, for use as the company's accounting and data processing center.

7. Western Hemisphere had an agreement to sell HSN's excess and unsalable merchandise at prices designated by HSN. HSN received a commission of 15 percent on the sales.

Any investor noticing all these related-party transactions would have been concerned about the integrity of management at HSN at that time and would not have been surprised when, despite a rapid run-up in the price of the stock, HSN's market value eventually declined by about 90 percent.

The Makeup of the Management Team: Be Wary of Nepotism

Integrity is often demonstrated by the makeup of the management team. In this regard, one of the problems affecting Kaypro Computer's demise resulted from the predominance of members of the Kay family as officers and directors of the company (referred to by some as "too many Kays and not enough pros").

One of the problems affecting Kaypro Computer's demise resulted from "too many Kays and not enough pros."

Similarly, at TCBY, another fast-growth company that later fell on tough times, top executives included CEO Frank Hickingbotham, his twenty-five-year-old son Herren, and Frank's brother-in-law Walter Winters; like the situation at Kaypro, there was an abundance of family members and a dearth of professional managers. It appeared that young Herren, with a B.A. in finance and seven months' experience as a government and municipal bond trader, lacked the credentials typically found in an executive vice president. Likewise, brother-in-law Winters previously was a vacuum cleaner distributor; he had no previous experience in franchising or in the frozen food business. It is possible that this weakness in management finally caught up with the company: despite a thirtyfold gain in its stock price over the first seven years of its being a public company, TCBY later lost more than 80 percent of its market value.

MIXING FAMILY AND BUSINESS. A more extreme example of problems arising from mixing family and business was evident at Vector Graphic, one of the many fast-growth computer makers of the early 1980s that is no longer in business today. When key executives fail to separate their business from their personal and family life, it often can be detrimental to both business and personal relationships. The husband-wife executive team at Vector Graphic was having serious marital problems around the time of its IPO. As the prospectus reported:

> the Company has been informed that an action seeking dissolution of [the] marriage [of Mr. and Mrs. Harp] has been filed. They have both indicated that regardless of their marital status, they intend to remain with the Company and have recently entered into three year employment contracts with the Company. No assurances can be given that either [Mr. Harp or Mrs. Harp] will remain with the Company for such three year period.

Marital problems are a touchy issue. Certainly some couples work out their differences and can even work together *after* a divorce. I have generally found, however, that (1) there is greater stress for a husband-wife executive team trying to run a fast-growing company than for other teams; and (2) when there are personal problems, such as a pending divorce, it places a greater strain on both the marriage and on the business. In the case of Vector Graphic and the Harps, this stressful relationship may have contributed strongly to the eventual demise of the company.

SOME FAMILIES CAN WORK WELL TOGETHER. Certainly there are potential problems in family-run businesses, as was seen with Kaypro and Vector Graphic. There are many notable instances, however, of successful family-dominated fast-growth businesses. For example, fast-growing pizza restaurant Sbarro included as executive committee members three Sbarro brothers (Mario, Joseph, and

Anthony), along with their mother Carmela. Similarly, King World Productions has been run by five of the children of the company's founding husband and wife. And up until the early 1990s Liz Claiborne's top management included the wife/husband team of Elisabeth Claiborne Ortenberg and Arthur Ortenberg. The "poorest" performer among these three fast-growth family-run businesses has been Sbarro, whose stock price appreciated by a mere tenfold in the five years subsequent to its IPO in 1985.

SOBs. The important question to ask is, despite the family relationship (which often affects only two executives out of the entire management team), is the *overall* makeup of management one in which commands confidence? In other words, does the management team have integrity and do they (regardless if they are husband and wife or father and son) have the capability as managers to foster the continued growth of the venture? If they are the right people for the job and are not there just because they are SOBs (sons of bosses), then the mere fact that some of the managers are related should not detract from the integrity of the entire team. Shrewd investors who adhered to this philosophy experienced a twentyfold increase in the value of their stock in King World Pro-

---

The important question to ask is, despite the family relationship, is the overall makeup of management one that commands confidence?

---

ductions and a thirtyfold increase in the value of their stock in Liz Claiborne.

Compensation Packages Should Be Realistic

Integrity of management is often illustrated in the compensation of key executives. In smaller fast-growth companies, the members of the management team are typically substantial stockholders of the company and therefore can have substantial input in their own compensation. By paying themselves excessive salaries or bonuses, they are often using proceeds that are best targeted to foster the growth of the business. Fortunately, for publicly held companies, information regarding executive compensation is included in a company's prospectus and proxy materials.

Of course, compensation by itself will not determine if a company's stock is going to rise or fall. Modest compensation, however, is a good signal to reinforce the integrity of the management team, as well as the company's long-range orientation. For example, in the early years of Apple Computer, a $100 million company at the time it went public, founders Jobs and Wozniak took home salaries of less than $50,000 apiece. Similarly, the executives at Cray Research were paid modestly to conserve capital for product development and other vital projects; Seymour Cray's compensation for 1975—the year before the firm went public—was $40,000. This same prudent philosophy was evident at Genentech, where CEO Swanson received a salary and bonus totaling $68,000 just before its IPO. Contrast that to the compensation of ZZZZ Best's CEO Barry Minkow, which included $300,000 per year salary plus $20,000 *"attributable to his use of a Company-owned automobile."* A prudent investor or prospective business partner could have found all this information on these companies in their prospectuses at the time of their IPOs, and he or she could have predicted that while Apple, Cray, and Genentech would go on to become superstar performers, ZZZZ Best would go out of business and Minkow would wind up in jail.

Running Away with Bonuses

A few of the more prominent athletic shoe manufacturers—which, despite their growth, have had their share of ups and downs in terms of profitability and stock price—illustrate the concerns raised by excessive compensation packages. Specifically, according to its prospectus at the time of its IPO, LA Gear awarded CEO Greenberg an annual base salary of $225,000 (plus an automobile) and an annual bonus of *"2 1/2% of that portion of the company's pre-tax net income over $2 million but less than $12 million and 5% of a portion of the company's pre-tax net income* *over $12 million."* The bonus totaled $1.5 million in the year prior to LA Gear's IPO.

In terms of bonuses, though, LA Gear could not quite keep pace with its archrival Reebok, whose CEO, Paul Fireman, earned $1.3 million in salary and bonuses in the year prior to going public. His compensation per his employment agreement was described in the company's prospectus: *"Mr. Fireman will receive a base salary of $350,000 and will be entitled to receive an annual bonus (pro-rated for 1985) equal to 5% of the amount by which the Company's annual pre-tax earnings exceeds $20 million."* The concern is that (1) the bonus was based on one factor, namely, dollars of income; and (2) it was completely open-ended. That could mean that even if the company's margins declined, if its debt rose precipitously, or if its liquidity eroded (all of which could weaken the company), Fireman could still receive an attractive bonus if aggregate sales and profits increased.

Interestingly, LA Gear and Reebok were both big winners immediately following their IPOs, suggesting that compensation alone should not be the sole basis for evaluating a fast-growth company. Later, however, both stocks realized significant declines due to disappointing earnings. In 1990 the board of directors at Reebok finally realized that their compensation plan made little sense, and they voted to limit CEO pay to no more than $2 million—quite a change for Fireman, who had been averaging $14 million during the previous five years. It is surprising that it took so long for the board to realize that the compensation formula was so inappropriate.

The Impact of the Board of Directors

A vital component of the management team for fast-growth companies is the board of directors. In many instances, an experienced board will partially offset some of the gaps in the knowledge or background of the management team. At a minimum, such a board will enhance the capabilities and experience of management in the eyes of the investor, which is critical at the early stages of a growth venture. Information about the backgrounds and experience of the members of the board is, like other vital information, contained in the prospectus and proxy materials of publicly owned companies.

Outside Representation Is Essential

The purpose of the board of directors is to aid, challenge, and if necessary replace the officers of the company. Thus a passive, unquestioning board (which is often the case if the board is composed primarily of either inside managers or friends and relatives) can have a disastrous impact on the business. Successful fast-growth companies will generally have several qualified "outsiders" (members who are not officers of the company—for example, experienced business executives with strong contacts) serve on the board. In the case of a start-up company, a strong external

---

Successful fast-growth companies will generally have several qualified "outsiders" serve on the board to aid, challenge, and if necessary replace the officers of the company.

---

board can give the company instant credibility, which in turn can assist in raising early rounds of financing, a key predictor of subsequent performance.

The Role of the Board

An example of the effective use of outsiders is illustrated in the case of Chester Kirk, founder, chairman, and CEO of Amtrol, a very successful privately owned manufacturing company in West Warwick, Rhode Island. Kirk has acknowledged that outsiders often possess expertise in areas where his own management team may be lacking. Outside directors with backgrounds in finance and international business were especially helpful in making recommendations related to selecting inventory accounting methods, choosing a computer system, developing an employee ownership plan, and in making general decisions on the long-term growth of Amtrol.

RAISING CAPITAL. Alejandro Zaffaroni, a Ph.D. chemist and former executive vice president of Syntex, invested $2 million of his own money to launch a pharmaceutical company, ALZA, in Palo Alto, California. Zaffaroni recruited a prominent board of directors, who were instrumental in giving the company the credibility to raise an additional $50 million (in multiple rounds of financing) while its products were still under development. ALZA, whose sales are only approximately $100 million (but with more than 20 percent net margins) has a market value of around $2 billion, which is comparable to the value of such multibillion-dollar revenue giants as Great Atlantic & Pacific Tea (A & P Stores), Super Valu Stores, Florida Progress, Chase Manhattan, and Travelers. Over the latter part of the 1980s ALZA's revenues were increasing by 30 percent per year while its earnings per share were growing at 70 percent per year, thereby accounting for its twentyfold increase in stock price during that decade.

Biotechnology company Nova Pharmaceuticals (of Baltimore, MD) has also had an impressive group of directors to complement its strong management team. They have included chairman John Lloyd Huck, former president of Merck; Solomon Snyder, a neuroscientist from Johns Hopkins Medical School who was chairman of Nova's scientific advisory council; Henry Wendt, CEO of Smith-Kline Beckman, a company that had invested $70 million in this venture; Ralph Gomory, retired chief scientist of IBM; Edward Hennessy, chairman of Allied-Signal; and former U.S. president Gerald Ford. Apparently, these influential directors were instrumental in enabling Nova to secure funding: aside from SmithKline Beckman, Nova received early-stage funding from Eastman Kodak, Marion Laboratories, and Celanese. Moreover, although Nova had yet to market a product (although several of its products were in clinical or preclinical studies), it was able to go public in 1983 without even a laboratory. Within two years, its stock price had increased fivefold. Nonetheless, it takes more than having a prominent board of directors to sustain stock price appreciation, and since 1986 Nova's stock has fallen in value considerably, largely as a result of its lack of earnings.

VENTURE CAPITALISTS AS BOARD MEMBERS. In order to gain access to external funding, often successful fast-growth companies will recruit venture capitalists and other investment professionals to serve as directors. Microsoft's board of directors includes David Marquardt, general partner of Technology Venture Investors, which provided Microsoft with funding prior to its IPO. Similarly, at Compaq Computer, Genentech, and Sun Microsystems, outside directors who were venture capitalists (and who were, consequently, early-stage investors), played important roles. Ben Rosen served as Compaq's chairman, and Tom Perkins, who was also chairman of fast-growth computer maker Tandem Computer, served as chairman of Genentech. Likewise, members of the board of Sun Microsystems included John Doerr, a partner at Kleiner Perkins Caufield & Byers as well as a director of Compaq, and David Marquardt of TVI.

Directors Should Add Value

Successful fast-growth companies generally devote the necessary time to recruit top-quality outside directors who could help the company. In contrast, most companies that have failed to enlist such outside support have performed poorly. At the time of its IPO, Kaypro lacked quality outside directors. The savvy business person or investor would have noticed this when reading Kaypro's prospectus. Likewise, the board of TCBY included no outside advisors or experts, other than a law partner in TCBY's law firm. Similarly, the board of directors of ZZZZ Best seemed to offer little if any synergy among the management team; they included an automobile wholesaler, a stationery and gifts manufacturer, and an associate superintendent of schools. It is questionable what knowledge and skills these directors offered to the already inexperienced management teams just cited.

The entrepreneur planning the growth of his or her company, or the investor seeking a generous return, must be able to rely on the expertise of a highly skilled and experienced management team and group of outside advisors. No matter how fine the product, without knowledge, experience and integrity at the helm, the venture is doomed to mediocrity or failure.

Management: Important Summary Points

1. Quality management (in the form of an effective management team) is an essential component for successful fast-growth companies; in fact, management is generally consid-

ered more important than the technology or product (for example, Compaq, Tandem, Apple, Echelon).

2. Leadership can have a dramatic impact on the success of a growing company (for example, Digital Equipment, Hewlett-Packard, Remington Products, Wal-Mart, Humana, Steelcase, Microsoft).

3. An effective management team is often a function of the knowledge and education of the managers (for example, Matritech, Oculon, Cirrus Logic), experience of the managers (for example, Data General, Data Switch, Amdahl, Oxygen Enrichment, Liz Claiborne, Costco, Home Depot), persistence of the managers (for example, Federal Express, Head Ski, ADP, LSI Logic), integrity of management (for example, Cray, Genentech), and quality of the external directors (for example, Amtrol, ALZA, Microsoft, Compaq, Genentech, Sun Microsystems).

Venture Capital Support

Venture Catalysts: Providing the Fuel
to Generate Growth

In the previous chapter I alluded to the importance of venture capitalists in shaping the management team of many fast-growth companies. As the reader will soon see, venture capitalists—the individuals and/or firms that provide the funding to fast-growth entrepreneurial ventures—have often been the catalysts behind the success of these companies.[1] Thus the term *venture catalysts* is often appropriate to describe the role that venture capitalists have played in fostering the development of these companies. The analogy is that of the automobile and the fuel necessary to sustain it.[2] The automobile is the venture, the true entrepreneurial genius. Venture capital, however, is the fuel to keep it going and to accelerate its movement; no matter how brilliantly the automobile is engineered, it needs the fuel to get anywhere.How important is this fuel? That is, how vital is adequate funding for a fast-growth business? As suggested by Alan Shugart, founder of two fast-growth companies, Seagate Technology and Shugart Associates, "Cash is more important than your mother."

Some entrepreneurs even go to great lengths to thank their investors for the contributions that they have made. Herman Miller, which has been consistently recognized as the most-admired company in the furniture industry (and one of the ten most-admired corporations of any kind, based on a survey in *Fortune* magazine), was not named after the company's founder, D. J. DePree. Rather, it was named after DePree's father-in-law, who provided the start-up capital for the venture in 1923. Seventy years later Herman Miller, Inc., generates nearly a billion dollars in revenues annually.

The venture, the true entrepreneurial genius, is the automobile. Venture capital, however, is the fuel to keep it going; no matter how brilliantly the automobile is engineered, it needs the fuel to get anywhere.

How can you determine how great an influence venture capitalists have for a given company? It may be difficult, but one clue comes from a company's prospectus and, to a limited extent, from its proxy material. There you will find the ownership position of all parties, including venture capital firms, delineated clearly in the section entitled "Principal and Selling Shareholders." You will see what kind of investment each investor has made and whether the investor is selling shares of stock in the company. In addition, in the "Management" section of the prospectus or proxy, you will get a brief biographical sketch of any of the investors who serve on the company's board of directors.

Venture Capital Is More Than Just Capital

As important as venture capital is in providing the necessary funding for a fast-growth business, the funding is only one small part of the entire venture capital process. Specifically, it is this *process,* rather than the capital itself, that fuels the growth of the venture. In essence, the venture capital process makes entrepreneurship better; it is this process that characterizes the importance of the role of "venture catalysts."

First, the process forces the entrepreneur to recruit a management team. It also forces entrepreneurs to prepare a business plan to delineate their objectives and to specify their financial projections. As noted by Nolan Bushnell, founder of Atari and several other fast-growth ventures, "Every time you prepare a business plan, you become a better entrepreneur."[3]

It should be emphasized that venture capitalists provide significantly more than capital to a fast-growth company. Venture capitalists will often assist in strategic planning, recruitment, and other critical areas. They will also usually bring a broad perspective of experience to the fast-growth company, thereby strengthening management's existing resources. It is just such a foundation that prompted the spectacular success of such companies as Compaq, Federal Express, Microsoft, and Sun Microsystems.

Venture capitalists provide expertise and capital to a fast-growth company.

Ideally, as a result of the venture capital process—which should be viewed as a long-term process, often lasting five to ten years—both the venture capital firm and the growing company should benefit. Moreover, the benefit should be significantly more than financial. The venture capital process ideally is structured in a manner that develops better entrepreneurs and better decision-making activity. As such, the investor and investee reap significant benefits.

Thus there *is* a difference between venture capital and conventional financing. Venture capital is more than investing and more than building personal wealth; it is building fast-growth companies.

"Vulture Capitalists"

Unfortunately, there is a somewhat commonly held perception that venture capitalists are a group of hungry investors looking for opportunities to gain control of young ventures. In fact, Lucien Ruby, a well-known venture capitalist, recounted a tale of his own entrepreneurial pursuits in which he was warned about the "vulture capitalists" and was told by his family, "Don't let those bloodsuckers near your company."[4]

Is there any basis for this? Traditionally, the role of the venture capitalist is to assist in the launching and growth of a business. That role was exceedingly apparent in such classic success stories among fast-growth companies as Digital Equipment, Federal Express, Apple, Compaq, and Genentech. Unfortunately, this traditional role is not always carried out appropriately. The reason for this is that the venture capital industry is a profession like any other, made up of good practitioners and bad ones. Furthermore, this is an industry that involves large investments of money, and any time money is involved, there is always the opportunity for greed to play a powerful role in decisions.

Bad Experiences

Wayne and Ron Erickson, founders of Microrim (Bellevue, WA), a developer of a data base system known as R:base, sought funding and assistance from several venture capital firms in the San Francisco area. Their experience with the venture capital community was far from satisfying. They were met with antagonism, arrogance, and a general feeling that the venture capitalists felt that they knew more about their business than they did. Eventually they sought a different route to raise capital.

Despite the bad experiences that Microrim and numerous other fast-growth companies have had with venture capitalists, the industry as a whole has a very strong track record, as evidenced by the successes of Tandem, Apple Computer, and countless other examples throughout this book. Moreover, the veteran professionals in this industry who have committed themselves to the goal of building companies have been instrumental in the success of these high-visibility firms and, to a large extent, of the entrepreneurial movement in our country. Yet the industry is not without its share of "professionals" whose contribution to and philosophy regarding building companies are, to put it mildly, questionable.

Assessing the Venture Capital Industry

On balance, the current state of the venture capital industry and its professionals can be viewed quite positively. I would hardly call the industry one of "vulture capitalists," although there are several individuals with whom I have had contact that certainly belong in this category). Moreover, in many regards, investors in small, growing privately owned companies are just like any other investors; they expect to be compensated (by high returns) for their risks and for the value added that they provide to the venture. Unlike a mutual fund manager's passive investment in a portfolio of publicly held companies, the venture capitalist makes active investments in high-risk, privately held ventures.

Although venture capitalists make active investments in fast-growth companies, they generally have no desire to control a venture. The reason they invest in a company is, first and foremost, because they like the management team. Why would they want to take control away from a management team behind whom they have put their faith? Also, venture capitalists are more than passive investors; they are experts in financing companies, in structuring deals, and in advising managers on critical long term decisions. Certainly their expertise is not in *running* the company, especially not on a day-to-day basis. And even if they were capable of running the company, they would not have the time to do it.

As noted by Benjamin Rosen, one of the most highly respected venture capitalists in the country (perhaps best known for his early-stage investment and involvement in Compaq, one of the most successful fast-growth companies in the 1980s), "We are catalysts in the process of creating new companies, new technologies, new products, new industries. What we try to do is to bring together talented entrepreneurs and technology, mix them together, and make this creative process happen."[5]

So it must be emphasized that venture capitalists are more than merely investors. The high potential returns for their investments should be viewed in light of the unusually high degree of risk, as well as the time needed to assist the management of the fast-growth company in strategic decisions.

Venture Capital's Impact on Entrepreneurial Growth and Success

Does venture capital enhance the success of individual entrepreneurial companies? One thing is very clear: The companies that receive venture capital or other such financial backing have a much greater likelihood of succeeding than companies that do not receive such financing. Several classic research studies showed that there is only a 10 to 20 percent failure rate for investments in a venture capitalist's portfolio (as compared to perhaps a 10 to 20 percent *success* rate for all new companies). Furthermore, as noted earlier, venture capitalists do more than merely fund ventures: they also tend to get involved in strategic planning, technology assessment, market analysis, risk/return assessment, and management recruiting, and therefore they provide added value for the emerging fast-growth company in such nonfinancing activities.

The Influence of Georges Doriot

Perhaps this philosophy of the value added provided by the "venture catalyst" is demonstrated best by Georges Doriot, an eminent professor at the Harvard University Graduate School of Business

---

Research studies show that there is only a 10 to 20 percent failure rate for companies backed by formal venture capital.

Administration during the 1930s and 1940s, as well as an astute investor. In 1946 Doriot founded American Research and Development (ARD) in order to foster the growth of exciting new businesses in the Boston area. ARD's most significant investment occurred in 1957, when Doriot was contacted by a thirty-one-year-old circuit design engineer at MIT Lincoln Laboratories named Kenneth Olsen, who had an idea for a device called an "interactive computer." This device, which was actually the forerunner of the minicomputer, would enable the user to communicate directly with the computer via a terminal or keyboard rather than punch cards. ARD invested $70,000 in Olsen's start-up company, which was called Digital Equipment Company (DEC). DEC set up its modest headquarters in an old wool mill in Maynard, Massachusetts.

Over the next fourteen years Doriot worked closely with Olsen, assisting him in establishing a strategic direction for DEC. Over that time, ARD's $70,000 investment grew to $350 million as DEC became one of the most successful fast-growth companies of all time. Doriot, who sold ARD to Textron in 1972, had other success stories, including Cordis, a pacemaker manufacturer; Cooper Laboratories, a pharmaceutical company; and Teradyne, an electronic test equipment maker. (As the reader will soon see, however, ARD's overall performance was far from stellar.)

Doriot's philosophy of "building men and companies" demonstrates the major differences between venture capitalists and other types of portfolio managers. Whereas the portfolio manager often avoids becoming too familiar with the companies in which he or she invests (because he or she may have to liquidate his position on very short notice in the case of deteriorating market conditions), the venture capitalist must establish a more personal relationship with the entrepreneurs over a much longer duration of time. Of course, as the industry has evolved and as new professionals have entered the venture capital arena, one can hardly expect that Doriot's guidelines will govern the behavior of *all* venture capital firms or *all* venture capitalists. The concern is probably much greater among the newer entrants in the industry than among its pioneers.

Enhancing Doriot's Principles

Doriot's philosophy, both as a teacher (of Thomas Perkins, founder of Kleiner Perkins Caufield & Byers, and numerous others who entered the venture capital business) and as a venture capitalist, has had a powerful impact. The creditable venture capitalists recognize their roles as nurturers of emerging growth businesses, rather than merely as passive investors.

In the mid-1970s, for example, Paul Wythes of Sutter Hill Ventures (of Palo Alto, CA) reviewed the business plan for Qume, a start-up computer printer manufacturer. When Wythes met with the company's founders, he suggested that Qume refine its focus in order to better meet the market's needs for a faster, more versatile, and higher-quality product. Within two years Qume was able to capture nearly one-fourth of a very competitive $80 million market.

Jerry Goodwin, a New York–based venture capitalist, sums up the relationship advocated by Doriot between the venture capitalist and the entrepreneur very well:

> Once one makes an investment in a company you are "getting into bed" with the other person. You are closely involved with somebody . . . for five or six years and there is virtually no way of getting out—you've made your commitment and you'd better make real sure that you like the people that you are involved with. . . . Otherwise you are going to lose your money in addition to losing a lot of sleep along the way.[6]

Venture Capitalists Can Build Management Teams

As suggested in the previous chapter, in some instances venture capitalists will even put together management teams with adequate funding in order to start ventures on their own. For example, in 1982 Art Caisse, a vice president for research at Tymshare, was approached by a partner at Sutter Hill Ventures. Caisse was offered a loan as well as office space to get started on any computer communications ideas that he felt were viable. Within six months Caisse's new company, Cohesive Network Corporation, received $2 million in funding for 50 percent of its equity from Sutter Hill Ventures along with Bessemer Venture Partners, which has an office in nearby Menlo Park, California.

Similarly, Onset, a small firm in Palo Alto, California, that invests solely in seed-stage and start-up ventures, has served as an "incubator" to several of its investments. For example, in addition to investing $650,000 (a typical investment for Onset) into Penederm, a skin medication company, Onset provided the start-up with office space at a reduced rent, recruitment assistance, and management guidance. Two of Onset's partners, Terry L. Opdendyk, the former president of VisiCorp (which is no longer in business), and Robert Kuhing, formerly with Sun Microsystems, are well equipped to provide the necessary guidance to the firm's early-stage investments.

The Importance of Experience of Venture Capitalists

Like Opdendyk of Onset, many successful venture capitalists have launched businesses of their own prior to entering the venture capital arena, thereby enabling themselves to help other entrepreneurs do the same. For example, Eugene Kleiner, a founder of Fairchild Camera and Instrument (which later gave rise to Fairchild Semiconductor, which in turn practically gave rise to the entire semiconductor industry) founded Kleiner Perkins Caufield & Byers in 1972 with Thomas Perkins, former director of corporate development for Hewlett-Packard. The venture capital firm, which is among the ten largest in the nation, is best known for its investments in Genentech, a leading biotechnology company, and Tandem Computer, a manufacturer of mainframe computers with backup systems.

As the venture capital industry has grown and as the financial rewards of venture capitalists have increased, this profession has become a high choice option among top business school graduates. The result has been that the venture capital firms have been able to choose some extremely bright MBAs from the likes of Harvard, Stanford, MIT, Wharton, Columbia, and Northwestern. Unfortunately, many have been lacking in experience. As one entrepreneur recently told me, "I have nearly thirty years of experience in the health care industry. Yet soon after receiving funding from a venture capital firm, I had a twenty-five-year-old kid with an MBA from Harvard acting like he knew more about the health care industry than I did. He wasn't even born when I began developing my client list."

A somewhat related concern is that as the funds have taken on less experienced (although extremely intelligent) associates to assist in investment decisions, the entrepreneurs have not necessarily received the kind of expert advice that is often more valuable than money. The problem is that the pool of available talent has not kept up with the dramatic growth of the industry itself; the venture capital industry has a large number of individuals with less than five years of experience actively involved in the capitalization process. The result is that a junior-level person will often be the contact person with an entrepreneurial company. As noted by John Hines of Continental Illinois Venture Capital, "It's like a large law firm. You can say you're with the greatest law firm in the world, but, if a junior person is handling your account, I'd say that's 'baloney.' The question is, who is your individual lawyer? This is not a profession for a lot of inexperienced, young people in their 20s and 30s."[7]

Entrepreneurs as "Angels"

Several successful entrepreneurs who have amassed sizable wealth from their own ventures have entered the venture capital industry on a more informal, yet powerful, basis. For example, several years after Henry Singleton founded Teledyne, he invested in several start-ups, including Apple Computer. H. Ross Perot, founder of Electronic Data Systems (EDS), which was sold to General Motors in 1984 for $2.5 billion, has invested in a few start-ups, most notably Steve Jobs's latest venture, NeXT.

Like Singleton and Perot, several other successful entrepreneurs have entered the "angel network"—a loosely structured network of informal investors who fund emerging businesses. Most of these investors invest between $100,000 and $200,000; they have varying levels of involvement. Some examples of these angels are William Poduska, the entrepreneur who founded Prime Computer, Apollo Computer, and Stellar Computer; Philip Romano, founder of Fuddruckers, a chain of hamburger restaurants that he sold in 1985; Robert Darvin, founder of Scandinavian Design, a $100 million furniture retailer; Mitchell Kapor, founder of Lotus Development (in which he sold his stake in 1986) and ON Technology (a software company he started with Peter B. Miller, a former Lotus executive); Warren Avis, founder of the car rental firm bearing his name; and Sophie Collier, founder of American Natural Beverage Corporation, which was sold to Seagram for $15 million in 1989.

Devilish Angels

One note of caution regarding the entrepreneur turned angel. In recent years, many entrepreneurs have accumulated greater and greater wealth and have had numerous opportunities to invest in emerging growth ventures. As informal investors, they represent a tremendous opportunity for other entrepreneurs, for themselves, and for the economy. It must be emphasized, however, that the examples just presented are of the ones who are "doing it right"; they are reputable and quite willing to assume the traditional role of venture capitalists as advocated by Doriot. Unfortunately, there are few restrictions for entering this industry. Consequently plenty of wealthy informal investors—whether they have accumulated their wealth through entrepreneurial pursuits, investments, real estate ventures, "wheeler-dealer" activities, scams, or any other means (honest or dishonest) have taken on the "angel" title. Some of them, however, have played a devilish role. Although many of these informal investors have provided significant benefits, several have been a discredit to this profession. Yet as I have already indicated, because their services revolve around something as emotional as money, entrepreneurs have often failed to exert the proper care in dealing with such individuals. This is particularly true during the earliest years of a venture, when the risks are highest and the entrepreneur is most vulnerable.

Angelic Roles

Nonetheless, in most instances the hands-on experience and knowledge of these entrepreneurs turned venture capitalists is extremely valuable for the emerging companies in which they invest. In 1980, when Wilf Corrigan had an idea for a company that would make semi-custom integrated circuits, he approached Don Valentine—who, with experience in the semiconductor industry, forced Corrigan to better define his ideas for his company, LSI Logic. Valentine earlier had assisted Altos Computer Systems with its marketing efforts, an area in which he was well versed as a result of his former position as marketing director at National Semiconductor. Valentine also recruited A. C. Markkula for his position with Apple Computer during Apple's early years. These episodes are consistent with Doriot's view of the role of the venture capitalist in building companies and is certainly consistent with the view presented here of the role of "venture catalysts."

Of course, many venture capitalists have similar accomplishments but on a smaller scale, thereby putting them in an ideal position to assist smaller, younger companies. For example, Kevin Kinsella, who has a management and engineering background from MIT and Johns Hopkins, launched Spectragraphics Corporation (a manufacturer of color workstations that operate with IBM software) prior to founding Avalon Ventures (a San Diego–based "feeder fund" that invests in early-stage technology companies). Avalon has since invested in NeoRx, a Seattle-based biotechnology company; Athena Neurosciences (of San Carlos, CA), which is in the health care business; and FASTech (of Waltham, MA), a computer software company.

Preferred Investments by Venture Capitalists: The Trend Toward Specialization

Since the late 1980s there has been a trend among venture capitalists toward greater specialization by geographic location, industry, and stage of development. Many focus on low-tech industries and

---

There has been a trend among venture capitalists toward greater specialization by geographic location, industry, and stage of development.

---

on leveraged buyouts (LBOs), although the investment community as a whole is less excited about LBOs today than it was during the mid-1980s. After all, if venture capitalists can obtain a fairly safe return of 35 to 50 percent on selected LBOs, why should they look for potential comparable returns in more risky start-ups?

A Niche Economy

More and more the United States has evolved into a niche economy. For example, Information America (Atlanta, GA) provides on-line public record information and services to lawyers; Roadshow Services (San Francisco, CA) provides trucks and drivers for performers; and Backroads Bicycle Touring (Berkeley, CA) markets van-supported bicycle tours. Each of these companies was founded after 1983 and less than ten years later is a multimillion-dollar business. They represent a widespread emerging trend of carving out small, specialized niches and then filling them better than anyone else can. As suggested in Chapter 5, nichemanship is an important characteristic of successful fast-growth companies.

The diversity of these niche-oriented businesses is startling. In an *Inc.* 500 listing of privately held fast-growth companies, in addition to the three companies just mentioned (which have grown by at least eightfold since 1988), there are other comparably successful companies in such specialized areas as archery equipment, handcrafted embroidery, Australian wines, parent education videos, and model racing cars.

Specialization Among Venture Capitalists

Therefore, just as there has been a trend toward specialization among fast-growth companies, it should not be surprising that there has been a similar trend among venture capital firms. This has been one of the most significant recent developments in the venture capital industry. It has also been a very positive development for fast-growth companies in that it has prompted venture capitalists to develop greater expertise in a given industry, thereby strengthening their role as catalysts. Oak Management Corporation (of Westport, CT), for example, has concentrated on three technology groups: computers, telecommunications, and biotechnology. Similarly, Battery Ventures, a Boston-based firm, concentrates on communications, information systems, and industry automation technology. Along with Accel Partners and others, these two companies have invested in Netlink (of Raleigh, NC), a manufacturer of data communications processors for IBM networks.

MedVenture, a San Francisco–based venture capital firm, is even more specialized; it limits its investments to the life sciences, (such as biotechnology, health services, and medical instrumentation). Julian Cole & Stein (of Los Angeles, CA) generally limits its investments to high-tech manufacturing companies on the West Coast, as evidenced by its investments in LaserCom, a manufacturer of detectors and transceivers, and Advanced Power Technology, a manufacturer of MOS transistors. As noted by David Brophy, professor of finance at the University of Michigan, *"There's an evolution going on in the structuring of the industry. . . . The old model, in which the venture capitalist was a generalist, confident that he could deal with any type of venture, is no longer possible. Because of the intense competition for money and deals, we're seeing much more targeting of specific areas of technology and growth."*[8]

This has required venture capital firms to become more specialized in their staffing needs and in the way that they raise funds from their own investors. Brophy adds that *"funds are tending to devote more people to specific areas of technology. . . . And there is an influx of people with operating backgrounds, people who have been successful in molding companies and getting products out the door."*

Even with specialization, though, many venture capitalists will deviate from their preferences. Some venture capitalists refer to this as their "liberal exception policy." For example, Brentwood Associates, a specialist in funding high-tech ventures, invested in Midway Airlines a few years ago. Why? Because, above all, the characteristics of the people involved in the venture are more important than the industry in which they operate.

Performance of Venture Capital Investments

The numerous successes of individual venture capital investments give the appearance that venture capital funds as a whole perform remarkably well. For example, American Research and Development's estimated $70,000 investment in Digital Equipment Corporation grew to roughly $500 million in twelve years,[9] which translates into a compounded annual rate of return of over 100 percent.

Of course, some venture capitalists have a way of overstating the performance of companies in their investment portfolio. One venture capitalist has provided the following humorous translations:[10]

What They Say	What They Mean
Product is 90 percent complete	We've got a name for it
Leading-edge technology	We can't make it work
Limited downside	Things can't get much worse

Possibility of shortfall	We're 50 percent below plan
Proven technology	It nearly worked once
We're repositioning the company	We're lost
Upside potential	It's stopped breathing

Nonetheless, the performance of several venture deals, as illustrated below, are noteworthy.

Success Stories

The investments made by our leading venture capital firms read like a "who's who" of successful fast-growth businesses.

KLEINER PERKINS CAUFIELD & BYERS. Thomas Perkins got into the venture capital industry in 1966 with a $15,000 investment in University Laboratories (of Berkeley, CA), a laser company. That investment grew to $2 million. In 1972 Perkins became a cofounder of the prominent San Francisco–based venture capital firm Kleiner Perkins Caufield & Byers, which has invested in Genentech and Tandem Computer, among others. Perkins has had an active involvement with his investments, having served as chairman of both Genentech and Tandem.

SEVIN ROSEN. Sevin Rosen Management, a venture capital firm founded by Benjamin Rosen (one of the most notable venture investors of the 1970s and 1980s) and L.J. Sevin (founder of Mostek, a semiconductor manufacturer), invested $2.1 million in Lotus Development (Cambridge, MA). That investment grew to $70 million when Lotus went public in 1983. Sevin Rosen also invested $2.5 million in Compaq Computer; when Compaq went public in 1983, that investment was worth $40 million.

ARTHUR ROCK. Arthur Rock's investments as a venture capitalist include Fairchild Semiconductor in 1957, Teledyne in 1960, Intel (an outgrowth of Fairchild Semiconductor) in 1968, and Apple in 1978. Rock's investment in Apple grew from $57,400 to $13.2 million when Apple went public in 1980.

ALLEN & COMPANY. Allen & Company is best known for its investment in Syntex, a small pharmaceutical company, in the late 1950s. Within a decade, when Syntex became one of the leading manufacturers of birth control pills in the world, Allen's investment grew to over $80 million. Allen & Company also invested in an early stage venture, Digital Switch, a developer of telecommunications equipment whose technology enabled MCI to become a major competitor of AT & T in the long distance telephone market.

HAMBRECHT & QUIST. Hambrecht & Quist, a venture capital firm that also provides such services as investment banking and underwriting of stock issues, is responsible for a good deal of the growth of high-tech companies in Silicon Valley. Among the firm's notable investments are Apple Computer and VLSI.

TA ASSOCIATES. TA Associates was formed by Peter Brooke, as the venture capital arm of Tucker Anthony and RL Day, a Boston-based investment banking firm. It eventually became an independent venture capital partnership and is now one of the largest venture capital firms in the country. TA Associates invested $1.7 million in Tandon Corporation between 1977 and 1980; by 1983 it had sold out their investment for $77 million. It also invested $171,000 in Biogen, a Boston-based biotechnology company. It subsequently sold out of this investment with a profit of more than $10 million.

Several other venture capital firms have had similar success stories. Sequoia Capital, for example, a Silicon Valley venture capital firm specializing in high-tech ventures, has invested in Atari, Apple, Tandem, Tandon, Altos Computer, LSI Logic, and 3Com Corporation. Burr Egan Deleage & Co., a Boston-based venture capital firm with $250 million in paid-in capital, has invested in Triad, Tandon, Genentech, Tandem, Federal Express, and Chiron. The Mayfield Fund, a comparably sized firm based in Menlo Park, California, has invested in Amgen, Atari, Businessland, Compaq Computer, Genentech, and 3Com. And Institutional Venture Partners, also of Menlo Park, has invested a portion of its more than

$200 million in committed capital to such companies as Borland International, Businessland, NBI, Seagate Technology, ROLM, Stratus Computer, and LSI Logic.

. . . and Failures

The most successful venture capital firms and venture capitalists also have their share of failures. For example, in addition to its investments in Compaq Computer and Lotus Development, Sevin Rosen invested $400,000 in Osborne Computer, which later went bankrupt.

Franklin P. Johnson, who manages Asset Management Company of Palo Alto, CA, a fund with approximately $100 million in paid-in capital, has realized tremendous returns from his early-stage investments in Amgen (a biotechnology firm based in Thousand Oaks, CA) and Tandem Computer (of Cupertino, CA). But even for one of Silicon Valley's most successful venture capitalists, there are significant risks that go along with the high potential returns of early-stage investments, as evidenced by Johnson's investment in now-defunct VisiCorp. Similarly, Fred Adler's investments in Data General, Daisy Systems, Life Technologies, and Advanced Technology Labs have made him a living legend in venture capital circles. But he was less successful in his investments in Tenet, a West Coast computer firm that ran into a major recession shortly after it started up in 1969, and Cogar Corporation, an upstate New York semiconductor memory systems company that never produced anything but publicity.

Osborne Computer, Fortune Systems, Pizza Time Theatre, Victor Technologies, and Diasonics also had experienced, intelligent venture capitalists supporting them. Yet all of those investments turned out to be losers for the firms that invested in them. The better venture capital firms try to limit their failures to one (or, at worst two) in ten. Their philosophy is that they cannot afford to have five or six losses that must be offset by a superstar performer.

Performance of Venture Capital Portfolios

Unfortunately, the investments in such fast-growth successes as DEC, Lotus Development, Compaq Computer, Apple Computer, and Syntex, are not at all indicative of the performance of venture capital portfolios (the overall groups of companies in which firms have invested) as a whole. For example, even with DEC in its portfolio, ARD's rate of return from 1946 to 1966 was only 14 percent. (Note: The investment in DEC had not reached its culmination by 1966. However, follow up research—after DEC had been harvested—reported that ARD's return had fallen to below 10% by the late 1970s.)[11]

Aside from ARD, studies have been made of the rates of return of the portfolios of other respected privately held and publicly held venture capital firms and small business investment companies (SBICs). The rates of return for a sample of such investments over the 1960s and 1970s, after deducting management fees, ranged from approximately 12 percent to less than 20 percent.[12] The returns of venture capital investments have varied somewhat in the 1980s and 1990s, both on an individual-year and on a long-term (ten to fifteen year) basis. Nonetheless, industrywide returns have rarely been better than 20 percent in any given year.

There have, however, been short-run "booms" (including 1961, 1967–1969, 1972, 1980, and 1983–1988) in which venture capital funds realized annual returns of approximately 30 percent or more. It is not surprising that these boom periods have coincided with favorable markets for IPOs, since the new issues market allows for liquidation of privately held venture capital investments.

Although there are short-run booms in which venture capital funds realized annual returns of approximately 30 percent or more, the overall rates of return have been less than 20 percent.

Given the fact that venture capitalists often invest in fast-growth ventures with high risk/return characteristics, the commonly held perception is that their portfolios would perform admirably. Many of these investments have low or negative returns, however, while few have substantial returns, thereby reducing the returns of the entire portfolio.[13] Research suggests that over the long term, 10 to 20 percent of the investments in a typical venture capital firm's portfolio are complete losses (compared to the 70 or 80 percent failure rate that is characteristic of new ventures throughout the population); 10 to 20 percent of the investments have annual rates of return of better than 40 percent; and fewer than 5 percent might be considered "superstars" with annual rates

---

Over the long term, 10 to 20 percent of the investments in a typical venture capital firm's portfolio are complete losses; 10 to 20 percent of the investments have annual rates of return of better than 40 percent; and fewer than 5 percent might be considered "superstars" with annual rates of returns of greater than 80 percent.

---

of returns of greater than 80 percent. The remainder are at best mediocre investments, typically characterized as "the living dead."

The Current Situation for Venture Capital Investing

First, the growth of the venture capital industry has failed to continue at its rate of the mid-1980s. From 1983 to 1988 there was about $4 billion of new venture capital raised per year; this slowed to about $2 billion in 1989 and 1990 and to about $800 million in 1991. More recently there has been a reversal of that downward trend—to about $2 billion in 1992—but the growth rates seen during the mid-1980s seem far behind us.

Second, it is getting tougher in the 1990s to realize the traditional returns expected by venture capitalists. When Intel, currently a $5 billion company, was started in 1968, an initial investment of $500,000 was all that was needed. Despite such a small investment, the returns to the investors were significant. Today the situation is quite different. For example, in the mid-1980s, venture capitalists invested *$21 million* in Convex Computer (of

Richardson, TX). This is typical of high tech start-ups; early-stage costs can often be $10 million to $50 million, with no guarantees of success. Convex was fortunate to have gone public in 1986 (before the 1987 stock market crash), so one may call it a success story. But despite the high risks involved with such a venture, the public offering only brought some of its early investors three times their original investment in a very strong IPO market. This is becoming more characteristic of the venture capital market. It is becoming more and more difficult to expect a tenfold return on an initial investment, let alone a hundredfold or greater return, as was the case with such fast-growth success stories as Syntex, DEC, Genentech, Apple, and Tandem.

Venture Capital: Important Summary Points

1. Successful fast-growth companies have often benefited tremendously from the financial assistance, as well as from the advice and direction, of venture capitalists.
2. Although some entrepreneurial growth-oriented companies have experienced the impact of "vulture capitalists" (for example, Microrim), many more have experienced the impact of venture catalysts (for example, Apple, Compaq, DEC, Genentech). There is a significant variance within the profession in the value of venture capitalists.
3. Companies receiving venture capital funding have a significantly higher success rate than those not receiving such funding.
4. Venture capitalists in the 1980s and 1990s have become much more specialized in their investment strategies (for example, Netlink, LaserCom, Advanced Power Technology).
5. Although many venture capital firms have had exceedingly successful individual investments in growth companies (for example, Apple, Compaq, Lotus, DEC, Syntex, Tandem), the overall portfolios of venture capital firms have generated long-term annualized returns of less than 20 percent.

Notes

Chapter 1

1. I took an in-depth look at several dozen fast-growth companies of the 1980s and 1990s. Included in the sample were companies from several different industries that have been included in listings of fast-growth companies in such publications as *Inc., Forbes, Fortune,* and *Business Week.* I followed up these companies over the ensuing years to assess their performance better.

   I limited the sample of companies primarily to publicly held corporations, which would provide us with considerably more—as well as more reliable—background and financial information than privately held corporations, due to reporting requirements. In addition, I examined primarily independent corporations that were not subsidiaries of larger corporations. I compiled whatever information I could about the companies included in the sample—including corporate reports, SEC filings, press releases, and newspaper and magazine articles—and then, when possible, spoke to industry experts as well as managers at these companies to learn what takes place at these companies and why they succeed or fail.

2. Generally, by the time these companies have become "alumni" of the Inc. 100, their growth has slowed down to the 20 percent to 40 percent range.

3. See Joel Kotkin, "Why Small Companies Are Saying No to Venture Capital," *Inc.,* August 1984, p. 67.

4. John Case and Elizabeth Conlin, "Second Thoughts on Growth," *Inc.,* March 1991, p. 50.

Chapter 2

1. See Jeffry Timmons, *The Entrepreneurial Mind* (Acton, MA: Brick House Publishing, 1989).

2. The *Fortune* survey ranks only the ten largest companies in each of a limited number of industries. Many of the companies mentioned throughout this book are not nearly large enough yet to be included in the *Fortune* survey.

3. Christopher Knowlton, "What America Makes Best," *Fortune,* March 28, 1988, p. 42.

4. *Dun's Business Month,* December 1987, p. 25.

5. Jeremy Main, "The Winning Organization," *Fortune,* September 26, 1988, p. 51.

6. From Louis Rukeyser, "Wall Street Week," February 8, 1985.
7. Joel Kotkin, "Why Smart Companies Are Saying No to Venture Capital," in *The Best of Inc.: Guide to Finding Capital* (New York: Prentice Hall Press, 1988), p. 94.

Chapter 3

1. See *Fortune,* March 26, 1990, p. 14.
2. Udayan Gupta, "Watching and Waiting," *Wall Street Journal,* November 13, 1989, p. R32.
3. Gary Slutsker, "Cloning Profits," *Forbes,* January 9, 1989, p. 152.

Chapter 4

1. See Peter F. Drucker, *Innovation and Entrepreneurship* (New York: Harper & Row, 1985).
2. The three largest American companies in terms of market valuation as of January 1, 1993, were Exxon ($77.6 billion), Wal-Mart ($74.6 billion), and GE ($74.2 billion).
3. Susan Caminiti, "The New Champs in Retailing," *Fortune,* September 24, 1990, p. 85.
4. Ibid., p. 90.

Chapter 5

1. See Michael Porter, "The State of Strategic Thinking," *Economist,* May 23, 1987, pp. 18, 22.
2. See Michael Porter, *Competitive Strategy* (New York: Free Press, 1980).
3. See Regis McKenna, *The Regis Touch.* Reading, MA: Addison-Wesley, 1986, pp. 21–23.
4. See Donald K. Clifford, Jr., and Richard E. Cavanagh, *The Winning Performance* (New York: Bantam, 1985).
5. I use terms such as *strategy, product/market focus, mission,* or *scope of operations* synonymously here.
6. Adam Smith, "How Liz Claiborne Designed an Empire," *Esquire,* January 1986, p. 78.
7. Susan Caminiti, "The New Champs in Retailing," *Fortune,* September 24, 1990.
8. See *Success,* January/February, 1989, p. 53.
9. Robert Wrubel, "Captain America," *Financial World,* May 29, 1990, p. 26.

Chapter 6

1. *Business Week,* November 19, 1990, p. 130.
2. Robert Wrubel. "Captain America," *Financial World,* May 29, 1990, p. 26.
3. *Business Week,* November 19, 1990, p. 76.

4. See "Nike" case, HBS #385-025, 1984.
5. Eric Severeid, *Enterprise* (New York: McGraw-Hill, 1983), p. 13.

Chapter 7

1. Jeremy Main, "Detroit's Cars Are Really Getting Better," *Fortune,* February 2, 1987, p. 95.
2. See "Formulating a Quality Improvement Strategy," *PIMSLETTER* no. 31, p. 5.
3. See Alex Miller and Bill Camp, "Exploring Determinants of Success in Corporate Ventures," *Journal of Business Venturing,* Winter 1985, pp. 87–105.
4. See *Consumer Perceptions Concerning the Quality of American Products and Services,* a study by the Gallup Organization for the American Society for Quality Control, 1985, pp. 12–13.
5. Donald Clifford and Richard Cavanagh, *The Winning Performance* (New York: Bantam Books, 1985), p. 9.
6. See Robert Levering, Milton Moskowitz, and Michael Katz, *The 100 Best Companies to Work for in America* (Reading, MA: Addison-Wesley, 1985).
7. Christopher Cerf and Victor Navasky, *The Experts Speak* (New York: Pantheon Books, 1984).
8. See *PIMSLETTER*, no. 33, p. 8.
9. John Case, "Customer Satisfaction: The Last Word," *Inc.,* April 1991, p. 90.
10. Regis McKenna, *The Regis Touch* (Reading, MA: Addison-Wesley, 1986), pp. 43–44.
11. See Jan Carlzon's excellent book *Moments of Truth* (New York: Ballinger Publishing Co., 1987) for some greater insight on the success of SAS.
12. See Tom Peters, *Thriving On Chaos* (New York: Knopf, 1988), pp. 89–90.

Chapter 8

1. Christopher Cerf and Victor Navasky, *The Experts Speak* (New York: Pantheon Books, 1984).
2. Paul Hawken, *Growing a Business* (New York: Simon & Schuster, 1988), p. 50.
3. James Botkin, Dan Dimanescu, and Ray Stata, *The Innovators: Re-discovering America's Creative Energy* (New York: Harper & Row, 1984).
4. Brenton R. Schlender, "Who's Ahead in the Computer Wars?" *Fortune,* February 12, 1990, p. 59.
5. MBWA, which refers to "management by walking around," was originally coined at Hewlett-Packard and is discussed in great length in such Tom Peters works as *In Search of Excellence, A Passion for Excellence,* and *Thriving on Chaos.*
6. Donald Clifford and Richard Cavanagh, *The Winning Performance* (New York: Bantam Books, 1985), p. 105.

7. George Gilder, *The Spirit of Enterprise* (New York: Simon & Schuster, 1984), p. 246.
8. Thomas Peters, *Thriving on Chaos* (New York: Alfred A. Knopf, 1987), p. 211.
9. Ibid., p. 221.

Chapter 9

1. "The Entrepreneur Series," *Hermes,* Fall 1984, p. 28.
2. Donald Clifford and Richard Cavanagh, *The Winning Performance* (New York: Bantam Books, 1985), pp. 32–33.
3. *Business Week,* October 8, 1990, p. 74.
4. *Fortune,* May 23, 1988, p. 33.
5. Donald Clifford and Richard Cavanagh, *The Winning Performance* (New York: Bantam Books, 1985), p. 13.
6. Ibid., p. 103.

Chapter 10

1. Donald Clifford and Richard Cavanagh, *The Winning Performance* (New York: Bantam Books, 1985), p. 94.
2. Ibid., p. 108.
3. Ibid., p. 108.
4. See Lynda Schuster, "Wal-Mart Chief's Enthusiastic Approach Infects Employees, Keeps Retailer Growing," *Wall Street Journal,* April 20, 1982, p. 21.
5. Ibid.
6. Ibid.
7. See Bill Saporito, "David Glass Won't Crack Under Fire," *Fortune,* February 8, 1993, p. 78.
8. Donald Clifford and Richard Cavanagh, *The Willing Performance* (New York: Bantam Books, 1985), p. 95.
9. Thomas H. Melohn. "How to Build Employee Trust and Productivity," *Harvard Business Review,* January–February 1983, p. 57.

Chapter 11

1. Jeffry A. Timmons, *New Venture Creation,* 3rd ed. (Homewood, IL: Dow Jones Irwin, 1990), p. 16.
2. *Venture,* May 1987, p. 96.
3. Lee Kravitz, "What Venture Capitalists Want," in *Venture's Guide to International Venture Capital* (New York: Simon & Schuster, 1985), p. 14.
4. Arthur Rock, "Strategy vs. Tactics from a Venture Capitalist," *Harvard Business Review,* November–December 1987, p. 63.
5. Bob Weinstein, "Boy Wonder," *Entrepreneur,* November 1990, p. 64.

6. See Robert Stuart and Pier Abetti, "Field of Study of Technical Ventures—Part III: The Impact of Entrepreneurial and Management Experience on Early Performance," presented at the Babson Entrepreneurship Research Conference, Calgary, 1988.
7. See Richard Teach, Fred Tarpley, and Robert Schwartz, "Software Venture Teams," in Robert Ronstadt, John Hornaday, Rein Peterson, and Karl Vesper (eds.), *Frontiers of Entrepreneurship Research* (Wellesley, MA: Babson Center for Entrepreneurial Studies, 1986), p. 546.
8. Thomas J. Peters and Robert H. Waterman, Jr., *In Search of Excellence* (New York: Harper & Row, 1982), p. 203.
9. Ibid.
10. Peter F. Drucker, *Adventures of a Bystander* (New York: Harper & Row, 1979), p. 255.
11. Cheryll Aimee Barron, "Silicon Valley Phoenixes," *Fortune*, November 23, 1987, p. 129.
12. Ibid.

Chapter 12

1. For an extensive discussion of the impact of venture capital on entrepreneurial growth and economic development, please refer to my book *Dream Makers and Deal Breakers: Inside the Venture Capital Industry* (Prentice Hall, 1991). In addition, a useful reference for entrepreneurs in search of venture capital is my earlier book *The Entrepreneur's Guide to Preparing a Winning Business Plan and Raising Venture Capital* (Prentice Hall, 1990).
2. Of course, I'm using the term *fuel* synonymously with the term *energy*; fuel for an automobile can be in the form of gasoline, electricity, or solar energy.
3. Jeffry A. Timmons et al., *New Venture Creation*, 2nd ed. (Homewood, IL: Irwin, 1985), p. 432.
4. George Kozmetsky et al., *Financing and Managing Fast Growth Companies: The Venture Capital Process* (Lexington, MA: Lexington Books, 1985), p. xi.
5. Louis Rukeyser, "Venture Capital: An Interview with Ben Rosen," *Wall Street Week*, February 8, 1985.
6. Robert C. Perez, *Inside Venture Capital* (New York: Praeger, 1986).
7. Joel Kotkin, "Why Smart Companies Are Saying No to Venture Capital," *Inc.*, August 1984, p. 67.
8. Lee Kravitz, "What Venture Capitalists Want," in *Venture's Guide to International Venture Capital* (New York: Simon & Schuster, 1985), p. 14.
9. The amount of the investment in DEC and the returns for ARD vary somewhat, depending upon your source of information. Please refer to G. Kozmetsky et al., *Financing and Managing Fast-Growth Companies: The Venture Capital Process* (Lexington, MA: D.C. Heath, 1985); P. R. Liles, "Sustaining the Venture Capital Firm," Management Analysis Center, Cambridge, MA, 1977; and W. A. Wells, "Venture Capital Decision Making," unpublished doctoral dissertation, Carnegie-Mellon University, 1974.

10. *Inc.*, August 1989, p. 22.
11. See W. Rotch, "The Pattern of Success in Venture Capital Financing," *Financial Analysis Journal*, September–October 1968, vol. 24, pp. 141–147.
12. For details of these studies, refer, for example, to B. Huntsman and J. P. Hoban, "Investments in New Enterprise: Some Empirical Observations on Risk, Return, and Market Structure," *Financial Management*, Summer 1980, pp. 44–51; and J. B. Poindexter, "The Efficiency of Financial Markets: The Venture Capital Case," unpublished doctoral dissertation, New York University, New York, 1976.
13. Refer to W. A. Carleton, "Issues and Questions Involving Venture Capital," in G. Libecap (ed.), *Advances in the Study of Entrepreneurship, Innovation, and Economic Growth*, vol. 1 (Greenwich, CT: JAI Press, 1986), pp. 59–70; and B. Huntsman and J. P. Hoban, "Investment in New Enterprise: Some Empirical Observations On Risk, Return, and Market Structure," *Financial Management*, Summer 1980, pp. 44–51.

Index

Company Index

Subject Index

About the Author

W. Keith Schilit is founder and director of the Program in Entrepreneurship at the University of South Florida College of Business Administration as well as an accomplished entrepreneur, consultant, author, and lecturer. He is an internationally recognized expert in the area of raising capital for and managing emerging growth businesses and has been featured in *USA Today, The Wall Street Journal, Business Week, The New York Times, Inc., Success,* and over 250 other publications.

He has founded three businesses and has assisted in the start-up of several others. He currently heads up Catalyst Ventures (Tampa, Florida), a consulting firm that assists small growth businesses.

He has consulted to or conducted training programs for numerous businesses in the United States and abroad and has served as an expert witness in the area of corporate valuation. His clients have included: The U.S. Civil Service Commission, Niagara Mohawk Power, Corning Glass Works, National Tire Dealers and Retreaders Association, Medcross, Intermedia Communications, Robbins Manufacturing, Business Video Productions, and Trinity Modular Technology Ltd. (U.K.). In addition, he serves on the board of directors of Chico's FAS and of Check Express (both publicly held, NASDAQ listed companies) as well as of the ASM Fund (a mutual fund that invests in large capitalization, blue chip companies). He is also a founding member of the Strategic Management Society, an international society of over 1,000 consultants, executives, and academicians.

He has written approximately three dozen articles on such topics as: investing in emerging growth companies, analyzing initial public offerings (IPOs), starting and financing new business ventures, preparing business plans, raising venture capital, strategic planning, and general management, and has given numerous talks to corporations, associations, and universities on these topics. He is also the author of three other recent books on venture capital and emerging growth ventures: *Blue Chip$ & Hot Tip$: Identifying Emerging Growth Companies Most Likely to Succeed* (Prentice Hall, 1992; which was a co-recipient of the "Best Investment Book of the Year" by the 1993 *Stock Trader's Amanac* and was one of only seven books included as a *Fidelity Investments* selection and was also featured on the ABC Nightly News), *Dream Makers & Deal Breakers: Inside the Venture Capital Industry* (Prentice Hall, 1991), and *The Entrepreneur's Guide to Preparing a Winning Business Plan & Raising Venture Capital* (Prentice Hall, 1990).

He holds an MBA & Ph.D. in strategic planning from the University of Maryland and has served on the faculties of Syracuse University and Keio University (in Tokyo). Currently, he is on the faculty of the University of South Florida (in Tampa).